# Principles
## of Traditional
## Archery

# Principles of Traditional Archery

## Thomas Grissom

SUNSTONE
PRESS

SANTA FE

Sunstone books may be purchased for educational, business, or sales promotional use. For information please write: Special Markets Department, Sunstone Press, P.O. Box 2321, Santa Fe, New Mexico 87504-2321.

Book and Cover design › Vicki Ahl
Body typeface › Basketville Old Face
Printed on acid-free paper
∞

_____

Library of Congress Cataloging-in-Publication Data

Grissom, Thomas, 1940-
Principles of traditional archery / by Thomas Grissom.
  pages cm
  ISBN 978-0-86534-948-3 (softcover : alk. paper)
1. Archery. I. Title.
GV1185.G725 2013
799.3'2–dc23

                      2013020896

_____

**WWW.SUNSTONEPRESS.COM**
SUNSTONE PRESS / POST OFFICE BOX 2321 / SANTA FE, NM 87504-2321 /USA
(505) 988-4418 / ORDERS ONLY (800) 243-5644 / FAX (505) 988-1025

$\mathcal{S}$o long as the new moon returns in heaven a bent, beautiful bow, so long will the fascination of archery keep hold of the hearts of men.

—Maurice Thompson,
*The Witchery of Archery*

*In memory of*

My Mother,
Who gave me my first bow

and

Al Slade,
Teacher, Scholar, Archer, Mentor, Friend,
With whom I long ago learned how to think about these things

and

Harold Groves,
Master Bowyer,
Who understood all of these things about bows, and more

# Contents

# *Prologue*

This is not a comprehensive manual on traditional archery. Many potential topics are left out entirely in order to focus instead on some topics that are generally omitted in other discussions of traditional archery, or, if included at all, are dealt with inadequately or incorrectly. The emphasis here is on the *basic principles* that underlie the *design, performance, and use* of all forms of traditional bows and arrows. It is not intended to be a book on the physics of archery but on the physical principles that are involved in the choices faced by every archer in selecting and using the implements of the sport. The goal is to present the reader with a new *way of thinking* about traditional archery, along with adequate examples of how this way of thinking can be applied in specific instances so that the reader will be able to extend the same ideas and the same approach to other questions as they arise. An ancillary goal is to dispel some of the incorrect notions and blatant misunderstandings that pervade traditional archery and its literature and that have become gradually ingrained in the lore of the sport, often going unquestioned because they have become so insidious and firmly entrenched. Even when these are not identified specifically in the narrative they are usually clear enough by implication.

Most traditional archers have little understanding of the principles that govern the performance of the bow and arrow. With that in mind the present text incorporates a number of unique and distinctive features.

In the beginning the narrative traces the probable origins and development of the bow and arrow in antiquity as the kinds of choices faced by earlier bowyers, choices dictated by the basic principles governing the mechanical operation of the bow and arrow. The design of the bow—and the arrow—are separately analyzed and discussed in terms of these same underlying principles that determine their performance and use. Central to all of this is the crucial concept of an *effective mass* assigned to the limbs of the bow, a concept generally glossed over or, more likely, ignored entirely in other treatments.

The manner in which the bow limbs store energy through elastic deformation and the efficiency with which they impart kinetic energy and momentum to the arrow are treated in detail, including the effects of limb shape and cross section, arrow mass, and effective mass of the limbs. The concepts of an ideal bow and an ideal arrow are introduced as useful ways of thinking about the design and performance limitations of real bows and arrows. The ability of a bow to impart velocity, energy, and momentum to an arrow is shown to be completely determined by the stored energy and effective mass of the limbs. And a convenient way of simultaneously determining both of these parameters by measuring the velocity imparted to two arrows of different mass shot from the same bow is given. The overall effect of draw weight on bow performance is discussed with the view of injecting some realism into the perennial question of how much draw weight is enough. A separate chapter is devoted to the problem of distance shooting, and another to clearing up the confusion surrounding the topic of arrow penetration. The effects of variations in arrow straightness, spine, and weight are analyzed in some detail to answer the question of when better arrows finally become good enough. The techniques of shooting and an in-depth discussion of the causes, and cures, of target panic are presented. And finally a separate chapter is devoted to a primer on the analytical design of bow limbs.

The topics in this book began as a series of informal articles written for news letters and magazines of archery organizations in the state of Washington. As I wrote them and talked with archers who read them, it became apparent that much of the sport of traditional archery and in particular questions concerning equipment and its use are so closely intertwined with the underlying physical principles that they cannot really be understood and addressed without at least a basic knowledge of those principles. It is to provide the reader with that necessary background that the present book was initially conceived. The final direction taken was shaped in part by comments I received from readers of those articles as well as readers of the present text.

The individual chapters are written so that each one can be read and understood by itself. Taken all together they reinforce one another and form a more comprehensive and complete picture; but each can be read separately to good effect by the reader who wants to approach the book as a series of individual topics from which to pick and choose what is most interesting or relevant at the moment. As a result there is a certain amount of redundancy and repetition of ideas. That is true for example of the concept of the effective mass of the bow limbs. Without this concept little else about the traditional bow can be understood. So it is introduced at each point where it is needed for the topic under discussion. There are two separate discussions of the shooting problems that fall under the heading of target panic, and two separate discussions about the question of draw weight, because of the relative importance of both topics. The resulting redundancy is deliberate and purposeful rather than careless. Another notion behind the individual chapters is that just so much can be absorbed at any one exposure to new ideas and new ways of thinking, and it is much better to break them up into more palatable chunks and use repetition to reinforce them. As a long-time college professor I am well aware of the value of repetition in promoting learning.

Although written by a physicist, the book and its treatment are aimed at the lay reader. I have eliminated for the most part the use of mathematical formulas, but not the use of numbers and numerical examples where they add to or reinforce the ideas. One of the main points that emerges is that traditional bows of all designs and all draw weights operate in a very restricted range of energy efficiency and arrow velocity. All traditional bows are, very roughly speaking, about the same. No really large differences can be achieved by design changes. The limits of performance are set by the properties of materials available for constructing the limbs and by the physical principles that govern the operation of the bow. No sophisticated mathematics is required to understand either of these limitations.

One exception is the chapter on measuring the performance parameters of the bow. There I have included the relevant formulas for the reader who might want to actually apply empirical measurement to the concepts. I have supplied just enough guidance to enable the reader to use the formulas without belaboring their derivation. Actually seeing the relationships between the various parameters might make them easier for some readers to understand. Anyone wanting to skip the equations can do so without any loss of continuity. Understanding the equations is not essential to reading and understanding the rest of the chapter.

The other exception is the chapter on limb design. There I give the design approach and the relevant equations for optimizing the actual design parameters of a laminated composite wood and fiberglass limb. The same ideas, and equations, can be applied to composite and self limbs made of any materials. The purpose is not to impress, or intimidate, the reader with mathematics, all of which is fairly elementary. The purpose is to give the reader a better feel for the complexity and some of the problems involved. Practically all bowyers approach their designs in a much more cut-and-try fashion in which mathematics plays little, if any, role. Many bowyers over the years have arrived at excellent, if not necessarily optimal, designs by trial and error. Analyzing limb design analytically with the use of mathematics however can help us better understand what they are doing. It can also enable the reader to look at a given design and begin to judge its merits for himself without having to simply accept whatever claims are made by the bowyer. Understanding the equations is not essential to reading and understanding the accompanying discussion of design principles. The equations are included for anyone wishing to consider them, along with a discussion outlining how they can be applied. Or they can be omitted if desired.

In the interests of brevity and compactness I have limited the use of figures and visual aids. Most of the readers for which the book is intended are archers with enough experience that basic visual aids are unnecessary. Figures are restricted to those instances where they are useful to illustrate or make clearer some point of the narrative. I realize that some learners are more visual than others, but the communication of the main ideas is through the text itself. I have found that although figures may enhance the visual appeal of the presentation, they often add very little in the way of understanding.

Finally, this is the sort of book that I would like to have stumbled on early in my pursuit of archery, but never did. In writing it I have not been guided by any conventional wisdom about what topics ought to be included. I have not done extensive research just to be able to include something. Instead I have written what I know. Otherwise, I have left it out. Much of my research has been done in idle time over the years with pencil and paper and mathematical equations. That has always been my starting point. In deciding what to include I have selfishly indulged my own whims and interests and passions. No record which does less deserves any reader's serious attention.

A note on terminology: I have adhered to the archer's practice of designating a bow by its draw weight, as in a *60 pound bow* for one requiring a force of 60 pounds to bring it to full draw. I have also used numbers for numerical values, as in the example above, instead of spelling out the numbers, in those instances when I thought that doing so made the point better or was more likely to be noticed and remembered by the reader. I have particularly done so in places with yardage, percentage, and weight values. Archery terms are not always standardized to the point where they are agreed upon by everyone, even those in the sport. In those instances, especially when there was no guidance in an unabridged dictionary of the English language, such as *Webster's Third New International Dictionary*, I have adhered to my own preferences for those terms commonly used by archers. For example, the limbs on a bow may be described as *recurved* but the bow itself is a *recurve bow*, to single out just one of the more obvious instances.

# Beginnings

*Not an actual history of the bow and arrow, but a story, a narrative, looking backward, by which we can organize and make sense out of the directions taken in the historical development of archery.*

The first bow was probably little more than a bent stick. It would have been thicker perhaps in the middle and tapered toward both ends to make it bend more evenly along its length. A stout cord of animal or plant fibers secured to both ends held it bent, or as the archer says, *braced*, so that it could be pulled and shot. It was held near the middle and drawn by extending the bow arm while pulling the string toward the chest or face with the fingers of the drawing hand. Aiming was by sighting along or over the arrow. Such a bow can be shot equally well right- or left-handed.

At first the limbs would have been left round or nearly so. The *thickness* of such a limb determines the force necessary to bend it and draw the bow. To be effective at killing even moderately small game a bow needs a *draw weight* of around thirty to forty pounds, meaning that a force that large is required to pull it to *full draw*, and this would have required a certain minimum thickness of limb. How far the limb could then be bent without breaking depends on its *length*. The longer the bow the farther it could be safely drawn. Short stout bows that couldn't be drawn as far would have been shot by holding them out in front of the archer and drawing to a point intermediate between the bow and the body, perhaps in front of the face to allow sighting along the arrow. This was the manner employed by Ishi when he taught Saxton Pope the techniques of Yana archery, and we can see this technique illustrated in Pope's photographs of Ishi shooting his bow. A short bow can be shot this way even when stooping or kneeling or squatting. Extending the bow arm fully and drawing all the way back to the face requires a longer bow, and this was the direction taken in arriving at the storied English longbow.

The quest for more powerful bows capable of shooting heavier arrows and greater distances led to thicker limbs which then had to be longer to be drawn as far without breaking. English longbows of sixty to ninety pounds draw weight, at the limit of what most archers could manage, with their thick, oval-shaped limbs must be about six feet long to be safely drawn the twenty-seven inches or more required to anchor the arrow beneath the chin or alongside the face in the manner of English archery. Bows of this length are usually shot standing and are held vertical, or perhaps slightly canted to give a clearer view of the arrow for aiming. It is to the use of these longbows of moderate to heavy draw weight that we owe the development of the techniques of English archery, and target archery in particular, techniques that continue to form the underpinnings of modern methods of shooting traditional bows.

Early bowyers would have soon discovered that a round stick too thick to be easily bent could be made into a useable bow by scraping it flat on the back and front, and that such a thinner-limbed bow could be drawn farther without breaking. The resulting loss in draw weight can be recovered by increasing the width of the limb. Instead of being nearly round or a thick narrow oval, the cross section of the limb becomes a thin flat oval much wider than its thickness. The wider limb also resists warping or twisting as the bow is drawn.

A thinner, wider limb allowed bows of heavier draw weight to be shorter while still capable of the same *draw length*. Thus came to be what is commonly referred to as the American flat, or semi-flat, bow, so named primarily because it was popularized in America in the early part of the twentieth century as a shorter alternative to the English longbow. The name has nothing to do with it being distinctly American. We find examples of it among primitive bows everywhere and it is a design that certainly emerged almost from the beginning. In fact it is one of the most common forms of aboriginal bows seen in museum collections. Thinner, wider limbs also produced a more efficient bow capable of shooting faster than a longbow of the same draw weight. And there are other distinct advantages to this approach. Shorter bows can be shot without having to stand upright, from a kneeling or squatting position, while still drawing the arrow to the face for greater draw weight and for ease and consistency in aiming. A shorter bow is easier to carry and maneuver in brush or to shoot from horseback or concealment. For any and perhaps all of these reasons flat or semi-flat bows were among the earliest forms of primitive bows.

The *English longbow* and the *American flat bow* then are the two generic forms of straight-limbed bows. They are fashioned straight, or nearly so, even though after being strung and shot a few times the limbs may, and generally will, take a permanent bend, or *set*, in the direction of the string. The bow is said to *follow the string*. This tendency results from a permanent deformation of the limb material when it is strained, or deformed, locally beyond its *elastic limit*. The thicker the limbs the greater the internal strain for a given amount of bend, and the more pronounced the permanent deformation. Bows made of a single material are termed *self bows*, and wooden self bows are especially susceptible to following the string. When unstrung the limbs do not return to their original shape even though we continue to term it a straight bow by design. Bows made of improved materials with elastic properties superior to wood, such as fiberglass or other composite laminates, usually do not exhibit a permanent set even when greatly overdrawn, sometimes right up to the *fracture limit*, or the point where the limb actually breaks.

There are also bow limbs that by design are not straight but are purposely curved. Curved limbs are one means of making the limbs slightly longer, allowing the bow to be drawn farther, without increasing the overall length of the bow from end to end. Limbs that angle or bend toward the *face* or *belly* of the bow (the string side, or the side facing the archer) are said to be *deflexed*. Limbs that angle or bend toward the *back* of the bow (away from the string) are termed *reflexed*. Limbs that start out slightly reflexed can end up straight after the bow is shot and takes a permanent set, as a means of countering the tendency of self bows to follow the string. Bows that are deflexed at the handle and reflexed toward the tips—the so-called *deflexed-reflexed* shape—can exhibit better limb speed and less recoil or hand shock and can be more pleasant to shoot than straight or purely reflexed bows.

A limb with a pronounced or increasing degree of reflex near the tip is said to be *recurved*. Recurved limbs offer some inherent advantages which we will go into later and the *recurve bow* is usually regarded as a distinct design separate from straight bows with reflexed limbs, although the distinction in many cases is mainly one of degree and is by no means absolute. The transition from straight bows to limbs that are deflexed or reflexed is likewise one of degree with many possible variations. Straight limbs can be either deflexed or reflexed abruptly at the handle or *riser*. Or they can be more gradually deflexed or reflexed along the length of the limb. English longbows were sometimes built reflexed with the straight limbs set back at the handle to offset the tendency of the thick oval limbs to follow the string. The difficulty of procuring six-foot lengths of straight, knot-free yew suitable for a bow often resulted in two shorter lengths dovetailed and glued together at the handle, where they could be set back away from the string into a reflexed shape of any desired degree. The American flat bow can equally well be made with limbs deflexed or reflexed in any combination.

Reflexed or recurved limbs have to bend farther in coming to full draw. As a result the limb is more highly stressed, meaning that a thinner limb with reduced limb mass can be used to achieve the same draw weight. Reducing the limb mass makes the limb faster and increases the *cast* of the bow, or the speed with which it propels an arrow. The same effect can also be achieved by merely shortening the limbs without reflexing them. Recurve bows can likewise be deflexed, with the limbs angled toward the string, which produces a bow with a smoother draw, better limb speed and stability, and reduced hand shock. As a result the deflexed shape is one of the most popular configurations for recurve bows.

It is sometimes customary to refer to all straight bows, whether reflexed or deflexed, as *longbows*, making no distinction between the design features of the English longbow and the American flat bow, lumping them all together as longbows, distinct from *recurve bows*. With that convention the two basic categories of traditional bows are *longbows* and *recurves*. There can still be a gradual transition from one to the other, with all sorts of variations in between. Any attempt to become dogmatic about the distinction between longbows and recurves fails because there is simply no single distinguishing feature to point to that can separate the gradual transition from one to the other. For that reason we sometimes see them all referred to as simply longbows to distinguish them from *compound bows*, a distinction about which we will be more specific later.

Another popular designation lumps them all together as *stick bows*, bows without pulleys, attributing the traditional bow to its origins as basically a bent stick in all of its myriad forms and refinements. Whether self bows or composite, they are still labeled stick bows. In many ways the latter designation is the preferable one. It is simple, clear and inclusive, and gets rid of a lot of pointless arguments about semantics. And it separates the traditional bow from compound bows.

As one can quickly see from the proliferation of nomenclature and the various schema used to categorize traditional bows there is the potential for far more confusion than enlightenment in the names by which we refer to the different types. That is partly because the names suggest sharp distinctions that are not really there. And it is equally pointless to try to artificially impose any particular scheme. One bowyer's reflexed limb is another bowyer's recurved limb, and one's longbow is another's semi-flat or recurve bow. Once we venture past the categorization *stick bows* we have to be alert as to what is actually meant in the designation of any particular type.

The recurve bow is often thought of as a modern innovation because of its refinement and popularization in American archery in the twentieth century. But like all other forms of traditional bows, it is in reality a very ancient design. We find drawings of bows with highly recurved limbs on ancient Greek vases and other artifacts from Greece and Asia Minor and Persia dating back to long before the Christian era. The bows depicted in these ancient artifacts are already highly refined and clearly have origins that date back to much, much earlier. Many of these bows are also highly deflexed in shape. Stories and myths mention the prowess of the Scythians and Lydians and Persians with these recurve bows. Homer in Book XXI of the *Odyssey* describes the bow with which Odysseus performs the "Test of the Bow" and slaughters the suitors as a *double torsion* bow, meaning one that curved or bent in two directions, or, in other words, was recurved. Greek drawings of Odysseus depict just such a recurve bow. The nomadic warriors of Tamerlane and Genghis Khan came storming out of the steppes of Asia shooting short recurve bows from horseback. Their use was already an ancient tradition with them. The exact origins of the recurve bow are forever shrouded in the mists of antiquity.

The recurve design is sometimes referred to as the Turkish recurve bow, because of a remarkable little book written in Arabic by one Mustafa Kani at the instructions of Sultan Mahmud II in 1847. In it is described the use of composite recurve bows for *flight,* or distance, shooting by Turkish archers over a period of four centuries. Firearms were introduced as weapons of warfare in Constantinople in the middle of the fifteenth century, at the highest point of development of Turkish archery. From then until the middle of the nineteenth century *flight shooting* with the bow and arrow became a national sport. Kani discloses in considerable detail the practices of the archery guilds in Constantinople at the zenith of Turkish archery, including the design and construction of the short recurve flight bows by which the Turks were able to shoot distances now known to have been as far as *half a mile.* These are incredible distances by English longbow standards and claims of such feats were for a long time dismissed in the West, in spite of a number of eyewitness accounts of distances well over four hundred yards. The best English longbows, by comparison, are capable of shooting only a little more than two hundred yards, and even with the lightest arrows not much beyond three hundred yards.

Mustafa Kani's book was discovered and translated in the nineteenth century by a German scholar who unfortunately was not an archer and did not understand a number of key descriptions in the text. Nevertheless it was clear from his translation that flight shooting by Turkish archers was a highly refined art and an important form of archery. In the twentieth century this little treatise came to the attention of Dr. Paul Klopsteg, an American physicist and avid archer. Klopsteg was able to handle only moderate draw weights, and as a physicist he became interested in ways to achieve greater arrow speeds with lower draw weights. Klopsteg retranslated the text and was finally able to correctly understand and document the flight distances found recorded on small stone pillars, or markers, on the *ok meidan* or shooting fields in Constantinople. Anyone interested in Turkish archery would do well to start with Klopsteg's book, *Turkish Archery*, originally published in a limited edition in the 1930's and recently reissued (*Turkish Archery and the Composite Bow,* Paul E. Klopsteg, The Derrydale Press, 1992).

These remarkable distances have been equaled using modern recurve bows similar in configuration to those shot by Turkish archers. The author owns one such flight bow made in the 1960's by Harry Drake, one of the Deans of American flight shooting. This bow is only a little over three feet long but has a draw weight of sixty-five pounds at a draw length of about seventeen inches and has shot an eighteen inch flight arrow fashioned by arrowsmith Riley Denton of Tacoma, Washington a distance of 860 yards. It is no longer possible to insist, as proponents of the superiority of the English longbow once did, that the Turks could not have accomplished the feats commemorated by the ancient records. We now understand that they had a bow equal in cast, if not in durability and reliability, to those of modern archers. Even if they *hadn't* shot so far, they easily could have.

As a result of what we now know about Turkish archery we can see that *the shorter composite recurve bow with laminated limbs is every bit as much a part of the historical traditions of archery as the English longbow.* When archery was revived in this country in the latter part of the nineteenth century, it was using English longbows and following the specific traditions of English archery in general, representing of course the European heritage and bias of Americans. The traditions of English archery were well known and readily available as a resource for anyone seriously wishing to pursue archery. But eventually our natural curiosity and ingenuity took over and led to improvements in the traditional longbow, notably by flattening the limb cross section and shortening the overall length to produce the American flat or semi-flat bow. Subsequent innovations included using laminated limbs to take advantage of the different properties of various woods in compression and tension, adding rawhide and sinew to the back and front of the bow, shaping the limbs by deflexing, reflexing and recurving them, and eventually using fiberglass as the elastic material on the back and front of the limbs. Yet each of these innovations already existed in some form or another in the history and past traditions of archery.

The culmination of all of these steps was the modern recurve bow in its present form. This bow owes as much to the traditions of Turkish and earlier archery as it does to English archery. Those purists who want to limit traditional archery to wooden self bows, or to any particular technology and tradition to the exclusion of any other, are merely sticking their heads in the sand and overlooking what we know about the history and richness of archery traditions as a whole. The composite recurve bow is as ancient as the earliest European and English longbows. There is no reason to exclude either one or the other from the proper traditions of archery. Much the same can be said about the move to a *primitive archery* as distinct from *traditional archery*. There is no definitive way to distinguish a separate meaning to primitive archery that doesn't simply make it a subcategory of traditional archery. And there is no reason to. Traditional archery by its nature should be inclusive of all its history and traditions.

These Turkish recurve bows—and much earlier recurve bows—are examples of *composite bows* made by laminating together two or more materials, as distinct from *self bows* made from a single material. Composite bows are also often mistakenly thought of as a modern innovation, again because of the extreme degree of refinement and popularity of this design in the twentieth century.

Turkish flight bows were fabricated by gluing a thin strip of buffalo horn to the face of the bow and joining layers of sinew from animal tendons to the back, with maple from Anatolia sandwiched in between as the core of the limb, remarkably similar in concept to the modern composite limb made by laminating fiberglass and maple. The Turkish design was also technically sound. Buffalo horn is strongest in compression and serves best on the face of the limb. Sinew is good under tension, or stretching, and thus works best on the back of the limb even though it is inferior to buffalo horn which compares more favorably to fiberglass. Modern studies have shown that gluing sinew to the back of the limb contributes little to the elastic properties or draw weight of the bow, but serves mainly to protect the back surface of the limb and helps prevent it from fracturing under stress.

We find numerous other examples of composite construction among earlier bows. In fact the traditional English longbow made of yew, even though fashioned as a self bow from a single piece of wood, was nevertheless a sort of natural composite. The bow stave was split from the yew log with the dark-colored heartwood on the face of the stave and the lighter-colored sapwood on the back. Tests have shown that the heartwood is better in compression and the sapwood in tension, probably because those are the predominant stresses encountered by each in the growing tree to support its weight and resist bending in the wind. Whether this was just a coincidence associated with cleaving the stave from the sectioned log or was actually discovered by a process of trial and error is less certain. English longbows were commonly made with a layer of fiber or cloth or very thin vellum or sinew glued to the back to protect it from damage. This practice was also supposed to help prevent fibers in the back surface of the limb from raising up, or *fretting*, and causing a fractured limb. Primitive flat bows were also commonly backed with sinew. Ishi constructed his bows this way and demonstrated the process to Saxton Pope. Many such examples of sinew-backed primitive bows are evident in museum collections.

As an interesting aside, Ishi's preferred glue for applying the sinew was made by boiling skin from the roof of the mouth of salmon native to the streams where he lived in northern California. Klopsteg's study of Turkish archery revealed that their preferred glue was made by boiling skin from the roof of the mouth of sturgeon from the Black Sea. A remarkable similarity to be sure, but one perhaps that points up the crucial importance of glues in being able to make composite bows, and the necessity to experiment and refine them to the utmost. The single most important ingredient in being able to exploit the advantages of composite limbs is the glue holding everything together. Turkish bowyers were trying to shoot as far as possible. Their composite flight bows were drawn to the very threshold of breaking on every shot. Otherwise they were leaving precious yardage in the drawn bow. To exploit the elastic properties of buffalo horn the glue joints had to be strong enough not to fail first. In this regard Turkish bowyers discovered the limits of what was possible and pushed it to the utmost. For Ishi, making a bow was time consuming and a lot of hard work. He didn't want to have to do it very often. Once he glued it together he wanted it to stay that way, a stringent requirement given the damp rainy climate of northern California.

What we have said to this point about early bows pertains as well to arrows and the rest of the archer's equipment. The first arrow too was probably little more than a simple stick, though in this case one that was reasonably straight. It would have been easiest in the beginning to choose for arrow shafts something that grew thin and straight naturally, such as a stiff woody reed or piece of cane. If it was hollow and light as well as stiff, so much the better. In the absence of suitable reeds or cane, small thin branches could have been peeled and scraped smooth then hardened and straightened over a fire. Birch, willow, and alder branches among others can all be used to make serviceable arrows in this manner. Both kinds of materials grow worldwide.

Solid shafts sharpened to a point and hardened in a fire could have been used in the beginning to kill very small game. Stone tools made of chert and obsidian, and the technique of shaping them into thin sharp cutting edges by pressure flaking, called *flint knapping*, made it possible to tip arrows with points capable of killing much larger game. Many of the stone points found in museum collections weigh less than one hundred fifty grains and are entirely suitable as arrow points for even a medium draw-weight bow, even though many of them are labeled as spear points. Some of those identified as spear points may actually have been arrowheads, mislabeled by catalogers unfamiliar with archery and the capability of primitive bows. Hollow reeds or cane could have had a short length of solid shaft inserted into the end and bound by wrapping with fine cord or rawhide, either to be sharpened as a point or for attaching a separate stone point.

Fletching was undoubtedly a later improvement, yet one every bit as innovative as the invention of the bow itself. An arrow without fletching will fly reasonably straight for short distances, particularly if it is heavier on the front end and balances well forward of the middle. But adding fletching causes arrows very different in stiffness and balance to fly more nearly alike. Fletching constituted a major innovation in the use of the bow and arrow. Arrows that no amount of care and attention could cause to fly the same, so that each arrow had to be aimed and shot individually according to its own peculiarities, suddenly would all fly the same and could all be aimed and shot the same way. Whether the first fletching consisted of the flight feathers of birds or were merely thin vanes fashioned from the wide stiff leaves of plants we have no way of knowing. But at first, fletching probably consisted of two simple vanes of some material placed symmetrically on either side of the shaft and bound in place at each end by wrapping thin cord of plant or animal fibers or strips of rawhide around the shaft. That arrangement would have served perfectly well, and at least in the beginning there would have been no advantage in going beyond that degree of sophistication. We still find arrows with such fletching among primitive cultures. Arrows fletched this way will sometimes fly in a kind of corkscrew motion. Adding additional vanes takes care of the problem and that too would have been discovered in time.

Arrows would have been fitted to the string eventually by cutting a shallow notch, or *nock*, in the back end and tightly wrapping the shaft below it with thin cord or rawhide to prevent it from splitting under the impact of the string. Again in the case of hollow reeds or cane a short length of solid shaft could have been bound into the end of the arrow in which to cut the nock for additional strength and durability. The exact course followed by the development of archery in all of these matters is forever lost in the illiterate ages before writing. All we can be sure of is that it progressed gradually somehow to the point where we begin to find specific evidence in the historical record. Everything before that is speculation no matter how reasonable it may appear to us in retrospect.

Perhaps the simplest way to pull a bow is to grasp the nock of the arrow by pinching it firmly between the thumb and forefinger of the drawing hand. This manner of pulling the bow is termed the *primitive release*. Contact with Stone Age cultures in the rain forests of modern Brazil has shown them drawing and releasing their bows in just this fashion. This is a perfectly good way to shoot a light draw weight bow. In some ways in fact it is ideal. It is extremely simple and fast and gives a quick, clean release without deflecting the string either left or right. Given our fingers and opposable thumb it is the most natural way to pull the string back and it is the one most beginners try naturally to use at first. If you hand a bow to a child and it has the presence of mind to try to shoot it, this is usually the way it will grasp the arrow to pull the string back. This *pinch draw* or primitive release is facilitated by making the nock bigger than the shaft and flaring it toward the rear providing a larger tapered surface to grasp and hold on to. But it is very difficult to develop a grip strong enough to pull even a medium draw weight bow this way without having the string slip out of one's grasp. And it is totally unsuited to heavier draw weight bows.

It is far more reliable to wrap the ends of the first two or three fingers of the drawing hand *around* the string and pull it back using the bent fingers as a *hook* of sorts. With three fingers even the heaviest bows can be drawn without danger of losing one's grip on the string. Relaxing the fingers gives a sudden, clean release. This manner of drawing the bow is termed the *Mediterranean release* and its use was widespread by the time archery had spread throughout Europe. It has long been the accepted way of shooting the English longbow.

With the Mediterranean release the arrow is placed against the left side of the bow for a right-handed shooter. *Right-handed means that the string is pulled with the right hand while the bow is held in the left hand.* Since pointing and controlling the bow are crucial to aiming and hitting the target, it might be thought more natural for a right-handed person to hold the bow in the right hand and pull the string with the left hand. Right-handed individuals can learn to shoot in that fashion from the beginning just as readily as holding the bow in the left hand. For a right-handed shooter the string rolling off the tips of the fingers twists the string clockwise (viewed from the top of the bow) and pushes the arrow against the left side of the bow rather than away from it. For a left-handed shooter the opposite is true. The arrow is placed on the right side of the bow and the string twists counter-clockwise coming off the fingers of the left hand to push it against the right side of the bow.

An alternative method of drawing the bow is to hook the end of the thumb around the string and wrap the second finger of the drawing hand around the thumb to lock it in place. The first finger then rests on or alongside the arrow to hold it in place. This technique is termed the *Mongolian release* and its use was equally widespread, particularly throughout Asia and Asia Minor. There is no reason to assume that its use was not as widespread throughout much of the ancient world as the Mediterranean release. With it a moderately strong bow can be comfortably drawn without fear of losing one's grip on the string. Relaxing the thumb and second finger gives a clean quick release, with the added advantage that only the thumb has to come off the string rather than three fingers as with the Mediterranean release. The Mongolian release was used by Turkish archers, as described by Klopsteg, and it may have been the way Odysseus shot as well. Interestingly enough, Ishi drew his bow this way, perhaps pointing to the introduction of archery into North America from Asia across the Bering land bridge. In more recent times Chief Compton, who hunted and shot with Saxton Pope and Arthur Young, is reported to have used this type of release.

With the Mongolian release the arrow is placed against the right side of the bow for a right-handed shooter, just the opposite of the Mediterranean release. The string rolling off the thumb twists the string counter-clockwise, viewed from the top of the limb, and pushes the arrow against the right side of the bow. For a left-handed shooter the reverse of all of this is true. This practice explains Pope's photos of Ishi, squatting, shooting his bow held out in front of him, the arrow on the right side of the bow with the upper limb canted sharply to the *left*, rather than to the right as would be natural with the Mediterranean release.

The Mongolian release also has the potential of functioning somewhat like a triggered release similar in principle to the non mechanical releases used today. The thumb hooked around the string can be relaxed and held in place by the second finger locked over the end of it much like having the ledge of a hand-held release hooked over the string. Instead of twisting or torquing the release off the string, the thumb could be flipped out from under the finger to trigger the shot.

To prevent injury to the fingers or thumb by the string, it is customary to wear some form of protection, though early archers might not have done so. With the Mediterranean release this is generally a leather *shooting glove* made of individual finger stalls that surround the tips of the fingers, joined together by a strap fastened around the wrist; or a thin leather pad or *finger tab* secured to the fingers and placed between the fingers and the string. With the Mongolian release it is customary to wear a solid *thumb ring* against which the string rests. Its use in Turkish archery is described by Klopsteg and was probably typical of its use elsewhere. Early thumb rings were carved from horn or bone with a hole in the center for insertion of the thumb. A leather band or stall around the thumb would undoubtedly work too.

At present in traditional archery the Mediterranean release is used almost exclusively. The author knows no one who shoots with the Mongolian release, nor has he ever encountered anyone using it as the primary method of shooting. The reason is partly because of our European traditions and partly, I think, because the Mediterranean release feels far more natural to the beginner. With three fingers it is easier and more comfortable to pull a heavy bow than with the thumb alone. That said, the Mongolian release using a thumb ring to hold the string resembles the hand-held releases commonly used in non-traditional archery and is a perfectly good way to draw and release the string. The use of non-triggered mechanical releases is a legitimate part of traditional archery for anyone wanting to shoot that way. They are not in any fundamental way different from the use of thumb rings and are therefore an ancient part of archery traditions. There are also many possible variations in the Mediterranean release, depending on how many fingers are used and how they are placed above and below the arrow. The usual configurations are one finger above and one or two below, or two or three fingers below, but any combination can be used.

Finally, an *arm guard* or *bracer* of some sort, worn on the inside of the bow arm to protect it from the painful slap of the string, and a *quiver* or other receptacle in which to carry arrows complete the essential tackle of traditional archery. The earliest quivers were probably made of animal skins or perhaps a section of hollow cane and were worn at the waist or across the shoulder for easy access in order to be able to quickly nock and shoot an arrow. All sorts of variations are possible.

All that was really essential for the earliest archers were a strung bow and adequate arrows to shoot. Everything else was optional and represents subsequent innovations and refinements to aid in the art of shooting the bow and arrow.

This then is the essential background out of which the traditional archery of today emerged. From thick-limbed bows strong enough to propel a heavy arrow and long enough to be drawn the full length of the traditional twenty-seven inch *cloth-yard* shaft evolved the English longbow, the historic prototype of modern longbows. The recent discovery of the "Ice Man," entombed in a glacier in the Alps some 5,000 years ago, reveals that the basic features of the longbow are very old. The Ice Man carried with him an almost completed bow made of yew and otherwise closely resembling the more modern English longbow. He also carried in his shoulder an arrow wound attesting to one of the earliest uses of such weapons. A recent photograph of a previously undiscovered tribe in the Brazilian rainforest shows the surprised natives menacingly pointing their bows and arrows upward at the helicopter hovering overhead. Their bows, interestingly enough, are quite long. It is clear from their immediate instinctive actions that they consider them weapons to be used against other human beings. From thinner-limbed bows that could be made shorter without breaking evolved the American flat bow. Examples of short flat-limbed bows are found among primitive cultures everywhere. Both types can be made as self bows or with composite limbs, and both can be either deflexed, reflexed, or any combination of the two.

From these innovations a third type evolved, the recurve bow, with limbs progressively reflexed near the tips. Self bows can be recurved by suitably heating, bending, and shaping the limb tips. But recurved limbs are generally constructed as composite laminations glued together, and are normally thin and flat in shape for ease and simplicity of construction, and wide to prevent twisting as the limb bends. Composite recurve bows are likewise a very ancient design and date back to long before the beginnings of history. For early bowyers they were much more difficult and technically challenging to construct. Their development at all is a tribute to human ingenuity and an indication of the significant role that archery must have played in these cultures.

To the newcomer to traditional archery it must almost seem at times that the bow and arrow are practically American inventions, so great have been the changes introduced into archery in the twentieth century by innovations made by bowyers and arrow makers in this country. In the first half of the 1900's engineers and physicists turned their attention to the bow and arrow and began to look for ways to improve performance. They modeled and measured the efficiency of the bow in storing and imparting energy and momentum to the arrow. And they analyzed those aspects of the design and construction of bows and bow limbs that limited things like the velocity, kinetic energy, and momentum of the arrow, the efficiency of bow limbs, and the reproducibility and consistency of bow performance. They analyzed stresses and strains in bow limbs and determined the optimum cross-sectional shape for limb design. And they analyzed and studied the flight of arrows. Out of these studies came innovations like the rectangular cross section of the American flat bow, recurved composite limbs of wood and fiberglass, and more uniform wooden and aluminum and fiberglass arrows. Among the principle pioneers in this effort were Paul E. Klopsteg, C. N. Hickman and F. Nagler.

A number of these pioneering studies were collected and reprinted in a book published originally in a limited edition of several hundred copies and recently reissued (*Archery: The Technical Side*, edited by C.N. Hickman, Forest Nagler, Paul E. Klopsteg, The Derrydale Press, 1992). Anyone wanting to read a more detailed treatment of these topics would do well to refer to this compilation of their studies. This was a landmark work in promoting interest in the technical aspects of archery. And it led to a spurt of activity among bowyers and archery manufacturers in the 1950's and 1960's to build new designs and make the most recent innovations more widely available to archers, as a result greatly stimulating interest in archery in this country. That interest quickly spread worldwide and today evidence of it can be seen in international competitions in target and field archery and in the Olympic Games where archery is now a regular event participated in by archers from all over the world.

We mention these things at the outset because most of the principles of traditional archery can be understood in terms of the evolution of present day bows and arrows from earlier forms. To get at these principles we are going to examine in more detail the simple technical reasons behind the choices made and the various directions taken in the design and fabrication of traditional bows and arrows. We will discuss these not in terms of the actual historical development but in terms of modern technology and present-day understanding. The detailed history of the bow and arrow except in more recent times cannot be reconstructed. Nor would doing so provide any special insight. *The way to understand traditional archery today is by examining the basic principles that govern the function of the bow and the arrow and by understanding how that function relates to the design of each and the materials out of which they are constructed.* That is what we have set out to do here.

No mention of archery traditions could be complete without acknowledging the special impact that several works and individuals in particular had on the popularity and subsequent growth of archery in this country. *The Witchery of Archery*, from which the epigram for this book was taken, was first published by Scribner in 1877 and consisted of a collection of stories and articles about archery and hunting with the bow and arrow, written by Maurice Thompson and published in various magazines. There had never been anything like it in the sporting literature. As Dr. Robert P. Elmer said in his "Introduction" to a subsequent edition published in 1928 and recently reissued (*The Witchery of Archery*, J. Maurice Thompson, The Archer's Company, Pinehurst Edition, 1928; The Derrydale Press, 1992), "The sport of archery, as we have it in America, practically owes its existence to the first edition of this book."

Maurice and his brother Will fought in the Civil War in the Confederate army and Maurice was shot in the chest and severely wounded at the battle of Cold Harbor in 1864. At the end of the war they returned home to the Cherokee Valley of Georgia to find their plantation in ruins and themselves greatly reduced in circumstances. For a period of several years, partly as a way to restore Maurice's health, they took to the outdoors where they subsisted partially by hunting with the bow and arrow. As boys they had made bows and arrows and learned to use them after a fashion. But as youths they had the good fortune to be correctly schooled in the standard techniques of English archery by a reclusive hermit named Thomas Williams who lived nearby, and they outfitted themselves with the proper implements of the sport. The stories of their hunting adventures with bow and arrow became the subject of magazine articles that Maurice wrote. Later editions of *The Witchery of Archery* also include one story about the same period written years afterward by Will Thompson. Together they hunted along the St. John's River and in the Everglades and Okefinokee Swamp. Both brothers were poets by nature and gifted writers, and the lyrical passages of their accounts remain as haunting and passionate today as when they were first written. It would be hard to imagine anyone falling under their spell and charm and not becoming enchanted by the "witchery of archery." Maurice became a naturalist and a novelist and served for a period as state geologist of Indiana, residing in Crawfordsville. He died in 1901. Will became an attorney and worked eventually for the railroads in the Pacific Northwest. Maurice was one of the founders and the first president of the National Archery Association in 1878; and Will won the first ever national archery championship in 1879 and four times thereafter, in 1884, 1888, 1901, and 1908. He competed a total of eighteen times. Will died in 1922.

In 1911 in northern California the last known Yana Indian untouched by civilization except for the decimation and disappearance of all of his people was discovered huddled and emaciated in a corral on the outskirts of Oroville. Befriended by the anthropologist T. T. Watterman, Ishi, as he referred to himself, went to live at the University of California Museum of Anthropology in San Francisco. He remained there for five years before finally succumbing to tuberculosis. He spent his time cheerfully working and teaching the museum staff about his history, his language, and his culture. During that time, Saxton Pope, a professor of surgery at the medical college, became Ishi's personal physician and close friend and admirer.

Ishi instructed Pope in the techniques of Yana archery and the making of bows and arrows, as well as Yana lore associated with each. As a result Pope became fascinated and interested in archery more broadly and went on to master the techniques of English archery and the making and use of the English longbow and arrows. Together with a few companions they returned to the Mount Lassen area where Ishi had spent most of his life undetected by the surrounding civilization, and there Ishi instructed Pope and his companions in the art of hunting with the bow and arrow. Saxton Pope along with Arthur Young and Chief Compton went on to further exploits with the bow and arrow, among them taking deer, mountain lion, black bear; grizzly bears in Yellowstone Park; moose, bighorn sheep and Kodiak grizzlies in Alaska; and even lions and other game in Africa. In 1923 Pope wrote a book on archery and hunting with the bow and arrow (*Hunting with the Bow and Arrow*, Saxton Pope, G.P. Putnam's Sons, 1923; The Derrydale Press, 1992) in which he told the story of Ishi and Yana archery, provided instructions on how to make and use bows and arrows, and recorded some of his hunting experiences. Pope had a fanciful, romantic turn of mind, and phrase, and this book quickly became a classic and was the inspiration for the continued growth of archery and the subsequent flourishing of hunting with the bow and arrow in America.

The first widely acclaimed "professional" archer in America was a young man from Alabama named Howard Hill, who began shooting the bow at age four and who after winning varsity letters in athletics at Auburn University pursued a career promoting archery and hunting with the bow and arrow. He became a trick shot artist giving public exhibitions and making feature films about shooting and hunting with the bow and arrow. His impressive skills and pinpoint accuracy with the bow, especially at close distances, captured the imagination of audiences who saw him perform, many of whom had never seen the bow shot before and were quite unprepared for the capabilities of this ancient implement in the hands of one as adept as Hill. He also captured the public imagination because he was physically powerful and routinely shot bows of 90 to 110 pounds draw weight. He is credited with having pulled the strongest bow on record, one of 175 pounds draw weight. He is also credited with having won 196 field archery tournaments without losing a single one. His two landmark books about hunting with the bow and arrow (*Hunting the Hard Way*, Wilcox and Follet, 1953; The Derrydale Press, 2000; and *Wild Adventure*, Stackpole Books, 1954; The Derrydale Press, 2000) were influential in shaping and keeping alive interest in traditional archery, especially among those hunting with the bow and arrow.

# What Is Traditional Archery?

*Or rather, what should it be? Formulating an answer to present a clearer choice and guidelines.*

**B**efore proceeding any further, let's start by being clear what we mean by *traditional archery*. There are lots of differing opinions about the proper answer to this question and some of them are divisive, or exclusive, in ways that are not in the best interest of traditional archery or the sport of archery in general. Unfortunately there is no universally agreed upon view of what should or should not be included as part of traditional archery. It depends somewhat on one's view of which archery tradition is meant or intended. For that reason, we tried to broadly sketch the basic elements of that tradition in the previous chapter. There is still ample room for discussing this question and coming up with some more reasonable and acceptable guidelines to what constitutes traditional archery. It isn't essential to do that of course. The alternative is that there will be several, even many, different versions of traditional archery. But part of understanding the principles of traditional archery is understanding what exactly those principles pertain to. And so we need to briefly outline what we will mean here by traditional archery.

Traditional archery is the broad all-encompassing term that has come to describe a sport based on the exclusive use of traditional bows. The discussion in "Beginnings" makes clear that traditional bows encompass a wide variety of types and design features. Fortunately, however, all of these various types have a common universal characteristic.

By a *traditional bow* we mean *one that has limbs made of elastic materials held bent and drawn by a string, and that stores energy and derives the force by which the string propels the arrow entirely from the elastic bending of the limbs, and not from the action of pulleys or eccentric cams.* Compound bows, in other words, are excluded.

So far, so good. We have said nothing here that would exclude any of the accepted ideas about what traditional archery should include. If it were up to me alone, I would draw the line right there, in the best interests of traditional archery and the best interests of archery in general. The basic distinction is between *traditional bows* and so-called *compound bows*. The latter are not truly bows at all in the traditional sense but instead are a modern form of ballistas and catapults and other types of hurling machines that employed various kinds of mechanical advantage and which have been in use from early historic times. Traditional bows store energy and propel the arrow solely by the elastic properties of the bent limbs, without the use of any mechanical advantage derived from the action of rotating cams or pulleys. Compound bows use rotating cams to obtain a mechanical advantage in bending the limb, thereby storing more energy for the same draw weight and draw length; or put another way, storing the same amount of energy at a significantly reduced final draw weight. In their more extreme form compound bows are more closely akin to crossbows than to traditional bows, the main distinction being one is mounted in a gun stock while the other is hand-held.

This kind of broad definition of traditional archery does two important things. *It makes the advent and adoption of the compound bow in the 1960's a defining moment in the history of archery. And it establishes the idea of drawing boundaries around traditional archery and placing limits on the technological innovations that are going to be included.*

This latter point is perhaps the more important one, for who can foresee what new inventions lie ahead? I recall a college conversation I had with Al Slade many years ago about how one might improve the performance of the bow. I responded by sketching a proposed curve showing how the force required to pull the bow initially increased as the bow was drawn and then at some point peaked and decreased as the bow was drawn farther. The potential advantages of such a bow were readily apparent. I had in mind some conceivable way to achieve this with traditional elastic limbs by shaping the limbs and riser section of the bow. (Unknown to me at the time such a possible scheme had been patented in 1935 by C. N. Hickman.) Little could I imagine that almost at the same moment someone else was achieving exactly the same result with pulleys and cams mounted to the limbs of a traditional bow. Who knows what conversations are taking place still and what new ideas will come along in the future.

Beyond that, the adherents to traditional archery (may their number increase) seem to agree on little else. Everyone acknowledges the distinction between traditional bows and compound bows that use pulleys and eccentric cams to store energy and shape the force required to draw the bow. "*Stick bow*" has become the term commonly used to describe traditional bows, namely a bow that is basically a bent stick in contrast to compound bows. But spend even a little time reading any of the traditional archery magazines or books and you quickly conclude that there are many different and often strangely conflicting ideas about what should or should not be included as part of traditional archery. And many of these contrary ideas are in conflict with the actual historical traditions of archery and are based more on ignorance than substance.

There are so-called traditional archery tournaments that exclude the use of clickers or other draw-checks; any kind of sight mounted on the bow; peep sights attached to the string; arrow rests other than an arrow shelf cut into the side of the bow; all arrows except wooden arrows; recurve bows or any bow other than a longbow (although I have yet to see an exclusive definition of a longbow that makes any sense or withstands close scrutiny); plastic vanes or any fletching material other than feathers; thumb rings and all other forms of hand-held non mechanical release devices; the list goes on and on. One can find other "traditional" archery tournaments where one or more of these banned items are allowed but others are not. In fact it seems possible to find almost any combination of excluded and allowed items, all purporting to represent "traditional archery."

The result of all this is a gradual splintering of traditional archery into more and more factions. Many of the exclusions make no sense at all and are just plain silly and arbitrary because they are not based on any kind of coherent rationale or underlying vision of what traditional archery is, or should be. Some of the things excluded have been part of archery traditions for centuries, as pointed out in the discussion of the previous chapter. Others make sense but the reasons for them become obscured in the maze of arbitrary choices about what is and is not to be allowed.

Clearly what is needed are a few guiding principles that express the underlying philosophy of traditional archery and that can serve as the basis for thinking about the sport and making choices about equipment. It is far better to choose beforehand than always be at the mercy of whatever happens to come along to take the sport in unwanted, or unintended, directions.

Although it is the obvious first step, *the restriction to traditional bows, that is, the exclusion of compound bows, by itself, is not enough.* There are many different kinds of traditional bows based on various shapes and materials and construction. There are straight bows and recurve bows, along with deflexed and reflexed combinations of each, and everything in between; bows with self limbs made of a single material like wood, and bows with composite limbs made of combinations of materials like wood and fiberglass and carbon composites; one-piece bows, and two-piece and three-piece take-down models; center-shot bows with the sight window cut past the center line of the bow, and those with no sight window or arrow shelf; and endless variations and combinations of these and other design features. Under the broad definition all of these are properly traditional bows. All of them derive the force by which the string propels the arrow solely from the bending of the elastic materials in the limbs. And all of these designs can be found somewhere in the long-standing traditions of archery. Restricting the bow itself does nothing to address questions about the other parts of the archer's tackle and about the various methods of shooting. To address all of these things there has to be some underlying vision or guiding principle of what traditional archery is trying to achieve. That is the question to which we want to turn next.

*The fundamental act of archery is shooting the bow.* That and that alone is the main point of the sport. The equipment is secondary. The archer and the athletic challenge of shooting a bow well are what are central to the sport: the strength and skill of the archer pitted against the physical challenges and demands of shooting a bow. The sport is ever diminished by always adopting technological solutions to the problems encountered in the archer's quest to shoot the bow well. Substituting technology for skill demeans the sport and transforms what should be an athletic feat into one of endless technology and gadgetry.

*The aim of traditional archery should be to keep the emphasis on the archer and the athletic nature of archery, not on technology.* This attitude seems to express the underlying motivation and intent behind the move to a traditional archery.

It is important to emphasize that this attitude is not anti-technology. *It merely seeks to choose technology that enhances the sport without replacing the skill of the archer and the focus on the athletic challenge of shooting a bow.* It is also important to emphasize that as a guiding principle it is far from clear-cut. It is not a formula. Human judgment is required to interpret it in each instance and to guide the choices that have to be made as new technology and innovations come along. These choices are always negotiable as a matter of judgment. Such an attitude is certainly in keeping with the restriction to traditional bows and the exclusion of compound bows.

How might we apply this principle to questions that go beyond the restriction to traditional bows? A good example might be the materials allowed in the design and construction of the bow. Improvements like better composite materials and improved glues for the limbs and better string materials should always be allowed. They improve the performance and life of the bow without significantly diminishing the skill required on the part of the archer. Improvements in the elastic properties of limb materials have been part of the traditions of archery from the very beginning to the present. Composite bows of horn and wood and sinew go back to the ancient Greeks and Persians and even earlier. They are mentioned by Homer in the *Iliad* and the *Odyssey*. Their use in Turkish archery had already reached a high degree of development and perfection at least as early as the fifteenth century, as documented by Paul Klopsteg in his book *Turkish Archery*. To achieve that level of sophistication they had to be already in use much, much earlier.

Improvements in arrow materials should likewise be allowed. Anything that makes all of the arrows the same and removes variations from arrow to arrow enhances the sport without in any way diminishing the skill required by the archer. Improvements in arrows actually highlight the ability of the archer since they remove one of the variables that can mask and obscure the archer's skill. It is equally true that beyond a certain point further improvements can become irrelevant. Once arrows achieve a certain degree of uniformity in straightness, spine, and weight, other variables of shooting become more important in limiting the minimum size of arrow groups. At that point it no longer makes any sense to strive for further improvements in arrow uniformity or to prohibit them. But this sort of thing takes care of itself without any need to meddle. Once further improvements don't lead to better shooting, they become irrelevant and no harm is done by allowing them. The archer's athletic ability remains the determining and limiting factor in the sport.

All innovations that are strictly improvements in materials technology should be allowed into the sport, no matter what part of the archer's equipment they affect, *if they enhance the sport by improving equipment without diminishing the importance of the archer's skill.* It is hard to conceive of an improvement in materials that would *not* be allowed under this criterion.

Mechanically triggered releases on the other hand should probably not be allowed for the same reason. Shooting a bow is a task relying on fine muscle and hand-eye coordination. Shooting the bow by pulling it back and releasing the string with the fingers of the drawing hand is an integral part of the task of coordinating muscles and eyes and brain. The mechanically triggered release offers a technological way of subverting the athletic challenge of that part of shooting a bow. By the same argument, one-piece non-triggered releases might be allowed since their use requires the same skills as that of shooting the bow with fingers. Such releases go way back and were part of Turkish archery in the form of the thumb ring, which functioned in basically the same manner as the present day non mechanical release. This is an area where judgment begins to take over. There are grounds for reasonable people to disagree and room for discussion in order to make those judgments.

Fixed sights should be allowed, since there is no effective way of preventing them from being made an integral part of the bow itself. Colored inlays and shapes built right into the sight window or the face of the bow can serve in effect as a fixed sight. A fixed sight can be as simple as a set of easily visible marks on the face of the bow. Adjustable sights should also be allowed unless there is absolutely no way of knowing the distance to the target. That never happens in essence, since the estimation of distance to the nearest yard or so is a skill that can always be acquired through practice. Once the range is known there is any number of ways of shooting that are equivalent to using a sight. Point of aim, string-walking and gap shooting are all the same in principle as using a sight, once the distance to the target is known or can be closely estimated. Purely instinctive, point-and-shoot aiming is possible, but it is impossible to impose by rule. Anyone who has shot a bow realizes this. The only form of purely instinctive shooting possible occurs when one is first learning to shoot. After that, experience inevitably influences how one aims the arrow at the target, and if it is based on experience it cannot be purely instinctive.

Clickers should be allowed since they enhance the sport by enabling the archer to overcome the problems of aiming and premature release without diminishing the degree of skill required, as anyone who has ever tried to master the use of a clicker soon realizes. In addition, the clicker teaches the fundamental elements of making a good shot. The inability to aim and hold on the target before releasing is perhaps the most serious threat that the sport faces in retaining new archers once they have developed a level of proficiency where this condition begins to show up. It as much as anything probably led to the rapid decline and almost total demise of archery after the boom of the mid 1950's, once all of those thousands of newly-recruited archers began to encounter the problem and found that it quickly destroyed all enjoyment of the sport and turned shooting into a perpetual nightmare of frustration. Banning the clicker is extremely shortsighted and indicates a woeful lack of understanding about what is involved in learning to execute a shot properly. The invention of the clicker is one of the most significant innovations in the recent history of the sport and should be awarded the archery Nobel Prize if there were one. It is certainly as significant as the mechanical release in non traditional archery, with which it has elements in common. If nothing else, the clicker has done more than any other innovation to make us think more deeply about the technique of shooting the bow properly, and for that it should be included as part of traditional archery.

Whether to allow other innovations, such as peep sights in the string, bubble levels on the bow, bow stabilizers, and how long and how many, are all things that have to be ultimately decided. Stabilizers are difficult to prohibit since they can be fabricated as an integral part of the bow, as they were in many cases when they were first introduced. Go back and look at some of the bows produced in the 1950's and 1960's. Off-center weights designed into the structure of the handle and riser were a common feature as their advantage in stabilizing the bow became apparent. There was at least one popular bow that had vials of mercury built right into the limb roots of the riser section for extra stabilizing weight that also acted as a shock absorber by breaking up into droplets and dissipating recoil energy. Peep sights and bubble levels represent very marginal advantages to anyone using them. Allowing or excluding them would be of minimal consequence either way. And for that reason, for inclusiveness if nothing else, they might easily be allowed.

Similarly, the question of separate categories of shooters and how many categories to have and how to define them are all matters about which there should be continuing discussion and judgment. The guiding principle should be keeping the sport as simple and unencumbered as possible. That means as few separate divisions and rules as make sense. A *freestyle* category that allows everything including adjustable sights, and a *limited* category that excludes sights but allows everything else might conceivably be enough. Or at the most only a couple of *limited* categories. Shooters in each category could then decide which of the allowed equipment they want to use.

Much of the present preoccupation with banning one thing or another from traditional archery grows out of an almost obsessive concern about making sure that no one gains any advantage over anyone else. Rather than just enjoying shooting the bow, the focus shifts to a mild paranoia over whether anyone has gained an edge over everyone else. *The real concern should be keeping the emphasis on the athletic challenge of shooting a bow, while excluding as few innovations as consistent with that aim.* Perhaps the emphasis on scores and tournaments is partly at fault. Archery is by nature an individual endeavor. The archer competes against himself and his own limitations. The object is to choose some type of equipment and learn to shoot it as well as it can be shot. If that becomes no longer satisfying then choose other equipment capable of greater precision and learn to shoot to its limits. Removing equipment limitations that obscure or hinder the athletic ability of the archer is in the best long-term interests of the sport and makes it more inclusive and welcoming to shooters. Whatever is settled on, it should all be embraced as part of traditional archery so long as it maintains the emphasis on the skill of the archer and the athletic nature of shooting a bow.

# The Bow

*An introduction to some of the physical principles that determine the design and performance of the bow.*

*I*n the first chapter we have traced some of the early practical considerations that probably helped shape the various directions taken by the bow in its evolution. There the purpose was mainly to identify and call attention to the different types of characteristics found in modern traditional bows. Now we want to go into these, and others, in more detail in order to better understand how specific design features affect performance. In the process we may repeat parts of some things we have already mentioned but our purpose here in doing so will be different. Besides, repetition is an effective way of reinforcing in another context what we have already said.

Before getting carried away with the technical aspects of bow design we should put this topic in some kind of practical context. The different types of traditional bows are far more alike in overall performance than they are different. As one measure of what we mean, even the least efficient bow of moderate draw weight will shoot a suitably matched arrow around 150 feet per second or better. And the most efficient design possible will not exceed a little over 200 feet per second. Almost all traditional bows of interest lie somewhere within this range. No amount of tweaking the design of the bow is going to achieve higher performance; nor should any acceptable design fall below these levels. The reason is straightforward. These values represent the practical limits of materials from which to fashion the limbs and the practical limits of the physics involved in limb design. The one exception is flight bows. These specialized designs can achieve arrow velocities of 300-400 feet per second with extremely light arrows made stiff enough by keeping them short. But these are not practical bows for most purposes, unless that single purpose is to see how far one can shoot without regard to accuracy, consistency, and the like. Of course there are other ways besides arrow velocity to characterize bow performance: things like stability, accuracy, smoothness of draw, ease of shooting, recoil, aiming, physical weight, and any number of others. But in all of these, the different types of traditional bows exhibit far more similarities than differences.

The main point being that there is not a lot of latitude in changing bow performance by design choices. The most so-so design will achieve about 150 feet per second, and the most optimum will not go much above 200 feet per second with the same arrows. Arrow velocity is an important measure of performance, in fact the most important, other things being comparable. Yet as a practical matter we cannot vary it by more than about thirty percent. And other things are never comparable. By the time we trade-off speed with other performance characteristics we end up having even less latitude over arrow velocity.

None of this is any reason not to be interested in bow design and performance. Only by understanding how physical characteristics affect performance can we understand the relative merits of the various types of traditional bows. There are bowyers today building very good bows who have no real understanding of what makes their designs good. As a result they have no idea how to change them to make an even better bow. There are other bowyers who tout a particular design feature or advantage that is either irrelevant or unimportant, or that in some cases actually *detracts* from the overall performance of their bows. Bowyers sometimes incorporate questionable or counter-productive features simply to satisfy some mistaken or misguided whim of their customers. Every serious archer should have at least some basic understanding of what goes into a good design and what the design trade-offs are.

At the same time not everyone is a physicist, or wants to be. So I have avoided any use of mathematics (though not numbers) in these explanations. That requires a bit of trust in accepting the conclusions (and the numbers) when the physics behind them may not be evident to the reader. This is especially true in several instances where the conclusions seem at first counter-intuitive. An excellent example is the important fact that a bow always imparts *more kinetic energy and more momentum* to a heavier arrow than to a lighter one.

As the mass of the arrow increases its velocity decreases, *but its kinetic energy and momentum both increase*. We shall in time see why. I try always to give an understandable physical argument, even to the point of belaboring the matter in those instances where the concept is especially important. But at times some readers will have to accept the conclusions even when they do not follow the reasons. I assure you that nowhere do I knowingly make assertions that are not physically justified. When I cannot be certain, I try to err on the side of caution and steer clear of questionable conclusions.

Bow design divides quite naturally into two categories. *The first concerns the properties of the materials from which the limbs are fashioned. And the second concerns the actual shape of the bow and limbs.*

These are the two basic choices one has to face in designing or selecting any bow. Innovations in each were undoubtedly ongoing right from the very beginning. The first bows would have been fashioned as simply and with as little effort as possible. The limbs were likely round in cross section, just the way the branch or sapling from which it was fashioned grew. A bow like this must be fairly long if it is to be drawn very far without breaking. If the cross section is uniform along its length so that the limbs are the same thickness throughout, the bow will bend too much in the middle and not enough nearer the ends. Probably the first innovation was simply to taper the limbs toward the tips to achieve more uniform bending of the bow along its entire length, allowing it to be pulled farther without breaking in the middle. If shot in the most natural manner, by holding the bow arm fully extended and drawing the string all the way back to the face or head to sight along the arrow, the bow would have been at least five or six feet in length. This is also the manner of shooting that allows the archer to pull a stronger bow. If shorter, then it would have been drawn not as far by holding it out in front of the body and pulling to a point well in front of the face to sight along the arrow. This was the manner employed by Ishi in shooting his bow.

Discovering which materials, as well as which shapes, make the best bows would have been among the earliest innovations, a search that has continued right down to the present moment. Archery flourished where there were natural materials available that made superior bows. Thus the English adopted yew as the wood of choice for their longbows. The Ottoman Turks used maple from Anatolia in combination with horn and sinew to build their composite recurve bows. The North American Indians found that hickory, ash, osage orange, and native yew all made good bows. One of the names given to osage orange was bois d'arc, or wood of the bow. Following the growth of archery in this country in the late 1800's, lemonwood, or dagame, from Cuba and split bamboo were added to the list. Many different kinds of wood have been used somewhere at one time or another to fashion usable bows and many are still in use today. In more modern times laminations of composite materials like fiberglass and carbon filaments have been combined with various woods to make improved bows and to make more attractive and beautiful limbs. Recently, limbs constructed from syntactic foam cores laminated with fiberglass and carbon composites have been introduced. These limbs have superior performance qualities And in the future still better elastic materials will be incorporated in building even more improved bows. This is still a fruitful area for further refinement and improvement.

When a bow bends, the front, or *face*, of the limb—the portion closest to the archer—is shortened or compressed, and the *back* of the limb is stretched. This is because the back, being farther from the string, bends along a slightly longer curve, one with a greater radius of curvature, than the face of the limb. Somewhere in between the front and back surfaces is a neutral zone where the transition from compression to stretching occurs and where the limb material is nearly stress free. For a symmetrical cross section, like a circle or an oval, the neutral zone is located on the *axis of symmetry* between front and back. The farther from the neutral zone, the greater are the forces of compression and tension in the material. The maximum forces occur at the front and back surfaces of the limb.

The thicker the limb the more the front is compressed and the back is stretched and the greater the forces at the front and back surfaces. If the limb is round in cross section the amount of elastic material is least just where the forces of compression and tension are highest, and the material will usually fracture there first and cause the limb to fail. In addition, a round cross section puts more of the limb material closer to the neutral zone where the forces of compression and tension are the least and where it does not contribute as much to the elastic forces that give the bow its draw weight and propel the arrow. For this reason a circular cross section is just about the worst shape possible, even though it may be the easiest and most convenient from the standpoint of using wood in its naturally occurring form. A bow with a round cross section must be relatively long to keep the front and back of the limb below the fracture limit. The stronger the bow the thicker the limb and the longer it has to be to prevent breaking. It is for this reason that the English longbow was typically six feet or more in length for moderate to heavy draw weights.

A round limb is thus the wrong shape entirely and early bowyers would soon have discovered that a bow could be safely drawn farther by flattening the limb on either the face or the back, or both. Thus we find that the back of the limb is flattened on an English longbow and that most of the shorter primitive bows had limbs with distinctly flattened oval cross sections, tapering in both width and thickness from the base of the limbs to the tips. Ishi's bow was of this shape, as were the short bows made by many of the North American Indians. An account of some primitive and early bows and arrows can be found in a study done by Saxton Pope (*Bows and Arrows*, Saxton T. Pope, University of California Press, 1974).

The English longbow adopted an oval cross section, but one with the back of the limb flattened much more than the face or belly which is prominently rounded. The result is a cross section that is a very unsymmetrical oval. This shape corresponds to making the bow out of a wedge- or pie-shaped billet split from the length of a yew log, with the back surface of the limb following the natural curvature of the growth rings of the tree, and the front or belly of the limb following the slope of the wedge rounded at the sides and front. The flattened back of an English longbow is sapwood from the outer portion of the log while the rounded front of the limb is heartwood from nearer the center. Although a decided improvement over a round limb, this shape is still not a particularly good one and the reason is instructive.

For an unsymmetrical cross section, the stress-free neutral zone is located on the *center of mass* of the limb. This means that for the English longbow the neutral zone is not at the center of the limb but is displaced toward the back surface where the center of mass is located. The compressive and tensile stresses at any point in the limb are proportional to how far from the neutral zone that point is located. Thus the compressive forces in the belly of an English longbow are greater than the tensile forces in the back of the limb. However wood is stronger in tension than in compression, and consequently the shape of the English longbow is just exactly backwards. The front of the limb is the side that should be the more flattened one. Why no one ever tried turning the shape around to make a better bow is hard to say, except that once tradition becomes established it is never easy to change and blindly goes its merry way, oblivious and heedless of knowledge or reason. The sapwood of yew is slightly stronger in tension and heartwood is slightly stronger in compression, so at least that part of the arrangement was in the right direction.

A much better shape would be a circle flattened on both the front and the back, or in other words something like a symmetrical oval with the long axis of symmetry along the width of the limb. But even that is not optimum since it still locates the smallest amount of material at the point of maximum stress at the curved front and back surfaces. A better shape still is a flat rectangular cross section. The limbs can be made wide enough to achieve the desired draw weight while keeping them thin enough to minimize the stresses in a relatively short bow. This is precisely the shape arrived at in the design of bows in this country in the early twentieth century. This is the cross-sectional shape of the American flat bow which carried to its logical conclusion the oval, or semi-flat, cross section of many primitive bow limbs and which subsequently became the basis for further improvements in limb design.

You may have figured out by now that the truly optimum shape is a trapezoidal cross section, with the front of the limb wider than the back. The stress-free neutral zone goes through the center of mass which is now located closer to the front of the limb. That means the compressive forces in the belly of the limb will be less than the tensile forces in the back, thereby taking proper advantage of the greater strength of wood under tension than under compression. In strictly practical terms however there is really no significant advantage to a trapezoidal cross section over a rectangular one if the limb is thin enough, though either is decidedly superior to an oval shape.

So far we have been talking about bows made of a single material, or self bows. We have also been talking about bows with limbs that are straight in the unstrung or unbraced condition. Straight-limbed self bows are the simplest and most basic and undoubtedly came first in the early development of archery. The prowess and effectiveness of the English longbow as a hunting and military weapon is adequate testimony to what can be accomplished with self bows. Since it is the simplest shape, the straight self bow can teach us a great deal about the kinds of technical limitations that are inherent in the design of a traditional bow. In traditional archery today there are those who still elect to shoot self bows made of various woods, particularly yew, osage orange, and bamboo, all of which can be used to make an excellent self bow. The challenge of the bowyer's art in this case is to understand how to make maximum use of the strength and elastic properties of a single material while working to minimize any effects of its limitations.

The limbs of a straight bow can be reflexed or angled away from the archer when the bow is unstrung. If the limbs angle towards the archer they are said to be deflexed. If the limbs curve away from the front of the bow along their length, or at the tips, we usually call them recurved instead of reflexed, although both terms are commonly used and the distinction is mainly one of degree. We would usually describe a straight limb that *angled* back as reflexed, whereas one that *curved* back away from the string would be described as either reflexed or recurved, with the term recurved usually reserved for limbs having a more pronounced degree of backward curvature. We can have all combinations of shapes, such as a deflexed-reflexed design to describe a bow whose limbs angle toward the archer near the *riser section*, or handle, and are curved away from the archer nearer the tips. Such a limb with a more pronounced recurved shape would be described as a deflexed-recurved limb. These two variations, in particular, are probably the most popular configurations at the present time for reasons that will become clearer as we continue.

The principal advantage of deflexed limbs is reduced recoil or hand shock, making a bow that is more comfortable and pleasant to shoot. This is partly because a deflexed limb has a slightly more pronounced vertical component to its motion and a decreased forward motion, lessening recoil when the limbs come to rest. This effect can be further enhanced by reflexing or, better still, recurving the limbs near the tip, providing an additional vertical component to the limb motion. For recurved limbs the effect can be pronounced and hand shock virtually eliminated. Limbs that are deflexed are not bent as far when fully drawn as straight limbs of the same length and cross section and therefore are not as highly stressed. That means to achieve the same draw weight requires a thicker (or wider) limb, which in turn means greater limb mass. And as we shall see, increasing limb mass makes for a slower limb and reduces cast. Reflexed limbs on the other hand are more highly stressed, since they are bent farther in coming to full draw, than straight limbs of the same length and cross section. The same draw weight can be achieved with a thinner, less massive limb, making it faster. By combining reflexed or recurved tips with deflexed limbs one can have the advantage of reduced hand shock without sacrificing speed. All of these effects are the most pronounced in recurve bows. Reflexed or recurved limbs with no deflex are in the direction of decreasing the limb mass and increasing limb speed, but at the penalty of a harsher-shooting bow. Besides which, the same limb speed can be achieved with deflexed-reflexed limbs properly shaped.

A wooden self bow bent far enough will exceed the *elastic limit* of the wood so that the wood fibers suffer a permanent deformation, referred to as *plastic deformation*, even though the *fracture limit* is not reached. The limbs in that case take a permanent bend, or set, and the bow is said to follow the string. Since wood is generally stronger in tension than in compression, plastic deformation is more likely on the belly of the bow than on the back, especially for a limb having the thick cross section of an English longbow. It is rare to find a wooden self bow of any reasonable efficiency that does not take a set after it has been shot for a while. Plastic deformation permanently alters the elastic properties of the limb material. The compressive and tensile stresses are reduced and as a result the bow stores less energy and loses cast. A permanent set can be minimized by thin, wide limbs having a rectangular cross section. Laminating a material with the superior elastic properties of fiberglass on the front and back of the limb, but especially on the front, can completely eliminate the problem.

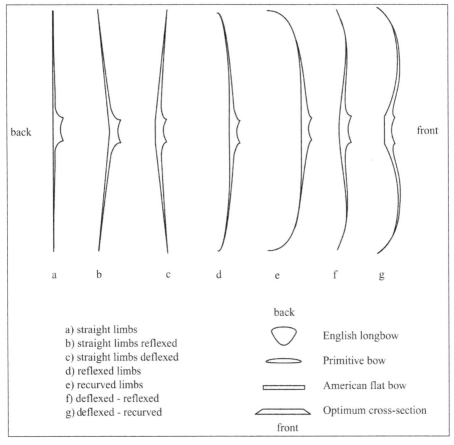

**Figure 1. Examples of traditional bow shapes and limb cross sections.**

The elastic properties of a material are described by its *elastic modulus*. This quantity is *the stress, or force per unit area, required to deform the material, divided by the resulting strain, or fractional change in the dimensions of the material.* Thus the stress, or force per unit area, in the material is equal to the elastic modulus times the strain, or fractional deformation, of the material. The higher the modulus the greater the force required to stretch or compress the material. The elastic modulus of fiberglass exceeds that of most bow woods by a factor of three or more. Carbon fiber composites have an even higher modulus. That means for the stresses encountered in a bow limb fiberglass deforms much less than wood and hence does not reach its elastic limit and take a permanent set. Gluing a thin layer of fiberglass to the back and face of the limb where the tensile and compressive stresses are highest can completely eliminate any permanent deformation. Such a composite limb can also be made thinner for the same draw weight since fiberglass requires a much smaller deformation to produce the same internal elastic force as wood. The tight bends of some highly recurved limbs are only possible because of the higher elastic modulus of fiberglass; otherwise the resulting stresses would generally exceed the elastic limit, and even the fracture limit, of wood.

Why not dispense with wood altogether and make the entire limb out of fiberglass? Solid fiberglass bows have been made but they are sluggish and disappointing to shoot, though they are rugged and relatively inexpensive to make. The problem is weight. Fiberglass is much heavier than wood. The fiberglass used on bow limbs has a density of about 2.0-2.1 compared to most bow woods which have a density around 0.6 or so, making fiberglass about three times as heavy per unit volume as wood. Even a thin fiberglass limb is much heavier than a comparable wood-and-fiberglass composite limb. And heavy limbs are slower. A heavy-limbed bow retains more of the stored energy and momentum and imparts less to the arrow, giving a sluggish cast and greater recoil and hand shock. Hollow fiberglass limbs with balsa wood cores have been tried also and these are lighter and perform better but are more difficult and more expensive to fabricate and still leave a great deal to be desired in performance, even when compared to wooden self bows to say nothing of much superior laminated wood and fiberglass limbs.

Laminated composite limbs allow one to combine the superior elastic properties of fiberglass and carbon fibers with the lighter weight and high shear strength of core materials like wood and syntactic foams. The thicker the limb, the more the thin layer of fiberglass on the front and back surfaces will be compressed and stretched as the bow is bent; so the thickness of the limb determines the final draw weight of the bow. To minimize mass, the limb should be no thicker than the minimum required to achieve the desired draw weight. Since a layer of fiberglass only 0.040-0.050 inch thick is able to support even very heavy draw weights, the material in the core of the limb does not have to have especially good elastic properties. Typically only about ten percent or so of the draw weight is provided by the elastic modulus of the core laminations, even in a relatively thick limb having a heavy draw weight. What is required of the core laminations is adequate *shear strength* to resist the opposing forces of compression and tension in the bent limb. In addition good gluing properties are needed. A material like maple is excellent in both regards but many other kinds of wood will work as well. In a wood and fiberglass limb the wood in the core is primarily there as filler to provide the right thickness and to glue the fiberglass to. The core laminations have a relatively minor effect on the performance of the bow limb in spite of conflicting claims and counterclaims by some bowyers to the contrary. Given two woods of adequate shear strength, in the absence of any other criterion we would always choose the one with the highest modulus per unit weight to minimize the physical weight of the limb and thereby decrease the amount of energy soaked up by the bow. Wood laminations that are chosen primarily for their beautiful and pleasing grain patterns and visual appeal, but which are heavier than other equally good choices, only slow down the limb speed and actually detract from the cast of the bow. Yew and bamboo, for example, would be better choices in that regard than osage orange or other exotic hardwoods.

We have determined then that a thin, wide limb with a rectangular cross section is the correct shape to balance the forces of compression and tension in the bent limb. We make the limb as *thin* as possible, consistent with the draw weight, to minimize stresses at the back and face of the limb; we make it *wide* enough to resist twisting and provide the desired draw weight; we make it *rectangular* to maximize the amount of material at the back and front surfaces where the stresses are greatest, and so that the forces of compression and tension will be equal at the back and front surfaces. *It is just as important that the stresses in the limb stay the same along its length as the bow is drawn.* If one section bends too little and another too much the limb may break where the bend is the sharpest, since that is where the deformation and stress are greatest. Every elastic material has a limit to how far it can be strained before reaching the point where it suffers permanent deformation and ultimately fractures. We always want to stay well below the fracture limit and well below the elastic limit too if at all possible.

The stress in any section of the limb is determined by the deformation of the material. The deformation in turn is determined by the ratio of its thickness to the *radius of curvature*. The radius of curvature, as the name suggests, is the radius of the curve which the bent limb follows at each point along its length. The larger the radius of curvature the less the limb bends. A sharp bend corresponds to a smaller radius of curvature and higher deformation. What we would like is for the radius of curvature to be roughly the same everywhere along the limb. We are speaking here of straight limbs, that is, limbs that are straight when unstrung. What we actually require is for the ratio of the thickness to the radius of curvature to remain the same. But since the thickness usually does not change much along the length of the limb, especially for thin flat limbs, that amounts to keeping the radius of curvature constant. Then no portion would be deformed more than any other. In other words, we want a straight limb to bend along the arc of a circle. What factors determine the actual curvature of a bent limb? The answer to that question can be complicated. Although it can be analyzed mathematically, to do so becomes fairly involved. At this juncture we have to decide just how deeply we want to delve into this subject; but without going too far into the details we can summarize the main points.

The radius of curvature at any point along the limb is proportional to the cube of the thickness at that point, multiplied by its width, divided by its distance from the tip of the limb where the bending force of the string is applied. To keep the radius of curvature the same we have to somehow make this quantity the same everywhere along the limb. Suppose the thickness of the limb stays constant. Then the width at each point divided by its distance from the tip would have to remain constant. We could in principle accomplish this by making the width of the limb at each point proportional to its distance from the tip. As that distance decreases, the width of the limb would decrease in the same proportion, and the ratio of the two would remain constant. The resulting limb would be a thin triangular beam of constant thickness tapering to a point at the tip. There are at least two practical limitations associated with this shape. One is that the tip of the limb where the string nock is located would have zero width, which of course is not feasible. The second is that a thin limb is prone to twist where it is narrow, making the limb unstable near the end. We can narrow the width toward the tip, but certainly not all the way to zero. For very thin limbs we want to maintain the width of the limb well out toward the tip to prevent twisting. This requirement becomes even more essential in a recurved limb.

We could also decrease the limb thickness toward the tip. Again, we can't make the thickness zero at the tip, so we can't strictly keep the radius of curvature constant that way either. What we do instead is to make the limb thick enough and wide enough at the tip to keep it from twisting and strong enough to withstand the sudden shock transmitted by the string as the limbs come to rest, and just thick enough near the riser to achieve the required draw weight. In between, we taper the thickness of the limb uniformly. For a composite limb this is achieved by tapering the core laminations.

Analysis shows that the proper rate of taper to minimize changes in the radius of curvature is one-third the ratio of the limb thickness, measured at the limb root, to its length. For limbs of say 40-60 pounds draw weight, this translates into a taper of approximately 0.002-0.003 inch per inch in the total thickness of the laminations, which is what one finds in most modern laminated limbs. This type of limb will still not bend everywhere the same and bends proportionately less nearer the tip. But the overall variation in radius of curvature is decreased, and the result is a reasonable and workable compromise between stability and uniformity. Many independent bowyers have discovered by trial and error that tapering the limb laminations in this fashion produces a better functioning limb. A more exact analysis indicates an advantage to tapering the thickness of the core laminations *parabolically* instead of uniformly, but the advantage is generally not enough to offset the greater difficulty of generating a parabolic taper.

We could also combine both of these schemes—decreasing the width *and* the thickness of the limb—to keep the radius of curvature even more constant along the limb. But stability is more important, especially for recurved limbs, than any gain in maintaining a constant radius of curvature.

So we compromise. We do not taper either the width or the thickness of the limb far enough to make it prone to twisting as it is drawn. The higher elastic modulus of fiberglass provides a margin of safety that allows us to make many such design compromises without exceeding the elastic limit of the material.

What we have said to this point, though it tells us something of what we need to understand about designing a bow limb without having it break or exceed its elastic limit, still doesn't tell us much about its performance in propelling an arrow, which is our real interest. *For that we have to start with what a bow is supposed to do.* A bow stores energy as it is drawn; holds it stored while the bow is aimed; and when the string is released, imparts kinetic energy to the arrow. That's three separate functions in all. There are a number of other characteristics that affect how accurately the bow propels an arrow along its intended trajectory and we have to consider them as well. Plus we want to be able to pull the bow with the least amount of physical effort. So we add the requirements of accuracy and ease of shooting to our list.

It all boils down to this. *We want a bow to store as much energy as possible for its draw weight; be able to hold it stored without having the energy diminish; and impart as much of that energy to the arrow as possible when the string is released; while propelling the arrow with a minimum of disturbance along its intended trajectory.* To this list we could add a number of other considerations, such as draw length, how the drawing force changes as the bow is pulled, length of the bow, stability, physical weight, materials, fabrication and cost. But all of these are connected one way or another to one of the four functions already identified and will automatically be taken into account as we consider those.

The force required to bring the bow to full draw is its *draw weight*. The actual distance the string is pulled in achieving full draw is the *draw length*. Note that draw length is not the same as arrow length. The two usually differ by at least the *brace height* of the bow, the distance between the string and some point on the handle or riser of the braced bow. This point is generally taken to be the front of the grip where the bow hand is placed, or the throat of the grip on contoured handles. This choice is a bit unfortunate. It makes perhaps more sense to measure the brace height from the string to the back of the bow, since that is the point to which the end of the arrow is most often drawn. In that case the arrow length and the draw length would differ by the brace height. Either point can be used so long as one is consistent. The arrow can be longer than the draw length by any amount the archer wishes. For bows with an overdraw shelf on the face of the handle the arrow can be almost as short as the draw length. If 28 or 29 inch arrows are shot in a bow with a brace height of 8 or 9 inches and pulled to where the end of the arrow coincides with the point from which the brace height is measured then the actual draw length would be about 20 inches. This is a fairly representative value which we shall use in our examples.

The *energy* stored by the bow is proportional to both the draw weight and the draw length, that is, to the *product of draw weight and draw length*. To store more energy we can choose a heavier draw weight, or pull the bow farther. But that brings us up against the practical limits of how strong a bow one can pull comfortably and shoot accurately. And draw length is fixed by the physical build of the archer, method of shooting, and the position of the rear anchor.

What we really desire is the greatest amount of energy stored for the lightest draw weight at a particular draw length, and that is determined by the *shape of the force curve*, or the manner in which the force required to pull the bow depends on how far it is drawn. If the force at each distance is plotted vertically and the corresponding distances horizontally, the result is the force curve. Its practical use is that *the stored energy is equal to the area under the curve*, that is, the area lying between the force curve and the horizontal axis out to the desired draw length. Just by inspecting the shape of the curve we can learn a lot about the stored energy.

The energy stored is the product of the draw weight, the draw length, and a factor that takes into account the *shape* of the force curve. A straight bow that isn't pulled too far has a linear force curve; the force is proportional to the distance the bow is drawn. The shape factor in this case is 0.5, and the energy stored is equal to one half the product of the draw weight and the draw length. That means that the energy stored by a 50 pound bow drawn 20 inches (1.6667 feet) is about 42 foot-pounds. Any straight bow that is long enough will have a linear force curve. The thicker the limbs and the greater the draw length the longer it has to be for the force curve to remain linear.

If a bow with a linear force curve is drawn far enough, eventually a point is reached where the force begins to go up faster with distance, and the force curve becomes concave upward. If the limbs are too short for their thickness, this point can occur well before the normal draw length is reached. We say that a bow exhibiting this characteristic *stacks*. In that case the area under the curve is *less* than it would have been if the curve had been linear all the way out to the full draw length. The shape factor for this type of force curve can be as low as say 0.45 so that the bow stores 10 percent less energy. That means a 50 pound bow drawn 20 inches might store only 38 foot-pounds of energy. In addition to storing less energy a bow that stacks is less comfortable to shoot, for the simple reason that the effort required to pull it increases fastest at the end of the draw where the force is greatest. Also, a small variation in draw length produces a correspondingly greater variation in the stored energy and the velocity imparted to the arrow.

For highly reflexed or recurved limbs, the force typically increases more rapidly at the beginning of the draw. Initially the string is pulling somewhat parallel to, or along, the surface of the recurved portion of the limb, and in that direction the ends of the limb are very stiff and resistant to bending. So at the beginning of the draw the thicker portion of the limb nearer the limb root bends first and the force rises faster than linearly. As the bow is pulled farther, the angle between the string and the end of the limb increases. Now the force begins to pull not as much along the limb but increasingly perpendicular to it, and the portions of the limb nearer the end begin to bend. As that happens, the string pulls on the end of the limb with an increasing lever arm so that the force required to bend it rises less steeply. This effect is accentuated if the recurved tips also straighten and bend toward the string during the last portion of the draw, so-called *working recurves*. The overall result is a force curve that is convex upward, rather than concave, and the area under the force curve is *increased* over that of a linear curve corresponding to the same draw weight. Even for limbs with a pronounced recurved shape the effect is not extremely large, but the shape factor for a recurve bow can easily be as high as say 0.55 so that the bow stores 10 percent more energy than a bow with a linear force curve. This means that a 50 pound bow pulled 20 inches might store 46 foot-pounds of energy.

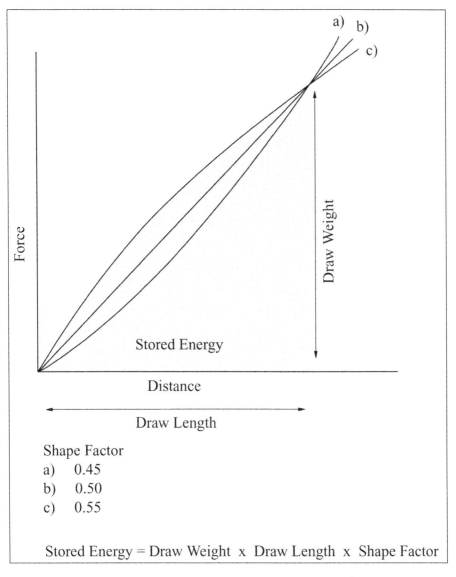

Figure 2. Types of force—draw curves for traditional bows showing how the force required to pull the bow increases with the distance the bow is drawn. The area under the force—draw curve represents the energy stored in the drawn bow. Curve b) is a linear curve typical of straight-limbed bows. Curve a) is typical of straight-limbed bows with thicker limb cross sections. Curve c) is more typical of thinner deflexed—recurved limbs.

So for the same draw weight and draw length, 50 pounds and 20 inches, the energy stored by the bow might vary all the way from 38 to 46 foot-pounds depending on the exact shape of the force curve, a variation of about ± 10 percent, or about 20 percent, around the mid-value of 42 foot-pounds. Thus the spread in stored energy varies by only about 20 percent from the best to the worst designs with regard to the shape of the force curve. This difference in stored energy corresponds to a variation of 10 percent in arrow velocity. This variation is due to the shape of the force curve alone and does not take into account other design differences that can increase the variation in arrow velocity.

The shape of the force curve depends on the shape of the bow and the limbs. The design storing the most energy is a recurve bow with the limbs set on the handle at a deflexed angle. The more pronounced the angle of deflex and the degree of recurve in the limbs, up to a point, the greater the area under the force curve and the greater the energy stored in the drawn bow. Even a bow of more modest deflexed-reflexed design will generally have a slightly convex force curve and store more energy than a straight bow of the same draw weight. The least desirable is a bow that stacks at the end of the draw. Any bow drawn far enough will begin to stack before it breaks. The way to prevent stacking is to make the bow long enough for the draw length and thickness of the limbs Thus the length adopted for the English longbow was six feet or more when drawing the full length of the traditional twenty-seven inch arrow. The thinner the limbs, the shorter the bow can be without stacking. By using thin layers of fiberglass on the front and back surfaces of the limbs, a bow can be made thinner and shorter without exceeding the elastic limit of the limb materials and without stacking. Composite limbs of wood and fiberglass are in the right direction to store more energy regardless of the bow design.

Some elastic materials exhibit a kind of internal friction against changes in shape. When these materials are stretched or compressed some of the energy is dissipated by internal forces of friction. Furthermore the energy dissipated can actually increase during the time the material is held stressed. For such materials not all of the stored energy is recovered when the string is released. This effect is termed *hysteresis*. It amounts to the fact that the force the string imparts to the arrow when it is released is actually less than the force required to pull the bow. The bow follows a lower force curve as the limbs relax. The area under this force curve is less than the area under the curve the bow followed when it was being drawn. The difference between the two areas represents the energy lost to internal friction. The only bow material today that exhibits any significant hysteresis is wood.

A wooden self bow that has taken a visible set will generally exhibit some hysteresis. The cast of such a bow will be slightly different if the bow is drawn and released rapidly, than if it is held for a prolonged time while aiming. Variations in aiming time will affect the speed and trajectory of the arrow. Shooting with exactly the same rhythm on each shot will, of course, minimize the difference. But hysteresis is a totally unnecessary nuisance. We can eliminate the problem entirely by simply using a superior elastic material like fiberglass on the front and back of the limbs. A composite wood and fiberglass limb does not exhibit any appreciable hysteresis; virtually all of the energy is recovered. For the purist who insists on shooting only a wooden self bow, however, it is helpful to be aware of the effects of hysteresis.

Even if none of the stored energy is dissipated by internal friction, *not all of the energy can be imparted to the arrow when the string is released.* If it were, the kinetic energy of the arrow would simply be equal to the energy stored in the bow at full draw. Then a heavier and a lighter arrow, though they would have different velocities, would both have the same kinetic energy. But that is never the case. The limbs and bowstring are still moving when the arrow leaves the string. As a result a portion of the energy is always retained by the bow as kinetic energy of the moving limbs and string. *This is the most important fact to understand about the operation of a bow.* In order to be able to quantify this amount of energy, we attribute to the bow an *effective mass*, sometimes referred to as its virtual mass following the designation suggested by Paul Klopsteg who introduced the idea. *The effective mass of the bow is the equivalent mass that, moving at the speed of the arrow when it leaves the bow, would have the same kinetic energy as the bow limbs and string.*

If it doesn't go to the arrow where does the kinetic energy retained by the bow go when the limbs finally do come to rest? It is dissipated as work done in stretching the bowstring; as vibrations of the limbs and string; as sound; and ultimately as heat imparted to the limbs, the string, the surrounding air and anything that absorbs the sound. We don't notice the effects of this heat since even if all of the energy stored by the drawn bow were converted to heat it would raise the temperature of the limbs and surroundings by only a negligible amount.

The formula for kinetic energy is one half the product of mass multiplied by speed squared ($\frac{1}{2}$ $MV^2$). The kinetic energy of the arrow as it leaves the bow is one half its mass times the square of its speed. *The kinetic energy retained by the bow is one half its effective mass times the speed of the arrow squared.* The energy stored in the fully drawn bow is thus shared between the arrow and the bow. The kinetic energy imparted to the arrow plus the kinetic energy retained by the bow equals the total energy stored in the bow before the string is released. *This is the basic principle by which a bow works.*

In this way we think of the stored energy as being divided between two objects, both moving at the speed of the arrow as it leaves the string. One is the mass of the arrow; the other is the effective mass of the bow. The energy imparted to each is proportional to its mass. Each receives a fraction of the total energy equal to its fraction of the total mass, obtained by adding the actual mass of the arrow to the effective mass of the bow. The usefulness of this idea is that the effective mass of the bow turns out to be constant and does not depend on the mass or speed of the arrow. As we shoot a lighter or a heavier arrow and change the arrow velocity, we find that the effective mass of the bow describing its share of the stored energy does not change. The effective mass is then a constant property characterizing the bow.

An immediate consequence is that *a bow always imparts more kinetic energy to a heavier arrow than to a lighter one.* The same is true of momentum. A heavier arrow will always leave the bow with greater kinetic energy, and greater momentum, than would a lighter arrow shot from the same bow. *This is the most important thing to understand about the performance of the bow in propelling an arrow.*

The reason why is straightforward. As the arrow weight increases the effective mass of the bow stays the same; a greater fraction of the stored energy is imparted to the arrow and a smaller fraction is retained by the bow. When the arrow mass is equal to the effective mass of the bow, one half of the stored energy is imparted to the arrow. When the arrow mass increases to twice the effective mass, two-thirds of the stored energy is imparted to the arrow. If the arrow mass is three times the effective mass, three-fourths of the stored energy goes to the arrow and only one-fourth is retained by the bow, and so on. As the arrow weight increases arrow velocity decreases, *but the share of the kinetic energy imparted to the arrow still goes up.* Decreasing the arrow velocity decreases the kinetic energy of the bow so that more energy is imparted to the arrow. This is completely contrary to what most archers intuitively think, even to the point where many simply refuse to accept it. But they are mistaken nevertheless.

A similar statement can be made about momentum. The energy stored by the bow is converted into a combined total momentum of the arrow and the moving bow limbs. Each receives a fraction of the total momentum equal to its proportion of the total mass. If the arrow mass and the effective mass are the same, the momentum of the arrow is the same as the momentum retained by the bow limbs. If the arrow mass is twice the effective mass of the bow, then the arrow gets two-thirds of the total momentum, the bow limbs one-third, and so on, just as in the case of the total energy. The heavier the arrow the greater the fraction of the total momentum imparted to it. Even though it is traveling slower, a heavier arrow always has more momentum than a lighter arrow shot from the same bow.

The concept of effective mass is the key to understanding how a bow works. Failure to take into account the portion of the stored energy and momentum retained by the bow has caused more wrongheaded and farfetched notions about the performance characteristics of bows than any other single misunderstanding.

The *effective mass* of a bow is not the same as the *actual mass* of the limbs and bowstring; but it is at least proportional to it in some fashion. Bows with long, thick heavy limbs, like the English longbow, have a relatively large effective mass. As a result they have greater recoil and a sluggish cast. The bow retains a larger share of the energy and momentum, which robs the arrow of energy, and velocity, and gives the bow its greater recoil when the heavy limbs come to rest. A thicker string must be used to stop the limbs and prevent the string from breaking when it snaps taut, which in turn contributes to increasing the effective mass.

As a boy I once had the unusual experience of shooting a bow whose limbs were made of spring steel. The bow came from a foreign land, brought home by a young man who was not an archer, the son of a local court judge, from his travels in the Middle East and Asia; from which country I no longer recall. Knowing that I was an archer and thinking to impress a youngster with the wonder of this weapon, he proudly showed it to me and invited me to shoot it. My naive notions led me to imagine that this powerful bow would surely cast an arrow with astonishing speed. Imagine my painful surprise when the recoil almost jarred my arm from its socket and left my shoulder and elbow stinging with pain. Although the draw weight was all that I could manage, the cast was unimpressive. Only later did I understand why. The large mass of the heavy steel limbs meant that most of the stored energy was retained as kinetic energy and momentum of the bow; relatively little went to the arrow. Everything about the idea of using steel to make bow limbs is all wrong. No one knowing anything about how a bow works would ever try it. The density of steel is approximately four times that of fiberglass. For exactly the same reason a solid fiberglass bow limb, in spite of the superior elastic properties of fiberglass, is greatly inferior to a much lighter, laminated limb of wood and fiberglass.

We can define an *energy efficiency* for the bow as *the fraction of the total energy stored by the drawn bow that is actually imparted to the arrow*. The efficiency is just the mass of the arrow divided by the sum of the arrow mass and the effective mass of the bow. So if the effective mass of the bow happens to be the same as the mass of the arrow, the bow would have an efficiency of 0.5, or one half. Most traditional bows will have an efficiency at least this large or greater when shot with arrows of the weight usually matched to the bow, that is, arrows not unusually light. The exception might be wooden self bows of heavier draw weights or bows shot with very light arrows. Higher draw weight bows have heavier limbs, and the effective mass might actually be greater than the weight of the arrows normally matched to the bow. Shooting very light arrows in any bow lowers its efficiency and imparts less energy to the arrow.

Most traditional bows will not have efficiency greater than about 0.80, or four fifths. Even that is a high value, achieved by only the most optimum designs.

We can always increase the efficiency of any bow by simply shooting heavier arrows. At some point heavier shafts will no longer fly properly, especially if they become too stiff as a result of making them heavier. Still, there are ways of increasing arrow weight without having them become too stiff, such as by making them longer or decreasing the diameter in the case of solid shafts; or by putting material inside them in the case of hollow shafts. If we normally shoot an arrow whose mass is equal to the effective mass of the limbs, then the starting efficiency is 0.5. If we double the arrow mass, the efficiency becomes 0.66. If we triple it, the efficiency becomes 0.75; quadruple it, 0.80; and so on. The arrow speed, of course, will decrease as the arrow weight increases. The heavier arrows will all fly slower than the original ones. In the example we have chosen, doubling the arrow mass results in a velocity about 0.82 as large; tripling it gives a velocity only 0.71 as great; and quadrupling it, a velocity about 0.63 of the original. We will return to these kinds of trade-offs later in connection with other topics.

To maximize the efficiency of a bow its effective mass should be kept as small as possible for its draw weight. That means reducing the actual mass of the limbs as much as we can. We want to minimize the amount of material in the limbs while still achieving the desired stiffness. All of the material should contribute to the elastic forces that give the bow its draw weight. Especially bad is inert material near the tips of the limb that are moving the fastest. Thick round or oval limbs like those of the English longbow are a relatively poor shape since much of the material is not being stressed in the bent limb and contributes to the overall mass but not the draw weight. Thin, flat rectangular limbs are much better. The optimum again would be a trapezoidal cross section since it minimizes the elastic material required to achieve a given draw weight. But as a practical matter a trapezoidal shape offers only a minimal advantage over a thin rectangle. Draw weight depends directly on the width of the limb, but is proportional to the cube, or third power, of the limb thickness. A small change in thickness gives a much greater change in draw weight than changing the limb width. A ten percent change in width will produce a ten percent change in draw weight. But a ten percent change in thickness changes the draw weight by about one third. To minimize effective mass the limbs should be no wider, especially nearer the tips, than required to keep them from twisting; and draw weight should be adjusted by changing limb thickness.

The more the fully drawn limb is bent, without of course exceeding the elastic limit, the thinner and lighter the limb can be while still achieving the tension and compression necessary to achieve the desired draw weight. One way of accomplishing that is to shorten the limb so that it bends farther at full draw. The working portion of a laminated limb doesn't have to be more than about sixteen inches or so in a proper design. The length of the handle or center section of the bow, including the portion of the limb root that doesn't bend, can be adjusted to achieve the desired overall length of the bow. The longer the bent limb the greater its radius of curvature and the less it is stressed. The unstressed material represents dead weight that contributes to the mass of the limb but not to the draw weight.

Another way is to reflex or recurve the limbs. The unbraced limbs curve away from the direction in which they are flexed in pulling the bow. When they are brought to full draw the material in the front and back of the limb is deformed more than if the limb had started from a straight position. Recurved limbs can be made stiffer for the same limb mass. As a result the limb can be made thinner for the same draw weight and the effective mass is reduced. The ability to make a stiffer limb with less mass represents probably the biggest single advantage of the recurve bow over a straight bow of equal draw weight.

Recurved limbs are glued together with a frozen-in radius of curvature. The tighter the bend the smaller the radius of curvature and the stiffer the recurved portion of the limb. If the radius of curvature is small enough the recurve may be so stiff that it does not bend at all. Any attempt to straighten the tight bend greatly deforms the fiberglass on the outer surfaces and produces compressive and tensile forces much larger than those required to bend the rest of the limb. The other parts of the limb that are not as stiff do all the bending as the bow is drawn. Such non-working recurves are a way of making the end of the limb stiffer with less mass.

Imagine that the outer portion of the limb is so stiff that it does not flex at all, so that all of the bending occurs in a short section near the limb root. The shorter the section, the sharper the bend and the greater the deformation. At the same time the short section has to be thick enough to generate the entire draw weight of the bow which adds to the amount of deformation at the front and back surfaces. As a result the strain in the bending section may exceed the fracture limit of the material and cause it to break. To prevent excessive bending at any point, the entire length of the limb should bend in such a way that the compressive and tensile forces are shared by all parts. To accomplish that the recurved portion of the limb should bend as the bow is drawn.

A related issue concerns the number of laminations in a composite limb. Is there any inherent advantage to multiple layers of wood laminations in the core of the limb? Why not just a single lamination? Clearly a single lamination will work and very good bows have been made that way by a number of bowyers, so long as the wood does not have to be too thick. But imagine bending a single lamination to form a recurved limb. Bending introduces tensile and compressive strains into the lamination, and the glued limb will have those strains frozen into the front and back of the wood core. Now imagine slicing that single lamination lengthwise between front and back into a number of parallel layers and allowing the internal strains to relax by having the layers slide past one another before gluing them together again to form the recurved shape. The resulting limb will have lower residual stress in the glued laminations. It is analogous to having the material in the single lamination flow plastically to relieve the internal stresses, only without the penalty of a permanent deformation. Two or more thin laminations will have lower stress than a single lamination of the same total thickness. In most cases a recurved limb will be thin enough that there is little practical advantage in using more than two laminations, though some bowyers use as many as three or four. Clearly there is a point of diminishing returns. The more laminations the greater the number of glue joints which increases the risk of failure in the glue.

So far we have considered three of the four functions of a bow. All that remains is to consider how the design affects accuracy and ease of shooting.

Up to the point where the string is released accuracy is the responsibility solely of the archer in choosing the correct trajectory for the arrow, whether aiming with a sight or some other way, and in holding the bow aimed until the release is accomplished. Even here design is a factor, since increased arrow speed produces a flatter trajectory which makes aiming easier and more accurate, especially when shooting without a sight or at unknown distances. Even with a sight the dispersion of the arrows at the target is less for a given sighting error if the arrow speed is greater and the trajectory flatter. Greater arrow speed also reduces the time required for the arrow to reach the target, which reduces how much it can be affected by wind as well as gravity.

Once the string is released the bow definitely begins to affect accuracy. The first issue is that of stability, especially the stability of the limbs. Thin recurved limbs in particular can be squirrelly, prone to twisting and to perturbations caused by varying the pressure of the fingers on the string. Pulling more with the bottom finger bends the lower limb more and effectively changes the *tiller* of the bow, by which we mean the amount each limb bends. The result is arrows that go high and low. A sloppy release that hangs up and doesn't come off the string smoothly can twist the limbs and result in an arrow that goes left or right. It was just such behavior that led to the early point of view by Howard Hill and others that recurve bows were inherently inaccurate or impossible to shoot well under hunting conditions. None of that is true of course. A properly designed recurve is inherently more accurate and easier to shoot if for no other reason than the increased arrow velocity at lower draw weights, which simplifies aiming and makes the bow easier to pull and hold drawn. It is true however that some recurve bows are sensitive to technique and make special demands on the form of the archer.

The worst offenders are recurve bows where the strung bow, viewed from the side, somewhat resembles a trapezoid with the riser section and the straight portion of the limbs being one parallel side and the string being the other. The string of such a bow can be moved up and down with little resistance and one can readily see how variations in finger pressure will lead to erratic arrows. The key is not to design a bow to have that shape when strung. The desired shape is that of a triangle, with the upper and lower halves of the bow forming two sides of the triangle and the string the third side. This is more closely the shape of a reflexed or recurve bow where the limbs are set on the handle deflexed. The string of a bow having this shape will not as easily move up and down because of the inherent rigidity of a triangle; this is the shape to be preferred, no matter claims by some bowyers to the contrary. This design also minimizes hand shock and produces a bow that is more pleasant to shoot.

The way to prevent thin limbs from twisting is to make them wider and to maintain the width well out toward the limb tip. A width of 1.75 inches at the limb root is usually adequate, even for a bow with longer than average limbs, but it is unwise to decrease the width of very thin limbs much below that. The result will be a lot of rejected limbs during fabrication, and twisted limbs later on, plus a bow that is very sensitive to any changes or mistakes in shooting form. There is no advantage to building a bow that is faster if the limbs are so unstable that it cannot be shot accurately and consistently, especially under less than ideal conditions. The compromise with stability is the one good reason for sacrificing limb speed.

An arrow that leaves the bow at 150 feet per second requires about 0.026 second to clear the bow, assuming the travel is 30 inches just to be safe. Even if the arrow velocity is 200 feet per second it still takes about 0.020 second. During that time the bow would fall as much as 0.13 inch if it were unsupported by the archer. Even if it actually dropped by that amount the effect on the impact point of the arrow would be negligible if no other forces exerted by the archer deflected the arrow. Slight variations in the force supporting the bow are then no more important than the effect of the other forces exerted by the archer on the bow. Sideways or up-and-down forces by the bow hand can deflect the arrow away from its intended trajectory. Some motion of the bow is going to occur even under the best of conditions and shooting technique. We want to minimize all of these motions by increasing the *inertia* or physical weight of the bow. The amount of deflection is proportional to the deflecting force divided by the mass of the bow. The greater the mass, the less it will move in the length of time it takes the arrow to clear the bow. The only limit is how heavy a bow the archer can support and hold steady during aiming, but a weight of three or four pounds is certainly well within that range. Some target bows, ready to shoot, are even heavier. Much lighter than that and we are sacrificing stability. Too much heavier and the bow begins to be uncomfortable or fatiguing to shoot. Even a weight of three pounds with a bow quiver is still reasonable for a hunting bow.

We want to make the bow heavy but without adding mass to the limbs. That means adjusting the mass of the center section to achieve the desired weight. This has become one of the major functions of the enlarged riser sections of modern recurve bows, but more recently of many straight bows too. The increased material in the handle allows very pleasing and aesthetic shapes, provides extra space for a contoured grip and sight window, and adds additional strength so that the sight window can be safely cut past the center line of the bow; but an important function of all that extra material is to add additional weight to stabilize the bow.

Making the bow center-shot is also a desirable design feature and one that contributes to accuracy. It is tempting to assert that the handle of all bows should be cut far enough that the center of the arrow can leave the bow along its center line. That isn't strictly necessary however. An unavoidable disturbance in the straight flight of the arrow is the bending of the shaft caused by the sudden accelerating force of the string. If the arrows are all identical each one will bend in the same way and they will all fly the same. Still it is desirable to cut the sight window in the handle of the bow past center to minimize any contact between the bow and the fletching and to reduce any effect of slight variations in stiffness of the arrows.

Not only does the bow move laterally after the string is released, it can also rotate under the influence of any torque exerted by the bow hand or any erratic sideways deflection of the string during release. We want to minimize these rotational motions as well. To do that we can increase the *rotational inertia* of the bow, its resistance to rotation, by adding additional weights displaced from the axis of rotation. The rotational inertia is proportional to the product of the mass and the square of the distance from the axis of rotation, so doubling the distance quadruples the effectiveness of the added mass. Or viewed another way, doubling the distance reduces the amount of additional weight needed by a factor of four. The addition of external weights to the bow as stabilizers may not always be a practical or even a desirable solution, particularly in the case of a hunting bow. They are aesthetically unappealing and cumbersome and really quite unnecessary in anything other than a target bow. A bow quiver mounted on a hunting bow however increases both the mass and the rotational inertia of the bow and has the dual effect of stabilizing it.

An additional step is minimizing the diameter of the bow grip, especially the throat of the grip where the web of the hand fits, to decrease the amount of torque exerted by the bow hand. A big fat grip is not only more difficult to place your hand on the same way every time, but even if you do, it magnifies any torque by the hand when the string is released and is just not conducive to accuracy. To minimize any unwanted forces and torques is also the main reason why the hand should contact the grip as lightly and over as small an area as possible. And that contact should be straight in line with the force exerted by the bow arm and shoulder to prevent any sideways deflection of the bow on release. Here we get into an area where bow design and shooting technique begin to impact each other. It should be the purpose of design to minimize any unwanted or unanticipated effects of faulty technique.

Practically the only thing we haven't mentioned so far is the length of the bow. There is an old adage that longer bows are more accurate, or that a bow that is too short cannot be shot as accurately. I have never been entirely sure what real evidence there is to support this contention, but it is well entrenched in the lore of the sport and there is perhaps some truth to it if we don't push it too far. The string on a longer bow makes a less acute angle at full draw and doesn't pinch the fingers together as severely. That supposedly leads to a cleaner release, and in extreme cases I suppose that is true. A longer bow has more rotational inertia and hence more resistance to rotational deflections about the two horizontal axes perpendicular to its length, but that's a relatively minor effect. Certainly a shorter bow combined with a long draw length will result in a bow that stacks; heavy draw weight bows that exhibit this behavior are unpleasant to shoot. Variations in arrow velocity and trajectory caused by small variations in the archer's draw length are accentuated with a force curve that increases rapidly near the end of the draw. On the other hand, a bow that is too long will not be pulled far enough to attain the necessary stress in the limbs for maximum efficiency. Somewhere in between these two extremes is a happy medium, and anything lying within several inches on either side is probably just fine. To find out where that is, don't be persuaded by what anyone says. Try it for yourself and be guided by your own experience. It is difficult to assess the adage about longer bows when everyone striving for higher scores is using a longer bow. Would they shoot just as well with a shorter bow? No one will ever know so long as no one is trying a shorter bow any more. Target archery, and archery generally, has become so guided by the prevailing fashion of what the top shooters are doing that it is often impossible to separate fact from fashion. This is true of the archer's equipment as well as shooting techniques. If someone wins a tournament by shooting from a kneeling position or sitting in a chair, then be assured that in the next tournament there will be others shooting that way.

What then is the ideal traditional bow? Each of the advantageous features that we have discussed can be thought of as leading us in the right direction. It is for the archer to decide how far he wishes to go in any given direction. Put them all together and you have what we recognize as the best features of the modern laminated recurve bow in its most refined form, whether strictly a target bow or one used for hunting. On the other hand there are a number of American flat bows of the deflexed-reflexed design that achieve comparable arrow speeds. In the hands of a good archer these designs make excellent bows for hunting and field archery and are every bit as pleasant and enjoyable to shoot. For those, like me, who admire their clean simple lines and classic beauty, they are a joy to behold. In addition they can be somewhat more stable and forgiving to shoot and are every bit as good a choice as the most refined recurve. It is still up to the individual archer to pick and choose from among these various design options, with personal preferences and the intended use of the bow in mind, to ultimately decide what the ideal design will be. Beauty and utility are in the eye and mind of the beholder, and nowhere is that more true than among archers.

# The Ideal vs. Real Bows

*What characteristics make up the ideal traditional bow and how do real bows compare?*

As a way of summarizing the ideas in the previous chapter about bow design it is useful to think about the attributes of an imagined ideal bow. There is of course no such thing as the ideal bow. There are only actual bows with their individual characteristics. The bow is an ancient invention. Its roots in antiquity mean that even today real bows still represent an early technology that is far from the ideal that can be imagined in more modern terms. The traditions of archery itself, so long as we choose to adhere to them, serve to limit what is possible or acceptable in bow design, in other words, what is to be allowed. But the concept of the perfect or ideal bow is still a useful way of thinking about the actual characteristics of real bows. It provides us a standard of comparison against which to gauge the design and performance of all bows. What then are the properties of an ideal bow?

The *ideal bow* must be able to do three things. It must store as much energy as possible for its draw weight. It must impart all of that stored energy to the arrow. And it should propel the arrow along its intended trajectory without disturbance or deviation.

The force required to pull a real bow increases as the bow is drawn. The farther the elastic materials of the limbs are bent the harder it becomes to bend them. As a result much more energy is being stored in the bow at the end of the draw than in the beginning. The build-up of stored energy mirrors the increase in the drawing force. In the ideal case, the force required to pull the bow would start off at its maximum value and continue that way throughout the entire distance the bow is drawn. That would result in the maximum amount of energy that could be stored in the bow for a given draw weight, which would just be the *product of the draw weight and the draw length,* or the draw weight times the draw length. In terms of the discussion of the force curve in the previous chapter, that would amount to a shape factor of 1.0, corresponding to a rectangular force curve. Then when the string is released the full draw weight of the bow would act on the arrow throughout its entire acceleration, instead of decreasing as the arrow is accelerated the way it does in an actual bow.

In a bow approaching the ideal, the force would rise abruptly at the beginning of the draw, quickly increase to its maximum value, and maintain that value during the remainder of the draw. No real traditional bow behaves in this ideal fashion. But it is possible to shape the limbs to be stiffer at the beginning of the draw so that the force increases faster initially than as the bow is drawn farther. A tapered limb with a stiffer limb root and a pronounced recurved shape, set on the handle deflexed sharply toward the string will exhibit just this kind of force. Initially the string pulls parallel to the recurved portion of the limb, and in that direction the limb is highly resistant to bending, forcing the section at the root of the limb to bend first so that the force rises quickly in the beginning. As the limb bends farther the string pulls at an increasing angle to the recurved section, straightening it and lengthening the effective lever arm through which the string acts on the limb, so that the force does not rise as fast. In effect the recurved section of the limb functions somewhat like a lever or a cam in which the point of application of the force is moving away from the root of the limb as the bow is drawn.

The first to point out the possibility and technical merits of such a design was C.N. Hickman in U.S. Patent 2,100,317 in 1935. He used an extreme form of this idea, consisting of very short limbs recurved backwards in a perfectly circular arc and deflexed at an angle of about 49 degrees to the handle or riser section. Hickman's bow, interestingly, suggests those highly deflexed recurve bows depicted in a number of ancient drawings, such as those of Scythian archers. The shape factor of the resulting force curve was in the vicinity of 0.75 for Hickman's bow. Considerations of fabrication, reliability and stability limit the practical usefulness of the more extreme version of these ideas. But a more modest version can be seen at work in any modern deflexed recurve bow. There practical limitations result in a shape factor as large as 0.55 or slightly more.

The ideal bow should be able to impart *all* of the stored energy to the arrow. In a real bow the limbs and the string are still moving at the instant the arrow leaves the bow. Not all of the stored energy goes to the arrow. Some of it is retained by the bow as kinetic energy of the moving limbs and string. The bow acts as though it possessed an effective mass that, moving at the same speed as the arrow, represents the kinetic energy of the bow. This energy is dissipated as work done in stretching the string when the limbs come to rest, as vibrations of the string and limbs, and finally as heat. Since the ideal bow can retain no kinetic energy but must impart all of it to the arrow, its limbs can have no mass.

Clearly the limbs of a real bow must have mass since it is the elastic materials of the limbs that provide the force necessary to propel the arrow. In a bow approaching the ideal the actual mass of the limbs should be as small as possible consistent with the desired draw weight. The limbs should use elastic materials that have the maximum stiffness for a given deformation, or the highest modulus of elasticity. Materials like fiberglass and carbon filaments are in this category.

The limb should also be constructed to achieve the greatest stiffness per unit weight. The back of the limb is stretched when the bow is drawn and the belly is compressed. In between is a zone where the forces of tension and compression are smaller. By placing a thin layer of fiberglass on the back and belly of the limb one can take advantage of the high elastic modulus of the fiberglass to minimize the amount of mass needed to provide the draw weight of the bow. The material in between that is not as highly stressed can be wood which is much lighter than fiberglass. The result is a composite limb that achieves greater stiffness per unit mass than a self limb made of either material alone. Reducing the actual mass of the limb reduces its effective mass.

The limb can also be stiffened by laminating it recurved, with the back of the bow concave. As the bow is drawn and the limb is bent in the opposite direction, the stresses in the back and belly of the limb are greater than if it weren't initially recurved. In this way a thinner limb and less mass are needed to generate the draw weight of the bow.

Finally, the limbs should be bent as far as possible without exceeding the elastic limit of the limb materials, in order to minimize the mass required to achieve the desired draw weight. The greater the deformation of the limb the greater the force required to bend it. This means the limbs should be kept as short as consistent with the allowable deformation of the elastic materials before reaching the fracture limit. The overall length of the bow can then be adjusted by choosing the length of the handle section or riser.

The ideal bow should propel the arrow along its intended trajectory without disturbance. This requires that nothing that happens to the bow after the string is released should cause any deviation of the arrow away from the point at which it was aimed. An arrow that leaves the bow even at 200 feet per second still requires about 0.020 second to clear the bow; 150 feet per second requires about 0.026 second. During that time the bow would fall only about 0.13 inch if it were not supported by the archer. So the deflecting forces exerted by the archer are at least as significant as the force of gravity. To minimize any disturbance to the arrow before it has time to clear the bow, the ideal bow should have infinite inertia, or resistance to motion, which means infinite mass. Here we face an obvious compromise since the heavier the bow the harder it is for the archer to support it and hold it still while aiming. The ideal bow has infinite inertia, but the actual bow can weigh only as much as the archer can comfortably hold and control.

We have already said that the limbs of the ideal bow would be massless, so the inertia of the bow has to be supplied by the mass of the handle section or riser. The bow should not only resist linear movements but also any twisting or rotational motion caused by torque from the archer's bow hand or from mistakes in releasing the string. The rotational inertia of the bow is increased by placing the mass of the handle section farther off-center, away from the axis of rotation. Some of the mass is there to supply structural rigidity and strength along the axis of the bow. The rest of it can be placed off-axis on stabilizer rods to add to the rotational inertia.

An unavoidable disturbance in the straight flight of the arrow is the bending of the shaft caused by the sudden accelerating force of the string. If the arrows are all identical each one will bend in the same way and they will all fly the same. The sight window in the handle of the ideal bow would be cut far enough past center to minimize any possibility of interference between the arrow and the bow, and reduce the effect of slight variations in stiffness of the arrows. The arrow rest would be adjustable to aid in tuning the bow and spring loaded to absorb the deflection of the arrow when it bends on release.

There is also the stability of the bow against mistakes in the archer's shooting form, particularly mistakes in the release. Varying the pressure on the string by the fingers of the drawing hand can change the tiller of the bow and deflect the arrow up or down. Plucking the string can twist the limbs and deflect the arrow sideways. The limbs of the ideal bow would be completely rigid against twisting and also rigid to up and down motion of the string when the bow is drawn. Here the recurve bow with its lighter, thinner limbs is at a disadvantage to a bow with heavier, more rigid, straighter limbs. The more energy efficient we make the recurved limb the easier it is to twist and to deflect up and down by changing the pull on the string. Making the limbs wider and maintaining the width well out toward the tips gives them greater resistance to twisting. Deflexing the limbs on the handle, angling them towards the archer, gives the strung bow a more rigid triangular shape and makes it harder to move the string up and down.

No real bow, of course, comes anywhere near these characteristics of the ideal bow. The farthest from the ideal is the traditional English longbow made of wood, with its rounded cross section peaked on the face of the limb and flattened on the back. This shape limb stores less energy for a given draw weight and imparts less of it to the arrow than almost any other traditional bow design. The force curve has a shape factor as low as 0.45 compared to that of 1.0 for the ideal bow. Flattening the limb cross section reduces the mass of the limb and improves the energy storage and energy efficiency. We refer to this design as the American flat bow and it is a decided improvement toward the ideal over the English longbow. A composite limb with a thin layer of high modulus fiberglass on the front and back allows a thinner limb and further reduces the limb mass and improves efficiency. Going from a straight bow to a deflexed-reflexed limb shape gives additional improvement in energy storage and efficiency. The best design with respect to both is a highly recurved limb set on the handle deflexed toward the string.

An English longbow or a straight bow with flat limbs will store no more than about 50 percent as much energy as the ideal bow. The best recurve bows might store as much as 55-60 percent, or about 10-20 percent more. This difference in energy storage alone can mean as much as 10 percent greater arrow velocity. An English longbow or an American flat bow will typically impart about 60 percent or so of the stored energy to an arrow of moderate weight, less for very light arrows and more for very heavy ones. The best recurve bows have an efficiency of about 70 percent or better for arrows of intermediate weight, again about 20 percent higher. This difference in energy efficiency amounts to an additional 10 percent greater arrow velocity.

Combining the two effects, the modern recurve bow will shoot the same arrow with as much as 20 percent greater velocity than an English longbow or straight flat bow of the same draw weight. As another way of stating the same comparison, straight bows typically shoot at about 50 percent the velocity of an ideal bow. The best recurve bows achieve about 60 percent the velocity of an ideal bow, or about 20 percent more. Of course here we are talking about the best recurve bow designs and typical longbows or flat bows, not specific individuals. These values should be taken only as guidelines, not as hard and fast rules.

A longbow with a mass weight of one and a half pounds will not be as stable a launch platform for the arrow as a three pound recurve bow with short limbs and a rigid center section, to say nothing of the possibility of hanging additional stabilizers on the latter. On the other hand many an archer has discovered that it is easier to shoot a longbow or a straight bow accurately, when forced to shoot quickly or under adverse conditions, than a more sensitive recurve bow. This is especially true of snap-shooting or shooting on the move under hunting conditions with cold fingers and shaky nerves.

What we learn from all of this is that, compared to the ideal bow, all real bows are really about the same. They all store about half, or slightly more, as much energy as the ideal bow. And all of them impart slightly more than half of the stored energy to the arrow. Thus real bows deliver only about 25-35 percent as much energy to the arrow as the ideal bow and propel an arrow at only about 50-60 percent as much velocity as the ideal bow. This is true across the entire spectrum of designs from the straight wooden longbow to the most refined composite-limb recurve bow. These limitations all stem from the same cause: *the traditional bow has to store energy and derive the force by which the string propels the arrow entirely from the bending of the limb* and not from the action of cams or pulleys as in the compound bow.

Looked at in this light the differences between all forms of traditional bows seem less significant. The difference in velocity attainable with the various designs is only a matter of about twenty percent, maybe as much as thirty percent if we include the best and worst examples of the various limb designs. This difference is really rather minor when shooting at distances typical of hunting. The bow is after all a very short-range weapon. There are however real differences in performance between the various traditional bow designs that are more apparent when comparing them to one another and not to the ideal bow. And these differences become very significant in using the bow as a precision target instrument. It is through the greater demands on precision and consistency inherent in target archery that improvements in traditional bows have always come. Target archery is the real laboratory for improving traditional bow design. These differences can best be understood as designing toward the characteristics of the ideal bow: *increased energy storage, lighter limbs, and greater stability.*

# Measuring Your Bow's Performance

*A simple measurement yields two parameters that completely characterize your bow's performance.*

By measuring the speed with which a bow shoots two arrows of different mass, we can determine the value of two parameters that completely describe every aspect of a bow's performance. With the value of these two quantities we can find the velocity, kinetic energy, and momentum the bow will impart to an arrow of any mass. Using this technique the archer can readily assess how any combination of bow and arrow will perform and will be able to directly compare the relative performance of different bows. Before discussing the actual measurements and how to use them, let's first briefly discuss these two parameters and how they characterize a bow's performance.

A bow stores energy as it is drawn and when the string is released delivers a portion of this stored energy to the arrow as kinetic energy. Clearly, one important measure of a bow's performance is the total amount of energy stored in the fully drawn bow. The greater the stored energy the greater the amount of energy potentially available to propel the arrow, and this stored energy is referred to as the *potential energy* of the bow. We would expect a bow that stores more potential energy to give more kinetic energy to the arrow and to propel it at a higher velocity, and that is generally the case.

But not all of the potential energy can be transferred to the arrow. It is interesting to find how many archers assume otherwise. They realize the energy stored in the fully drawn bow. Once the limbs are at rest following the shot, the bow no longer has either stored energy or kinetic energy, and the arrow is speeding away, so all of the energy that was originally stored in the bow must have gone to the arrow. But it doesn't work that way. No bow is one hundred percent efficient in transferring potential energy into kinetic energy of the arrow. At the instant the arrow leaves the string the limbs and string are still moving so that a portion of the stored energy is retained as kinetic energy of the bow itself. As the limbs finally come to rest this kinetic energy is dissipated as work done in stretching the string, as vibrations of the limbs and string, as sound, and ultimately as a negligible quantity of heat imparted to the limbs, the string, and the surroundings.

Any assessment of a bow's performance has to include some measure of how the stored energy is divided between the kinetic energy imparted to the arrow and that retained by the bow. The parameter that describes how much kinetic energy the bow retains is its effective mass, sometimes also referred to as the dynamic or virtual mass of the bow. The kinetic energy of the arrow as it leaves the bow is one half the mass of the arrow times the square of its velocity ($\frac{1}{2}MV^2$). We can describe the kinetic energy of the bow as one half its *effective mass* times the square of the arrow velocity ($\frac{1}{2}M_{eff}V^2$). The effective mass of the bow is not the actual mass of the limbs and string. *It is the equivalent amount of mass that, moving at the same speed as the arrow, would have the same kinetic energy as the moving bow limbs and string.* A good way to think about this is the following. When the string is released the potential energy stored in the bow gets divided between two objects, both traveling at the same speed. One is the arrow; the other is the effective mass of the bow.

The effective mass of a bow is constant over a wide range of arrow velocities, which is what makes it a useful concept. As we vary the mass of the arrow and change its initial velocity, the effective mass of the bow stays roughly the same. The value of the effective mass is determined by the design of the bow and the materials used in its construction. Once we select a bow we are stuck with whatever effective mass its design and construction dictates. There is nothing we can do to change it, except to choose a bow of a different design or limb materials. Since the effective mass is constant, the only way to reduce the kinetic energy retained by the bow is to decrease the arrow velocity by shooting a heavier arrow. This is the reason why a bow always imparts more kinetic energy to a heavier arrow than to a lighter one.

The same argument holds for the momentum imparted to the arrow. Not all of the stored energy can be transferred to the arrow as momentum. Some of it is retained as momentum associated with the effective mass of the bow. Decreasing the arrow velocity by shooting a heavier shaft has the effect of decreasing the momentum retained by the bow and increasing the momentum imparted to the arrow. The result is that a heavier arrow also has greater momentum than a lighter arrow shot from the same bow.

Both of these parameters—the stored energy and the effective mass of the bow—can be determined experimentally by simply measuring the speed with which a bow shoots two arrows of different weight. Suppose we measure that a bow shoots an arrow of mass $M_1$ at a velocity $V_1$, and an arrow of a *heavier* mass $M_2$ at a velocity $V_2$. Then the effective mass of the bow is given by equation (1):

$$M_{eff} = \frac{M_2 V_2{}^2 - M_1 V_1{}^2}{V_1{}^2 - V_2{}^2}$$

The numerator of this expression is positive since the heavier arrow always has the greater kinetic energy; the denominator likewise is positive since the lighter arrow always has the higher velocity. As a result the value of the effective mass given by the equation is always positive.

Once we have calculated the effective mass from the above expression, the potential energy stored by the bow is given by the expression:

$$E = \frac{1}{2}\left(M_1 + M_{eff}\right)V_1{}^2$$

In this last expression we can also use the measured values of $M_2$ and $V_2$ in place of $M_1$ and $V_1$, and the result should be the same value for $E$. Equation (2) states that the potential energy stored by the bow is shared between the kinetic energy of the arrow and that of the bow.

*One note of caution*: the arrows used in this measurement should differ in weight by as much as possible. The greater the weight difference, the greater will be the difference in velocity and the more accurate will be the calculation of the effective mass in equation (1). The difference should be at least 200 grains or more, say a 350 grain and a 550 grain arrow. Since equation (1) contains differences between large numbers *squared* in both the numerator and denominator, small errors in the measured values of the arrow velocity will lead to much larger errors in the effective mass; so the measurement of arrow velocity should be done carefully and even repeated a number of times to get a more reliable average value. Also, the amount of potential energy stored by the bow depends on how far it is drawn. So the value calculated from the formula above pertains only to the draw length used in measuring the arrow velocities, which should be the same in every measurement. If the draw length changes, the stored energy will change and the arrow velocities will also change.

In equation (1) we can use any units we wish to express the mass or weight of the two arrows, and the value of the effective mass will be expressed in the same units. If the measured values are in grains, which is customary in archery, then the calculated value of the effective mass that results from equation (1) will also be in grains. The only restriction is that both the measured arrow weights have to be expressed in the same units. If the arrow weights are measured in pounds, ounces, kilograms, grams, or any other units, then the calculated value of the effective mass will be in the same units. It also does not matter what units are used to express the measured arrow velocity so long as the same units are used for both values. This is because the velocity units squared occur in both the numerator and denominator of the right hand side of equation (1) and cancel out. It is customary to use feet per second and most chronometers used to measure arrow velocity will give the measurement in those units; but meters per second will work equally well so long as the same units are used throughout.

We have to be a bit more careful in using equation (2). The units we wish to use for the stored energy E determine the units that we have to use in the right hand side of equation (2). It is customary in archery to express energy in foot-pounds. To make the value of E come out in foot-pounds, we have to measure arrow velocity in feet per second. In addition, if the arrow weights are measured in grains we have to multiply those values by the conversion factor 0.00000446 to make the units of energy be foot-pounds. If instead the arrow weights are measured in ounces, the conversion factor is 0.00195. If arrow weights are in pounds, the conversion factor is 0.0312. If you wish to be a purist and measure energy in the physicist's unit of joules, then arrow velocity must be measured in meters per second, and arrow mass must be expressed in kilograms (or in grams multiplied by 0.001). That is all you need to know about units to use these two equations.

In some cases you may be able to get a good estimate of the effective mass of your bow without making any measurements at all, using information already provided by the bowyer. Suppose your bow comes with a claim that the same bow in a draw weight of 60 pounds shoots a 400 grain, 29 inch arrow 190 feet per second. That is typical of the form such claims by bowyers take. And suppose the normal brace height is about 8-9 inches. Then the draw length will be about 20 inches and at that draw length the bow will store about 50 foot-pounds of energy. We obtain this value by multiplying the draw weight in pounds (60) times the draw length in feet (1.6667) times the shape factor, which for purposes of estimation here we take to be 0.5, as a value typical of many bows. According to equation (4) given below, this amount of stored energy will impart a velocity of 190 feet per second to a mass of 620 grains, which is the combined mass of the arrow plus the effective mass of the bow. Subtracting the 400 grain arrow mass gives an effective mass of 220 grains. If your bow has a lower or higher draw weight, then the effective mass may be slightly lower or higher than this. It is often possible to obtain a fairly good estimate this way.

Once you have determined the value of these two parameters—the effective mass and the stored energy—for a particular bow, you can completely characterize how that bow will perform when shooting an arrow of any weight. This includes finding the arrow velocity and the kinetic energy and momentum imparted to any weight arrow. We will consider each of these in turn, starting with the simplest.

The easiest parameter to use and interpret is the effective mass since it tells us immediately how the stored energy will be divided between the arrow and the bow. *The fraction of the stored energy imparted to the arrow is just the weight of the arrow divided by the sum of the arrow weight and the effective mass of the bow.* Similarly, the fraction of the energy retained by the bow is the effective mass divided by the sum of the effective mass and the arrow weight. If the effective mass and the arrow weight are equal, then half of the stored energy is imparted to the arrow and half is retained by the bow. If the arrow weight is twice the effective mass, then two thirds of the stored energy goes to the arrow and only one third stays with the bow. If, as in a more efficient bow, the arrow weight is about three times the effective mass, then three fourths of the energy is imparted to the arrow and only one fourth is retained by the bow. And so on.

Even the most efficient traditional bows have an effective mass somewhere in the range of 100-200 grains. If we assume 100 grains as the best case, such a bow would still retain 1/5, or 20 percent, of the stored energy when shooting a 400 grain arrow. The same bow shooting a 500 grain arrow would retain 1/6, or about 17 percent, of the stored energy. By shooting a heavier arrow we can increase the share of the energy imparted to the arrow; but as a practical matter, unless we are willing to shoot much heavier arrows than normally used even in hunting, we never go much beyond recovering somewhere around 3/4, or 75 percent, of the stored energy as kinetic energy imparted to the arrow, and that only in the more efficient bows. An effective mass of 200 grains or so is probably more representative of a majority of the bows, especially hunting bows, in use today. If a 400 grain arrow is shot from such a bow, only 2/3 of the stored energy is given to the arrow and 1/3 stays with the bow. With a 500 grain arrow about 0.71 of the energy is imparted to the arrow. And that is about the best one should expect in most cases.

We can define the *efficiency* of the bow as *the fraction of the stored energy that is imparted to the arrow*. The efficiency when shooting an arrow of mass $M$ is just

$$e = \frac{M}{M + M_{eff}}$$

where we use the measured value of the effective mass expressed in the same units as the weight of the arrow. The fraction of the stored energy retained by the bow is just $1 - e$. If we put 200 grains for the value of the effective mass and 400 grains for the weight of the arrow in equation (3), we obtain an efficiency of 2/3, or 67 percent; 2/3 of the energy is imparted to the arrow and 1/3 is retained by the bow. Once we know the effective mass of a bow we can use equation (3) to find its efficiency when shooting an arrow of any weight. The stored energy multiplied by the efficiency gives us the value of the kinetic energy, in foot-pounds, imparted to the arrow.

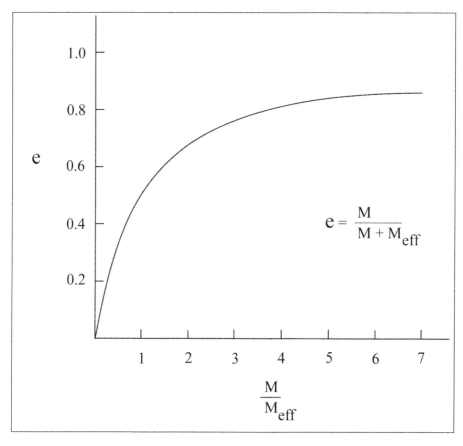

Figure 3. Curve showing how the efficiency $e$ of the bow depends on the ratio of arrow mass to the effective mass of the bow.

Figure 3 shows how the efficiency depends on the ratio of the arrow mass to the effective mass of the bow. The efficiency of course goes from 0 towards 1 as the weight of the arrow goes from 0 to ever-increasing values. Note from figure 3 that the efficiency initially rises fairly steeply as the arrow mass increases, until the arrow mass becomes a few times the effective mass, and from there the efficiency increases much more slowly as the arrow mass continues to increase. To keep the efficiency of the bow 0.7 (70 percent) or greater, we have to make the arrow mass at least 2.5 times the effective mass of the bow. Or stated another way, we have to keep the effective mass of the bow no greater than 0.4 (40 percent) of the arrow mass. That means if we are shooting 400 grain arrows the bow should have an effective mass of only 160, which is a very low value. Otherwise we may achieve good arrow velocity but poor energy (and momentum) efficiency.

We can change the arrow mass fairly easily and far less expensively than we can buy a new bow to reduce the effective mass. So we usually choose arrows that are greater than 2.5 times the effective mass of whatever bow we are shooting. For typical effective mass values of 200-250 grains, that means we should be shooting arrows of 500-625 grains in order achieve efficiencies of 70 percent of greater. Note also from figure 3 that the efficiency increases relatively little once the arrow weight is 3-4 times the effective mass of the bow. There is not much point in shooting arrows heavier than that since doing so primarily sacrifices arrow speed for relatively little increase in energy or momentum.

The velocity of an arrow of any mass can be found with the aid of the equation

$$V^2 = \frac{2\,E}{M + M_{eff}}$$

where we have to take the *square root* of the right hand side to obtain the arrow velocity. This is just equation (2) solved explicitly for velocity instead of energy. Note: To obtain arrow velocity in feet per second the energy must be in foot-pounds, and we have to multiply the arrow weight and the effective mass by the appropriate one of the conversion factors given previously. As an example, suppose we have a fifty pound bow that stores 42 foot-pounds of energy for a draw length of 20 inches and has an effective mass of 150 grains. The appropriate conversion factor to multiply the arrow mass and the effective mass by is 0.00000446 from above. Then such a bow will shoot a 400 grain arrow at 185 feet per second and a 500 grain arrow at 170 feet per second. If instead the effective mass of this bow is 250 grains, these values are reduced to 170 feet per second for the 400 grain arrow and 158 feet per second for the 500 grain arrow.

| M \ M$_{eff}$ | 100 | 150 | 200 | 250 | 300 | 350 | 400 | 450 |
|---|---|---|---|---|---|---|---|---|
| 100 | 321 | 287 | 262 | 243 | 227 | 214 | 203 | 194 |
| 150 | 287 | 262 | 243 | 227 | 214 | 203 | 194 | 185 |
| 200 | 262 | 243 | 227 | 214 | 203 | 194 | 185 | 178 |
| 250 | 243 | 227 | 214 | 203 | 194 | 185 | 178 | 172 |
| 300 | 227 | 214 | 203 | 194 | 185 | 178 | 172 | 166 |
| 350 | 214 | 203 | 194 | 185 | 178 | 172 | 166 | 160 |
| 400 | 203 | 194 | 185 | 178 | 172 | 166 | 160 | 156 |
| 450 | 194 | 185 | 178 | 172 | 166 | 160 | 156 | 151 |
| 500 | 185 | 178 | 172 | 166 | 160 | 156 | 151 | 147 |
| 550 | 178 | 172 | 166 | 160 | 156 | 151 | 147 | 144 |
| 600 | 172 | 166 | 160 | 156 | 151 | 147 | 144 | 140 |
| 650 | 166 | 160 | 156 | 151 | 147 | 144 | 140 | 137 |
| 700 | 160 | 156 | 151 | 147 | 144 | 140 | 137 | 134 |
| 750 | 156 | 151 | 147 | 144 | 140 | 137 | 134 | 131 |

**Table I. Arrow velocities in feet per second for values of arrow mass (M) and effective mass (M$_{eff}$) in grains for a stored energy of 46 foot-pounds. Each row corresponds to the arrow mass shown at the beginning of the row. Each column corresponds to the effective mass shown at the top of the column.**

Table I shows the values of arrow velocity (in feet per second) calculated using equation (4) for various combinations of arrow mass (*M*) and effective mass (*M$_{eff}$*) of the bow (in grains) The table is generated for a value of 46 foot-pounds for the stored energy of the bow. This is the energy stored, for example, in a typical 50-55 pound bow drawn about 20 inches, depending on the shape of the force curve. Each row in the table corresponds to the arrow mass shown at the beginning of the row. Each column corresponds to the effective mass shown at the top of the column. Arrow mass values are given in 50 grain steps from 100-750 grains; and effective mass values from 100-450 grains. Both of these ranges include essentially all of the values of interest in traditional archery. As an example of how to use the table, the velocity for an arrow mass of 450 grains and an effective mass of 250 grains is 172 feet per second, which can be found from the intersection of the row corresponding to 450 grains and the column corresponding to 250 grains. Note that the velocity values are all the same on any diagonal corresponding to a constant value of the total mass obtained by adding the arrow mass and the effective mass. From equation (4) we see that the arrow velocity stays the same if the total mass is constant.

Most values of practical interest are in the central portion of the table, between an effective mass of say 150 and 400 grains and an arrow mass of say 300 and 600 grains. In this region the arrow velocity doesn't change much as either the arrow mass or the effective mass change from one value to the next. We can estimate intermediate values by interpolating between the values shown in the table. For example, we can estimate the arrow velocity for a 425 grain arrow (half way between 400 and 450 grains) and an effective mass of 250 grains to be about 175 feet per second (half way between 172 and 178 feet per second). Similarly, the estimated value for a 425 grain arrow and an effective mass of 200 grains would be about 182 feet per second From these two values we can then estimate the velocity for a 425 grain arrow and an effective mass of 225 grains to be about 178-179 feet per second. The exact value calculated from equation (4) in this case is 178 feet per second. Generally the values estimated in this fashion are close enough for any comparisons we wish to make.

A more accurate way of obtaining values intermediate between those in the table is the following simple rule: The fractional (or percentage) change in arrow velocity is exactly *one half* the fractional (or percentage) change in the total mass (arrow mass plus the effective mass) as we go from one value in the table to any other value. As the total mass increases, the arrow velocity decreases, and vice versa. If we *reduce* the arrow mass, for example, from 450 to 400 grains for an effective mass of 250 grains, then the fractional change in the total mass is 50/700, or .071, and the fractional change in the arrow velocity would be half that amount, or about .036. Since the total mass decreases, the arrow velocity would *increase* by that fractional amount, from the value of 172 feet per second to 178 feet per second, as shown in the table. An exact method of finding the fractional change in the arrow velocity is to take the *square root* of the ratio of the two values of total mass. For the example above that would be the square root of 700/650 or 1.037

The fractional change in arrow velocity is likewise *one half* the fractional change in the stored energy. As the energy increases, the arrow velocity increases and vice versa. We can use that rule to convert the arrow velocities given in table I as the stored energy changes from 46 foot-pounds to some other value. If the stored energy goes from say 46 to 52 foot pounds, corresponding to a fractional increase of 0.13, then the arrow velocities shown in table I would increase by one half that fractional value, or about 0.06. Thus to obtain the arrow velocities corresponding to 52 foot pounds we would multiply the values in table I by 1.06. As before, an exact way of finding the fractional change in arrow velocity is to take the square root of the ratio of the two energy values. In this example that would be the square root of 56/42 which is 1.06. For convenience, I have listed in table II the appropriate factors by which to multiply the velocities in table I for various values of the stored energy. Each of these factors is just the square root of the corresponding energy value divided by 46. For energy values between those shown in the table one can use the factor that is half way between the ones listed in the table.

| Energy in Foot-Pounds | 26 | 30 | 34 | 38 | 42 | 46 | 50 | 54 | 58 | 62 | 66 |
|---|---|---|---|---|---|---|---|---|---|---|---|
| Multiplication Factor | 0.75 | 0.81 | 0.86 | 0.91 | 0.96 | 1.00 | 1.04 | 1.08 | 1.12 | 1.16 | 1.20 |

**Table II. Multiplication factors by which the arrow velocities in Table I have to multiplied for different values of the stored energy in foot-pounds.**

All of the numbers that I use in the examples in this book can be obtained from the values listed in table I in the fashion discussed above. This is all one needs to know about how arrow velocity depends on arrow mass and the effective mass and stored energy of the bow.

Equation (4) can be used to understand another result encountered by the archer. Increasing the draw weight of a bow often does not produce an equivalent improvement in arrow velocity. Increasing the draw weight should increase the stored energy in the same proportion, and that in turn should lead to greater arrow velocity as indicated by equation (4). But the only way to achieve greater draw weight is to increase the thickness or the width of the limbs or use thicker fiberglass, in short to increase the physical mass of the limbs. But that also increases the effective mass which means that more energy will be retained by the bow and less imparted to the arrow. The result is that the increase in the effective mass in the denominator of equation (4) partially offsets the increase in stored energy in the numerator. To see how this works, suppose we increase the draw weight from 50 pounds to 65 pounds while also increasing the effective mass from 200 grains to 250 grains. Then if we shoot a 450 grain arrow in both bows, the arrow velocity will increase by only a factor of 1.10, or 10 percent. The same increase in draw weight alone would have produced an increase in arrow velocity by a factor of 1.14, or 14 percent. Part of the expected increase in arrow velocity is lost to the increased kinetic energy retained by the bow.

Momentum is likewise divided between the arrow and the bow. We can choose to define a total momentum as the sum of the momentum imparted to the arrow and the momentum retained by the effective mass of the bow. *The fraction of the total momentum imparted to the arrow is the same as the bow's energy efficiency.* In other words the arrow receives the same fraction of the total momentum as it does the total energy. With the total momentum defined this way, the momentum efficiency and the energy efficiency are the same. One difficulty with this definition of total momentum is that, unlike the total energy, it is not constant, but increases proportional to the square root of the total of the arrow mass plus the effective mass of the bow. The total momentum and the maximum momentum that can be imparted to an arrow increase as the mass of the arrow increases. Since the efficiency of a bow improves as the weight of the arrow increases, a bow always imparts more momentum to a heavier arrow than a lighter one.

The potential energy stored by a bow, and its effective mass, depend in a complicated way on the details of the bow design, primarily on the shape and material properties of the bow limbs. Still it is possible to make some general comments about how these parameters are affected by the design features of the bow. The more steeply the force increases at the beginning of the draw, the greater will be the amount of energy stored in the fully drawn bow. Another way of saying the same thing is that any leveling off of the force during the draw will result in more stored energy for the same final draw weight. This is because there is more area included under the force curve. One way of accomplishing this is by using the deflexed-reflexed shape in which the limb bends toward the archer at its root (deflexed) and away from the archer toward the tip (reflexed). The extreme form of this is a highly recurved limb sharply deflexed where it joins the handle, and such a design will store more potential energy for the same draw weight, as much as 10-25 percent more. However, this shape limb tends to be unstable and is prone to twisting, which makes it more difficult to construct and tiller. The deflexed-recurved limb found on the modern recurve bow is a more modest version of this design and accounts in part for the improved performance of this type of bow.

The other part of that improvement is related to the effective mass. Reducing the effective mass means keeping the actual mass of the bow limbs as small as possible. Although the effective mass is not the same as the actual mass of the limbs, it is proportional to it in some fashion. Making the limbs physically heavier will increase the effective mass and result in less energy going to the arrow and more of it being retained by the bow. The ideal bow would have massless limbs, something which of course cannot be achieved. The closest we can come is to make the limbs as stiff as possible for the least amount of limb material. So we use very thin limbs, only wide enough to keep them from twisting, and make them stiff by recurving them and by using a thin layer of high modulus fiberglass laminated on both sides. For this reason the modern laminated recurved limb generally has a lower effective mass and is more efficient at imparting energy to the arrow than other limb designs.

We can use the same idea to distinguish between different recurved limbs. A limb that has very heavy recurved tips that do not bend, or bend very little, will not be as efficient as one with thinner, lighter tips that do bend. The latter design will have less actual weight in the limb and as a result will have a smaller effective mass. Any extra weight in the tips is a liability, soaking up kinetic energy that otherwise would go to the arrow and impart higher velocity. A limb that is more severely bent at full draw to stress the fiberglass laminations closer to the elastic limit will also require less limb material and will exhibit a smaller effective mass. The way to stress the limb more is to bend it farther, which means making the limb as short as possible for a given length bow. The modern recurve bow achieves this by using relatively short limbs, at least for the portion of the limb that actually bends, together with a riser section that gives the desired overall length to the bow. The same length limbs can be used to make a bow of any desired length by simply changing the length of the handle section. The same limbs on a longer handle will not bend as far and will not be as highly stressed and will have a lower draw weight on the longer handle than they would on a shorter bow.

It is also easy to see why it is better to change the thickness rather than the width of the limb to change the draw weight. Draw weight is directly proportional to the width of the limb, but depends on the thickness cubed, or raised to the third power. To double the draw weight of a bow the width of the limbs would have to be doubled everywhere, whereas increasing limb thickness by a factor of 1.26, or only 26 percent, would double the draw weight. Much smaller changes in limb thickness than in width are required to produce the same change in draw weight, and lead to much smaller increases in the effective mass of the limbs.

These are only some of the design features that one can relate to the stored energy and effective mass of a bow; but they illustrate just how useful these two concepts are in understanding the way a bow imparts velocity, kinetic energy, and momentum to an arrow, and how that performance depends on the various design features of the bow. A measurement of the velocity of two arrows of different weights at the same draw length is all that is required to find the value of both of these parameters. And with that you have all the information you need to assess your bow's performance or to compare the relative performance of different bows.

# What Do You Gain by Shooting a Heavier Bow?

*Should you pay the price to shoot a heavier hunting bow or is the one you are already using adequate? Here are some of the tradeoffs.*

Suppose you have been shooting a traditional hunting bow of say 50 pounds draw weight at your particular draw length. The bow is comfortable for you to pull and shoot even on the field range over a complete twenty-eight target course. Better still you can pull and hold it comfortably enough to let you shoot accurately. When you do miss it is because you misjudged the aim and not because you hurried the shot or released prematurely due to the bow's draw weight. As a result you have developed a reassuring degree of confidence that you can shoot this bow well. When you do get a shot under hunting conditions there are no negative feelings beforehand about missing. You expect to hit what you are shooting at and to make a clean kill, and you have a number of successes to reinforce that feeling.

Not only have you learned to shoot well by not overbowing yourself, you have learned that success means staying within the limitations of your equipment. Realizing (as most archers do not) that *a bow always imparts more energy and momentum to a heavier arrow*, you have chosen to shoot the heaviest shafts that will match your bow in spine and still give a reasonably flat trajectory over the limited distances that most hunting shots are made. That way you have assured the greatest possible penetration from your arrows. To compensate, you simply limit your shots when hunting to those distances at which the higher trajectory of the heavier arrow still allows accurate shooting.

On the face of it this sounds like pretty much the ideal situation. Yet you still wonder if you might not be better off with a heavier bow. The heavier bow would store more energy, and that means it would impart more energy and momentum to the arrow at a higher velocity. That in turn would mean greater penetration and a flatter trajectory, both of which could be a distinct advantage in a hunting bow. You do not shoot your bow that often when hunting, you reason, and you can always do most of your practicing with a lighter bow, only tuning up with the heavier bow long enough to learn to compensate for its flatter trajectory. That way you can prevent a lot of the bad shooting habits that come from being overbowed. Besides, you can comfortably pull a 60 pound bow to full draw and a 70 pound bow with manageable difficulty.

Everyone who hunts with a traditional bow faces this same dilemma in one form or another at some time. Perhaps you have been hunting deer for years and now you want to try elk. An elk is a much larger and heavier boned animal than even a big whitetail or mule deer, requiring potentially more penetration to achieve a sure kill. Maybe you have in mind eventually hunting moose or even species other than North American animals. Maybe you are simply tired of turning down shots that you feel you could make with a flatter trajectory. Or maybe you have seen an arrow stopped, and an animal lost, by hitting a shoulder or other bone in even a smaller animal like a deer, and you want as much penetrating power as you can command. Or perhaps you simply want to try a heavier bow as part of broadening your experience of bowhunting. Whatever the specific reason, every one of us asks at some point, "How heavy a hunting bow should I shoot and what are the possible tradeoffs?"

To try and get a handle on answering this question, let's compare your present 50 pound bow with what you should expect from a 60 pound bow and a 70 pound bow of the same design. To do that of course we will look at the velocity that each will impart to hunting arrows of various weights, along with the factors determining that and the effect on the trajectory of the arrow.

A 50 pound bow with a draw length of 20 inches, corresponding to an arrow length of about 28-29 inches, typically stores about 42 foot-pounds of energy. A straight-limbed bow might store a little less than this and a recurve bow a bit more, but this is a good nominal figure with which to make comparisons. No bow is one hundred percent efficient in imparting all of the stored energy to the arrow. When the arrow leaves the string the bow limbs and string are still moving and some portion of the stored energy is retained by the bow as kinetic energy. The quantity which describes the amount of energy retained by the bow is its *effective mass*. The effective mass of the bow is just the amount of mass that traveling at the same velocity as the arrow has the same kinetic energy as the moving bow limbs. Let's assume that you are already shooting a fairly efficient bow with an effective mass of 200 grains. The most efficient bows might have a value less than this, but there are also a lot of traditional bows of this draw weight that have an effective mass greater than 200 grains.

Let's assume that you are shooting 450 grain hunting arrows in your present bow. Then the stored energy of the bow will be imparted to a total mass of 650 grains, the 450 grain mass of the arrow *plus* the 200 grain effective mass of the bow. So 450/650, or 0.69, of the energy will be imparted to the arrow, and 200/650, or 0.31, of the energy will be retained by the bow. That's how it works, and why it is so important to know the effective mass of your bow and to take it into account when thinking about its performance.

A stored energy of 42 foot-pounds will give the 450 grain arrow an initial velocity of 170 feet per second. That is a respectable value for a traditional bow with a draw weight of 50 pounds shooting a 450 grain arrow. The kinetic energy of the arrow will be 29 foot-pounds, and the bow will retain 13 foot-pounds of the stored energy. If instead you were shooting 500 grain arrows in this bow, then 5/7, or 0.71, of the stored energy would be imparted to the arrow, giving it a kinetic energy of about 30 foot-pounds. But in that case the arrow velocity would be reduced to 164 feet per second. An arrow weight of 450 grains in this case seems like a reasonable compromise between trajectory and arrow penetration.

How are these values going to change as we increase the draw weight of the bow? We will assume that the design of the bow does not change, only its draw weight. You simply choose a stronger version of the same bow you have been shooting, since we do not want to compare apples and oranges.

The energy stored by the bow is directly proportional to the draw weight. If we increase the draw weight from 50 pounds to 60 pounds, then the stored energy will increase by the same proportion, or 20 percent, to 50 foot-pounds. Increasing the draw weight by 40 percent to 70 pounds will increase the stored energy to 58 foot-pounds. If nothing else changed, and the arrow weight and the effective mass of the bow stayed the same, then the *percentage* increase in arrow velocity would be *half* the percentage increase in the draw weight. The 60 pound bow would shoot 450 grain arrows at a velocity of about 186 feet per second; the 70 pound bow would shoot the same arrows at a velocity of about 200 feet per second.

But the stronger bow has heavier limbs and so the effective mass of the bow, even a bow of the same design, will increase a little. A rough rule of thumb is that the minimum *percentage* increase in the effective mass should be about *one third* the percentage increase in the draw weight. The effective mass of the 60 pound bow will be about 215 grains and that of the 70 pound bow will be about 225 grains. We should stress that these are optimistic values achieved by only the more efficient reflexed and recurved laminated limbs. Using these values, the velocity of a 450 grain arrow will be 184 feet per second for the 60 pound bow, and 196 feet per second for the 70 pound bow, only a slight decrease.

If our primary aim in going to the heavier draw weight is to achieve a flatter trajectory by obtaining greater arrow speed, then this is probably the right approach. We would keep the arrow weight the same and take advantage of the full increase in arrow speed that the greater draw weight gives us. With all of the choices of arrow shafts available to us we can easily keep the same arrow weight while still achieving enough stiffness to match the arrows to the stronger bow in each case.

However, in all fairness, we should put the potential advantage of the higher arrow speed and flatter trajectory in some kind of perspective. The quicker the arrow reaches the target the less time it has to drop under the influence of gravity and the easier it will be to estimate the aim if shooting without a sight. Or the less accurately the distance has to be estimated if using a sight. At a distance of 40 yards an arrow going 170 feet per second will fall an extra 14 inches more than one traveling 184 feet per second; and about 24 inches more than one traveling 196 feet per second. The corresponding differences at 30 yards are 8 inches and 13 inches. At 20 yards the differences are only 4 inches and 6 inches. The differences in each case represent how much higher the slower arrow would have to be pointed to hit the same spot as the faster arrow.

These latter values mean that there is virtually no advantage in trajectory and aiming at a distance of 20 yards for the fastest arrow over the slowest. A difference of 4-6 inches is just not that important in any indirect, or point-and-shoot, method of aiming a bow. The brain quickly learns to adjust for differences of that amount, and much larger, or point-and-shoot aiming wouldn't work in the first place. I would argue similarly that the differences are not really important at 30 yards. Even at 40 yards these differences are still not nearly as large as the amount by which even the fastest arrow falls in traveling that far. However they quickly become more significant at distances beyond that.

Another way of getting a handle on this is to look at the differences in trajectory at 20 to 40 yards for an arrow of each speed. At 170 feet per second an arrow will drop about 24 inches at 20 yards, 54 inches at 30 yards, and 96 inches at 40 yards; at 184 feet per second the drop is about 20 inches at 20 yards, 46 inches at 30 yards, and 82 inches at 40 yards; at 196 feet per second the drop is 18 inches at 20 yards, 40 inches at 30 yards, and 72 inches at 40 yards. Each of these values represents how far above the intended impact spot the arrow has to be pointed when aiming. Although these distances may seem alarmingly large at first sight, they represent elevations of only 2-4 degrees in the worst case. And that means the arrow will still look practically horizontal to the archer in point-and-shoot aiming. They don't look quite so unrealistic when converted to feet instead of inches. In the worst case the drop is 2 feet at 20 yards; 4.5 feet at 30 yards; and 8 feet at 40 yards.

For all of these arrow speeds the drop is already appreciable at 20 yards and becomes quite large at 40 yards. This drop has to be compensated for in the process of aiming. In assessing the importance of arrow speed, the *additional* drop between the fastest and slowest arrows has to be compared with the normal drop of the fastest arrow. Looking at these values that way we can see that all three arrows drop about the same amount in the first 20 yards so that all three bows will shoot virtually the same at that distance; and that no one could shoot any of them very accurately beyond 40 yards unless the exact distance was known beforehand, usually not the situation in hunting. The trajectories beyond 20 yards are in reality worse than the values given because we have not taken into account any slowing of the arrow due to friction, which becomes worse beyond 20 yards. Somewhere in between is the effective limit of accurate shooting with any of these three draw weights. Viewed this way there really is no inherent advantage in the heaviest bow over the lightest; all three are limited to about the same effective range. The message is that going to either of the heavier bows just to improve the trajectory is probably not a good idea at practical hunting distances.

Suppose on the other hand our main concern is to achieve greater arrow penetration. Then we might opt instead to choose the heaviest arrows that allow us to achieve the same arrow speed with the heavier bow that we were getting before from the 50 pound bow. Heavier arrows will always have greater kinetic energy and momentum, and hence greater penetration, than lighter arrows shot from the same bow. The 60 pound bow would shoot a 560 grain arrow 170 feet per second; the 70 pound bow would shoot a 674 grain arrow at that speed. We could choose to shoot arrows up to the heavier weight in each case and still achieve the same arrow velocity that we were getting with the 50 pound bow. In this way we could take advantage of the greater penetration of the heavier arrows without any sacrifice in trajectory.

Or we could compromise somewhere in between. We could trade a little of the potential increase in arrow speed for better arrow penetration by increasing the arrow weight more modestly, somewhere in between 450 grains and the values indicated above. By shooting a 500 grain arrow in the 60 pound bow we could improve arrow speed to 177 feet per second and still take advantage of increased arrow penetration. Shooting a 500 grain arrow in the 70 pound bow would improve the arrow speed to 189 feet per second while improving arrow penetration. A 550 grain arrow in the 70 pound bow results in an arrow speed of 183 feet per second with improved penetration.

As you see we really don't increase arrow speed by all that much in going to a heavier bow, even if we keep the weight of the arrow the same. With the 50 pound bow we were able to shoot a 450 grain arrow 170 feet per second. With draw weights of 60 and 70 pounds, the same weight arrow had speeds of 184 and 196 feet per second. But most hunting shots are at relatively close range, the vast majority at 40 yards or less, most of the time at half that distance. At those distances, the difference between 170 and even 196 feet per second is insignificant for the most part. Sure it is a bit easier to aim and shoot with the flatter trajectory, but out to about 40 yards the difference in trajectory between an arrow traveling 170 feet per second and one traveling196 feet per second is just not a big factor. No one ever failed to make a kill because of that kind of difference in arrow speed.

Couple that with the greater difficulty of shooting a heavier bow accurately and you can see that it is hard to justify going to the heavier draw weight just to gain a flatter trajectory.

The same is not true however for arrow penetration. The 70 pound bow allows us to shoot 674 grain arrows at 170 feet per second, corresponding to a kinetic energy of 43 foot-pounds. This is an increase of almost 50 percent over the 29 foot-pound energy of 450 grain arrows shot at the same speed from the 50 pound bow. And that 50 percent increase in the kinetic energy of the arrow translates into a potential 50 percent increase in arrow penetration, which might very well be the difference in whether you make a clean kill on a really large animal. Similarly, the 60 pound bow shooting 560 grain arrows at 170 feet per second corresponds to a kinetic energy of 36 foot-pounds, which is a 25 percent increase in kinetic energy and a potential 25 percent increase in penetration.

The same is true of the improvement in momentum. The percentage increases in momentum are the same as those for kinetic energy, so that it doesn't really matter whether penetration in any given instance is controlled more by kinetic energy of the arrow or by its momentum. The potential improvement in penetration is exactly the same in either case. But to be fair, arrows this heavy are not required on any but the largest, thick-skinned and heavy-boned animals, which most of us will never have an occasion to hunt. In all but those instances there is really no significant advantage to be gained by the greater draw weights.

More than one bowyer who sells hunting bows to traditional archers has told me that the average draw weight of the bows being purchased has crept up in recent years. It is not clear why but if generally true it is probably a bad sign. It probably means less hunting success and more frustrated bowhunters, and more who will give up archery over the kinds of shooting problems that being overbowed almost always leads to. If anything, improvements in bows should allow the average draw weight to decrease.

The message here is clear. The only compelling reason to go to a heavier hunting bow is to achieve greater arrow penetration. And even that has to be weighed against the difficulty of handling the increased draw weight. No one ever killed an animal that he couldn't hit, and too many animals are lost because they are not hit in a vital spot. It is always a better idea to shoot 'em where you know you can kill 'em. A bow too heavy in draw weight to shoot accurately is a poor choice under any circumstances. Better to limit the distance at which you are willing to shoot, and to use a bow that you can shoot with confidence and accuracy out to that distance under all conditions. Then choose the heaviest arrows that still allow you to shoot well at that range. When you have done that you have made all the right choices.

# How to Shoot Far

*Have you ever wondered about shooting a quarter of a mile, or even half a mile? Here is what it takes.*

The bow is by no means a long-range weapon. It is decidedly a short-range instrument. Anyone who has ever shot a bow quickly becomes aware of that particular limitation. As a hunting weapon the bow is most effective at distances less than thirty to forty yards. The majority of successful shots at game are made even closer than that and as a practical matter its use in hunting is limited to no more than fifty or sixty yards under the best conditions. As a precision target instrument, even in the hands of the best archers in the world, its effective use is limited to no more than 100 yards. The range of the storied English longbow, one of the foremost military weapons of its day, which determined the outcome of battles at places like Crecy and Agincourt was limited to about 250 yards. At distances less than that, archers could rain down deadly swarms of bodkin-pointed arrows on massed troops; but they had to wait until they were at least that close. Beyond that range they could not shoot arrows heavy enough to be effective no matter how powerful the bow.

The reason is simple. Even neglecting air resistance an arrow must have a velocity of 155 feet per second to travel 250 yards. With air resistance, a velocity of 170-180 feet per second is required, and that is about the limit of an English longbow even one with a very heavy draw weight. Even the most efficient modern recurve bow capable of achieving 200-210 feet per second will only shoot a heavy hunting arrow with typical fletching about 300-350 yards.

To understand why, one has to realize that a bow, even a relatively strong one, is capable of storing only a modest amount of energy. The stored energy is the product of the force required to pull the bow to full draw (the draw weight), the distance through which the string is actually pulled (the draw length, not the arrow length), and a factor that depends on the exact shape of the force curve, or how the force increases as the bow is drawn. These three quantities have to be multiplied together to find the stored energy. For an English longbow the shape factor can be as low as 0.45. For the most efficient recurve bows the shape factor only increases to about 0.55-0.60, with 0.50-0.55 probably being more representative. So across the board we can use a shape factor of 0.5 as representing the typical energy storage of traditional bows.

That means that a bow of either type with a draw weight of 60 pounds will store only about 50 foot-pounds of energy, assuming a draw length of 20 inches corresponding to an arrow length of about 28 inches. If all of that energy could be imparted to a 500 grain arrow, it would propel the arrow with a velocity of about 212 feet per second, which would be enough to get us out to 350 yards or so. Unfortunately, when the arrow leaves the bow the limbs are still moving and a fraction of the stored energy is retained by the bow as kinetic energy of the limbs and string. That fraction is determined by the *effective mass* of the bow, *an equivalent mass that, moving at the same speed as the arrow, would equal the energy of the moving limbs and string.* The energy is divided between the arrow and the bow in proportion to the mass of each divided by the sum of the arrow mass and the effective mass of the bow.

For an English longbow with a draw weight of 60 pounds, the effective mass will likely be as much as 300 grains or more. So when shooting a 500 grain arrow, only 5/8 of the stored energy actually goes to the arrow and 3/8 is retained by the bow. Instead of 212 feet per second, the arrow velocity is only 167 feet per second and the range will be more like 200 yards. Suppose we could decrease the effective mass of the bow by a factor of 2, down to 150 grains. This value is achieved by the most efficient recurve bows with wood and fiberglass laminated limbs. Then the velocity of a 500 grain arrow shot out of our 60 pound bow would be 186 feet per second, which would be capable of reaching 225-250 yards.

Suppose we try to solve this problem by increasing the draw weight of the bow, from 60 pounds to say 90 pounds, which would still have been within the capability of a well-conditioned and practiced English archer. Then the energy stored by the bow would go up by the ratio of the draw weights, or by the ratio of 90 to 60, a factor of 1.5. Increasing the stored energy by a factor of 1.5 would give us a theoretical increase in arrow velocity by the square root of 1.5 which is about 1.22, or a little over 20 percent. But two things happen to partially offset the advantage of the greater draw weight. The first is that we have to shoot a stiffer arrow in the stronger bow, which generally means a heavier arrow and less velocity. The second is that the stronger bow will have heavier limbs and a greater effective mass.

Imagine that we increase the arrow weight by only 150 grains, from 500 to 650 grains. The increase in draw weight from 60 to 90 pounds would increase the effective mass of the bow from 300 grains to perhaps 350 grains. The result of these two changes is that the arrow velocity increases not by 20 percent but by only 10 percent, from 167 feet per second to 184 feet per second, and we still can't shoot beyond about 250 yards. Regardless of how we try to manipulate the numbers, we are still always stuck at something around 250 yards.

We could of course always shoot a lighter arrow, to achieve a higher velocity. But the English archer could not do that. A lighter arrow would not have enough energy or momentum to penetrate the armor or protective clothing of his adversary. For the same reason, a lighter hunting arrow to achieve greater velocity and a flatter trajectory is not a wise choice for the bowhunter. As we have seen a better choice is to limit the range to those distances at which one can accurately shoot a reasonably heavy arrow that will have adequate penetration.

How then did the Ottoman Turks, as far back as the fifteenth century, manage to shoot distances of half a mile? There were in Constantinople shooting fields with stone markers commemorating individual feats of distance shooting that far surpass anything that can be done with the English longbow and that have only been equaled in recent times using modern technology. A short answer is that they used a combination of powerful bows with low effective mass, and light arrows with low air resistance, to achieve the necessary velocity to shoot these amazing distances. Anyone interested in an account of Turkish archery and their distance records can find them in *Turkish Archery* by Paul Klopsteg, recently reprinted by Derrydale Press.

What then does it take to shoot a quarter of a mile (440 yards) or half a mile (880 yards)? Neglecting air resistance, an initial velocity of 206 feet per second would propel an arrow 440 yards. With air resistance, even making the fletching as small as possible and the cross-sectional area of the shaft a bare minimum, a velocity of about 230 feet per second is required. To shoot 880 yards would require 291 feet per second, neglecting air resistance, and about 340 feet per second taking even minimal air resistance into account. The exact value depends on whether we assume that the air resistance is proportional to the *momentum* of the arrow or its *kinetic energy* (proportional to the velocity of the arrow, or to the velocity squared). For even the most streamlined flight arrows with the area of the fletching held to an absolute minimum, the coefficient of friction is about 2.7 percent (0.027) of the momentum of the arrow, or about 0.045 percent (0.00045) of the kinetic energy of the arrow. Let us see how we might go about achieving these arrow velocities with a bow.

We can quickly convince ourselves that shooting 440 yards is not all that difficult. To illustrate why, assume a stored energy of 50 foot-pounds. This amount of energy will impart the necessary velocity of 230 feet per second to a total mass of 425 grains. That means the combined mass of the arrow and the effective mass of the bow together can be as large as 425 grains. If we design a bow to have an effective mass as low as 150 grains, then we can shoot a 275 grain arrow at the required velocity of 230 feet per second needed to achieve 440 yards. How do we design a bow storing 50 foot-pounds of energy (65 pounds drawn about 18 inches) to have an effective mass of only 150 grains? By keeping the limbs as light as possible. And that means making them thin and short, recurving them to increase the stress in the material on the back and face of the limb, and bending them as close to the fracture limit as practical. A good flight bow should be almost broken when it is fully drawn. We also have to reduce the arrow weight to 275 grains while keeping it stiff enough to shoot out of a bow pulling 65 pounds or more. That means a short arrow, to keep it both light and stiff, and that in turn suggests using a bow with some sort of overdraw shelf on the front and a handle extension on the back. We don't want to waste any energy by having the arrow flex and bend around the bow, so we make the arrow stiff and make the bow completely center-shot. A keyhole design is the optimum here in which the arrow is shot through a hole cut out in the center of the bow handle. To assure a clean departure of the arrow from the bow we use a double flipper or some other type of release aid to prevent twisting or deflecting the string as it is released. A double flipper pulls the bowstring by wrapping the two ends of a long strip of leather around the string in opposite directions. The strip of leather loops around the fingers and the two ends are pinched together between the thumb and forefinger of the drawing hand. The Turks employed a thumb ring very much like a modern non mechanical release.

Of course we could also reach 440 yards with a bow having an effective mass as high as 200 grains if we further reduce the arrow weight to 225 grains to achieve our goal of 425 grains. With arrows as short as 18 inches or so, arrow weights this low while still maintaining adequate stiffness to shoot out of a 65 pound flight bow are no problem. So we see that the task of shooting 440 yards is relatively straightforward.

What about a distance of 880 yards? Can it be attained the same way? In this case we need an arrow velocity of 340 feet per second, or more, and that is a formidable challenge. A stored energy of 50 foot-pounds would impart this much velocity to a mass of 194 grains. The combined mass of the arrow and the effective mass of the bow can be no larger than 194 grains. It is possible to make 18 inch flight arrows out of specially selected Port Orford cedar that weigh less than 150 grains and are still stiff enough to shoot properly out of a 65 pound bow. The author has some arrows like this which were made by the noted arrowsmith Riley Denton of Tacoma, Washington over thirty years ago. They were fashioned from a special cedar log designated Ulrich Number Nine which he had found to yield the highest quality and most uniform dowels. The lightest of them weighs only 127 grains and shoots well in a 65 pound flight bow made by Harry Drake, so long as the shooter's form is flawless. Let's assume an arrow weight of 130 grains. Then the effective mass of the bow would have to be no bigger than 64 grains. This is attainable, but probably just barely. The author's Harry Drake flight bow has been chronographed at 341 feet per second shooting a 127 grain arrow, which translates into an effective mass of about 66 grains. I say about because I have never bothered to measure the stored energy exactly. Here we are probably nearing the limit of what can be achieved using fiberglass and wood and traditional bows.

If we want to improve on these distances then we probably have to go to stronger bows with higher draw weights. If we increase the stored energy to 60 foot-pounds by increasing the draw weight 20 percent, then to achieve an arrow velocity of 340 feet per second the combined arrow mass and effective mass of the bow can be as high as 230 grains, which means an effective mass of 100 grains for an arrow weight of 130 grains. An effective mass of 100 grains is probably within the limits of what can be achieved by proper design, even with a stronger bow. Hand-held bows like this have shot beyond a half mile in flight competition.

Beyond just having a bow and arrows capable of these kinds of speeds, there is also a great deal of skill and refinement in shooting technique required to wring the maximum yardage out of the shot. The shot has to be executed at the correct angle of elevation (around 42 degrees) while the bow is being drawn, without ever coming to a complete pause in the draw, all the while pulling the arrow right to the very tip on the arrow rest. The motion of the bow has to be still forward in a straight line without any twisting while the motion of the draw has to be smoothly rearward when the release occurs; and the arrow has to leave the bow straight without fishtailing or porpoising. If you can see the arrow leave the bow it is probably because it did not leave cleanly. The same bow and the same arrows in the hands of two different shooters may achieve very different results depending on the form of the archer. There is a fair amount of risk involved too. During my first foray into flight shooting, a friend, using my flight bow, pulled the arrow off the end of the rest and shot it cleanly through his bow hand. It looked like he had impaled himself on a knitting needle. Seeing that happen quickly leads to the development of a full-blown flinch.

What place does all of this obsession and fascination with distance have in traditional archery? Why be concerned at all about how far a bow will shoot? Even if we can shoot a traditional bow half a mile that doesn't alter the fact that the bow is still a short-range instrument. The kinds of bows and arrows required to shoot that far have no practical place in the rest of archery, especially not as hunting weapons or as implements of precision shooting. A 130 grain arrow is useless for anything except achieving higher arrow velocity to see how far one can shoot. A short, sensitive flight bow, with a handle extension on the back and overdraw shelf on the face of the bow for shooting short arrows, is impossible to use with any degree of accuracy. The only thing required in flight shooting is that the arrows go in the forward direction. The sole objective is distance.

Besides being an integral part of archery traditions—and hence an important part of traditional archery—dating back to the fifteenth century and before, distance shooting is valuable for what it teaches us about improving the design of bows and the materials from which they are constructed. It is by pushing any technology to its ultimate limits that one learns the most about what is necessary and most important in improving it further. Flight archery plays a role in the technology of traditional archery somewhat analogous to that of racing in the technology of automobiles. It is equally important, and beneficial, for the deeper understanding it gives us about the limits to our traditional bow designs, even if we are not interested in improving them further but only enjoying them the way they are. There is a deep pleasure and satisfaction in understanding these things, even if that pleasure is our only real objective.

# The Plain (and Simple) Truth about Arrow Penetration

*Why a heavier arrow will always penetrate better than a lighter arrow shot from the same bow.*

*D*oes a heavier arrow penetrate farther than a lighter one shot from the same bow, or is it the other way round? Which is more important in determining arrow penetration, kinetic energy or momentum? Shouldn't it be possible to achieve greater kinetic energy—and greater penetration—by shooting a lighter arrow at higher velocity? Or is it better to shoot a heavier arrow at slower speeds but with greater momentum?

These are typical of the questions that come up whenever the conversations turns, as it invariably does among bowhunters, to the subject of arrow penetration. It is a topic that generates probably more confusion and controversy than any other between those who advocate the virtues of heavier hunting arrows and those who are addicted to faster arrow flight and flatter trajectories. After reading article after article on the subject, some of which even managed to arrive at the right conclusion though usually for the wrong reasons, I have yet to see one which pointed out the obvious. Far from clearing up the confusion, they generally end up adding to it.

The argument usually bogs down around the question of whether penetration depends more on the kinetic energy of the arrow or its momentum. As we will see, this controversy between kinetic energy and momentum is a bogus issue based on a complete misunderstanding of how a bow works.

Let's state the answer right up front. The plain and simple truth is that *a heavier arrow will always penetrate better than a lighter arrow shot from the same bow*. This assumes, of course, that all other conditions stay the same: same shape and size of broadheads, same degree of sharpness, same fletching, same shaft diameter, and so on. It is to be emphasized that we are comparing arrows shot from the same bow. I mention these other factors at the outset just to keep the discussion honest.

The last point is especially important. Several times I have seen comparisons of penetration between arrows that differ in energy or momentum in such a way that they could not have been shot from the same bow. The laws of physics made it impossible. Such comparisons are completely pointless and irrelevant since you can only shoot one bow at a time. The question here isn't whether to shoot a heavier or lighter draw weight bow. The only question facing the bowhunter is whether to shoot a heavier or lighter arrow out of whatever bow is chosen for use.

And here's the obvious part. Heavier arrows penetrate better for a very simple reason: *a bow always imparts greater kinetic energy and greater momentum to a heavier arrow than to a lighter one.* It really doesn't matter whether one argues that kinetic energy or momentum is more important for penetration. The heavier arrow always has more of both than a lighter arrow shot from the same bow. That's the important point. Furthermore, the heavier arrow not only starts out with more energy and momentum, it also arrives at the target with more of both. When it comes to penetration lighter arrows always lose. The only advantage of a lighter hunting arrow is higher arrow speed and a flatter trajectory, but both come at some sacrifice of kinetic energy and momentum—and less penetration.

If this is true, then why all of the disagreement and controversy? The source of confusion is that few archers realize *why* a bow imparts more kinetic energy and momentum to a heavier arrow. The mistaken argument one most often hears—and even sees in print—is that the heavier arrow can have more momentum but the lighter one more kinetic energy. Momentum is the mass of the arrow multiplied by its velocity (or MV); kinetic energy is one half the mass multiplied by the square of velocity (or ½ MV$^2$). The idea, presumably, is that the heavier arrow, though traveling slower, can have greater momentum because of its larger mass; while the lighter arrow, even though it has less mass, is traveling faster and can have greater kinetic energy since that quantity depends on the *square* of the velocity. But it just doesn't work that way. This argument, no matter how many times it has been repeated and made its way into the archery literature, is simply wrong. The lighter arrow will indeed have higher velocity than a heavier arrow. *But the heavier arrow will have both more kinetic energy and more momentum and as a result will penetrate better.*

Why then does a bow always impart greater kinetic energy and momentum to a heavier arrow? The key is that not all of the energy stored in the drawn bow can be transferred to the arrow. At the instant the arrow leaves the string, the bow limbs and string are still moving and posses kinetic energy. A portion of the stored energy is retained by the bow and this energy is not available to the arrow. This portion can be described by the effective, or dynamic, mass of the bow, which is the equivalent amount of mass that, moving at the velocity of the arrow, would have the same kinetic energy as the moving limbs and string. The kinetic energy retained by the bow is finally dissipated as work done in stretching the string when the limbs come to rest, as vibrations of the limbs and string, and ultimately as heat.

The point then is that the energy stored in the fully drawn bow is converted to kinetic energy, but this kinetic energy has to be *shared* between the arrow and the bow itself. Any energy retained by the bow is lost to the arrow. The effective mass of the bow is a measure of how much of the energy stays with the bow. It tells us how the bow behaves dynamically. At the instant the arrow leaves the string, the moving parts of the bow have a combined kinetic energy equivalent to that of the effective mass traveling at the velocity of the arrow. This kinetic energy is given by one half the effective mass multiplied by the square of the arrow velocity (or $\frac{1}{2} M_{eff} V^2$).

The effective mass of a bow remains constant over a wide range of arrow velocities, so that as we change the weight and speed of the arrow the effective mass doesn't change. The effective mass is fixed by the bow design and limb materials, primarily by the shape and mass of its limbs. In general, the less the actual physical mass of the limbs for a given draw weight, the lower the effective mass and the more efficient the bow will be in transferring kinetic energy to the arrow. This is the primary reason why the fiberglass and wood composite limb is more efficient than the self wood limb. The composite limb usually requires less physical mass to achieve a given draw weight and as a result has a lower effective mass.

Once we have chosen a particular bow to shoot, we are stuck with whatever effective mass its design dictates. We can't change that except by changing bows. If we want to decrease the energy retained by the bow and increase the kinetic energy imparted to the arrow, there is only one option available, *and that is to decrease the arrow velocity by shooting a heavier arrow.* It's that simple. The heavier arrow has a lower velocity, and that in turn decreases the kinetic energy of the bow at the instant the arrow leaves the string. Although the arrow velocity decreases, the *share* of the kinetic energy imparted to the arrow actually increases. Failure to understand this is what creates all of the confusion whenever the subject of arrow penetration comes up.

A good way to think about this is the following: When the string is released the energy stored in the bow is divided between two objects, both traveling at the same speed. One is the arrow; the other is the effective mass of the bow. Since both have the same velocity, the kinetic energy of each is proportional to its mass. As the mass of one increases relative to the other, its share of the total kinetic energy goes up in proportion. The fraction of the total energy that each receives is just its mass divided by the total mass of the two together. We can't change the effective mass of the bow. All we can do is increase the weight of the arrow to increase its share of the kinetic energy.

The effective mass of even the most efficient bows is generally in excess of 100 grains; a typical value might be somewhere in the range of 100-200 grains. A lot of the traditional hunting bows that archers are shooting these days have an effective mass greater than these values. The effective mass has to be added to the arrow mass to get the mass of the two combined. The arrow mass divided by the combined mass gives the fraction of the energy imparted to the arrow, or its energy efficiency. The effective mass divided by the combined mass gives the fraction of the energy retained by the bow. That's the way it works. And that's the point overlooked in the controversy about arrow penetration.

A bow whose effective mass is 200 grains will impart only 2/3 (400/600) of its energy to a 400 grain arrow. But the same bow will impart 5/7 (500/700) of its energy to a 500 grain arrow. The 500 grain arrow will thus have 1.07 times as much kinetic energy as a 400 grain arrow. This is true even though the heavier arrow will have the lower velocity. For example, a 60 pound bow with an effective mass of 200 grains and a stored energy of 50 foot-pounds would shoot a 400 grain arrow at a velocity of around 193 feet per second, and a 500 grain arrow at only about 179 feet per second. But the slower arrow will still have about 7 percent more kinetic energy than the faster one. The specific values I have chosen in this example are representative but they are less important than the point being made. Any other set of values would make the same point just as well.

Exactly the same argument holds for momentum. Increasing the weight of the arrow increases its momentum by decreasing its velocity, and thereby decreasing the momentum retained by the bow. A heavier arrow always has more momentum as well as more kinetic energy. The fraction of the total momentum (momentum of the bow and arrow combined) imparted to the arrow is the same as the fraction of the total energy. The greater the mass of the arrow, the greater its share of the momentum.

Just as an interesting aside, how would any of this change *if* a bow could impart all of its stored energy to the arrow? I hesitate to even bring this up because I don't want anyone to get the mistaken impression that what I am saying here is at all possible. The only bow which could impart all of its stored energy to the arrow would be the ideal bow with massless limbs that we discussed in an earlier chapter. And such an ideal bow is of course an impossibility. But what if it could be possible? Then the kinetic energy of the arrow would *always* be the same as the energy stored in the drawn bow. The weight of the arrow would not matter. All of the stored energy would be imparted to the arrow. A heavier arrow would have less velocity than a lighter one, but both would have exactly the same amount of kinetic energy. That would not be true of momentum. A heavier arrow would *always* have more momentum than a lighter one. Now the archer could shoot a lighter arrow to take advantage of a flatter trajectory without sacrificing any of the kinetic energy of the arrow. But the lighter arrow would have less momentum than a heavier one. And now there would be a genuine controversy about which was more important for penetration, kinetic energy or momentum. If kinetic energy was the determining factor it wouldn't matter whether you shot lighter or heavier arrows. Both would have the same amount of kinetic energy. If momentum was more important, then a heavier arrow would penetrate better. It is this hypothetical—but impossible—situation that most writers on this subject mistakenly address.

As a footnote to all of this, we can ask what physics does tell us about the relative importance of kinetic energy and momentum in determining how far an arrow will penetrate. The answer hinges on how the resistance encountered by the arrow varies with its speed. If the force of friction is *constant* and does not depend on how fast the arrow is moving, then the depth of penetration is directly proportional to the *kinetic energy* of the arrow. If the friction depends directly on the *arrow velocity,* then the penetration is proportional to the *momentum* of the arrow. If the resistance depends on the *square of the arrow velocity,* the penetration is not directly proportional to either kinetic energy or momentum but is proportional to the *mass* of the arrow.

There is no reason to expect the force of friction encountered by a broadhead cutting through tissue to be *exactly* constant, or to depend *exactly* on either arrow velocity or the square of arrow velocity. But from what is known about sharp pointed bodies moving through various kinds of materials, the friction encountered by an arrow falls somewhere in this broad range, between being constant and varying as the square of the velocity. I suspect, but don't really know, that for a sharp broadhead cutting through soft tissue at the relatively slow speeds of an arrow, the friction is fairly constant, and in that case it is the kinetic energy of the arrow that primarily determines its penetration. On the other hand, cutting through a bone or pushing soft tissue out of the way of the penetrating arrow once it has cut a path is more like colliding with a heavy object, and in that case it is the momentum and mass that determine whether the arrow makes it through or not. But in either case it really doesn't matter. I don't have to know whether energy or momentum is the determining factor. *The heavier arrow has more of each and has the advantage in penetration over a lighter arrow shot from the same bow.*

How should you use these results? In the first place, to avoid being misled by the false claims of those who don't really understand the subject, but whose advice too often finds its way into the archery literature. *And clearly you should think before choosing the lightest hunting arrow that can be matched to your bow, or the lightest arrow legally allowed where there are minimum weight restrictions.* That choice always carries with it some sacrifice in penetration. Lighter arrows may still be all right, unless you are shooting at an animal the size of a moose or a large elk, or you happen to hit a rib or a bone that a heavier arrow would have gone through or glanced off of and continued on through the animal. Just as clearly, you can't increase the weight of the arrow beyond a practical limit. The stiffness of the arrow has to match the draw weight of the bow. And the trajectory has to be flat enough to allow accurate shooting.

The most sensible, *and ethical,* advice for the bowhunter is to place some upper limit on how far you are willing to shoot, the closer the better, and then choose the heaviest shaft whose trajectory still allows you to shoot well out to that distance. When you do that you've done the best you can, and you know all that you need to know about arrow penetration. You can leave all of the arguments about whether kinetic energy or momentum matters most, to others, while you enjoy your elk steaks.

The discussion to this point has focused on arrow weight. Even after selecting the heaviest shafts that you can shoot accurately out to a reasonable distance, there are still some other things that you can do to improve arrow penetration.

For one thing, an arrow flying straight when it hits the target, without fishtailing from side to side or porpoising up and down will penetrate better than one flying erratically. Transverse motion of any kind represents energy and momentum lost to penetration. Since most hunting shots are taken from quite close, any oscillation of the arrow should damp out in the first few yards. That means that the arrows must be well matched to the bow, neither too stiff nor too limber to clear the bow cleanly without interference. And the fletching must be large enough to damp out the unavoidable oscillations as quickly as possible. This can be easily checked by shooting through a sheet of paper at a distance of a few feet. When the resulting hole is perfectly round except for the slits made by the point and the fletching, then the arrow is flying straight. If the spine of the arrow is correctly matched to the bow and the fletching is large enough, it shouldn't take more than a few feet to achieve straight arrow flight.

Whether or not you get clean arrow flight also depends on shooting technique. Even properly matched arrows will not leave the bow cleanly if the string is deflected sideways or up and down, or if the bow is severely twisted on release. I have spent hours trying to tune arrows to my bow only to find that my shooting technique was the real culprit.

The type of broadhead has a lot to do with penetration. Two bladed points penetrate better than those with three or more blades, the possible exception being small razor blade inserts that don't substantially increase the frontal area of the point. The worst are multibladed points that because of the way the blades are joined together result in an enlarged frontal area between the blades, particularly if the frontal area exceeds that of the ferrule and the shaft itself. So-called bodkin points are of this type. Any frontal area, in addition to the blades, extending beyond the diameter of the shaft effectively represents a blunt cylinder which impedes and quickly slows the motion of the arrow. Two bladed points with both blades in the same plane are every bit as effective as multibladed points, even more so when penetration is considered

If a razor-sharp broadhead hits a vital region where it will cause fatal hemorrhaging, it doesn't much matter whether it has one cutting edge or more; the eventual outcome will be the same. The same is true if it doesn't hit a vital spot. More cutting edges will not make up for poor arrow placement. Viewed point on, the blades and ferrule should present as small a frontal area as possible. The blades should open up a hole for the ferrule and the shaft. Small razor blade inserts at right angles to the main blades produce a four-slit opening for freer passage of the ferrule and arrow shaft. Also detrimental is a shaft significantly larger in diameter than the ferrule. The frontal area of the central region of the point, exclusive of the blades, should closely match that of the shaft to minimize any friction caused by the transition between the two. The shaft diameter if anything should be less than that of the ferrule. Then the shaft will have adequate clearance in any hole through which the ferrule passes.

The angle of the cutting edge to the direction of motion also makes a difference. The steeper the angle, beyond a certain point, the poorer the penetration. The optimum angle is somewhere between about 10-15 degrees, corresponding to a point 2-3 times as long as it is wide. That translates into an angle of 20-30 degrees between the cutting edges at the front point of the blades. For this configuration the blades cut forward 2-3 inches for every inch sideways so that cutting is more by a slicing motion rather than a blunt punching motion. There is less resistance to slicing than punching through soft tissue. The two motions become roughly equal at a frontal angle of about 50 degrees, resulting in a point equal in width and length; we want to stay well below that limit.

There is no particular advantage to using a wider broadhead. On the one hand it might be imagined that the size of any vital area would be slightly larger for a wider blade since the arrow would not have to pass quite as close for the cutting edge of the blade to hit it. A wider blade has a greater reach. And a wider blade makes a bigger cut and potentially produces more hemorrhaging when it passes directly through a vital area. Neither of these possible advantages outweighs the poorer penetration of the wider point. Without adequate penetration to reach a vital area no blade can be effective. It is far more important for it to get there than for it to make a bigger cut once it does.

There are a number of broadheads on the market that are designed to reduce the frontal area to a bare minimum by having cutting blades that fold somehow against the sides of the point. The end of the ferrule is hardened steel or some other alloy sharply pointed and shaped to punch through hide and muscle and even bone. The cutting blades unfold after the point makes initial contact and has begun penetrating. There are several different configurations of these. The common idea seems to be that they have a smaller frontal, and side, area and hence fly cleaner, presumably meaning straighter, than larger points, and that they also penetrate better. Such points do not represent a better idea. It requires more energy to punch a hole through hide and muscle that it does to cut one. And any broadhead that depends on mechanically moving parts to function has no place in bowhunting. These points definitely do not improve penetration over a well designed and properly shaped head with fixed blades. And no one should ever use a point that can malfunction mechanically. Neither idea makes much sense.

# The Arrow

*What are the attributes that go into making a good arrow
and how do we go about achieving them in practice?*

The most important piece of the archer's equipment is the arrow, by
far more important than the bow. The bow merely propels the arrow
toward the target. Almost any bent stick can be made to do that after a
fashion. It doesn't even need to do it very efficiently. In the final analysis all
that is required is that it be able to propel an arrow with sufficient velocity to
get it there and penetrate the target, and even that is not especially difficult,
easily within the capabilities of any stave of sufficient elasticity and draw weight.
The broad range of traditional bows of widely varying designs and efficiencies
testifies to the great latitude possible in the choice of a bow and its level of
performance. But to fulfill *its* purpose the arrow must get there, and to do that
it has to fly unerringly, straight and true to the target. Not any old stick will do
for an arrow, or even make a serviceable one. The theory of archery tersely
uttered long ago by the Seminole Tommy to Maurice Thompson, remains as
apt now as then, "Any stick do for bow—good arrow dam heap work!"

The archer's prospect would be simpler if it involved shooting but a
single arrow, that is, the same arrow shot over and over. Then any deviations
from shot to shot could not be the fault of the arrow, which stays the same each
time, but would be due to variations in the archer's technique. Granted, that
one arrow would have to be correctly designed to fulfill its intended function,
but we would not have to concern ourselves in addition with minimizing
variations from arrow to arrow. So we want to consider what is involved in
making one good arrow; and then what is involved in making all the others just
like it. Actually the two questions are not independent but are related.

Likely this is exactly the problem faced by early archers. They would
have quickly discovered that in order to fly properly an arrow needed to be
straight as well as possess a certain degree of stiffness or elasticity. Fletching

was not essential to make it fly straight for short distances. All that was required was a straight shaft of the proper stiffness that balanced a bit forward of the midpoint. Even now the best way to detect problems in shooting technique and to find out how well a shaft of a given stiffness, or *spine*, matches your bow is to see how well it flies with no fletching at all. Any interference between the arrow and the bow caused by incorrect spine, any plucking of the string, any variation of finger pressure will all cause erratic left-right or up-down arrow flight that might be damped out by fletching and go undetected. The ultimate test of correct spine is when a bare shaft can be made to hit the same spot on the target as an identical shaft with fletching. Only then can one be reasonably certain that the fletching is not masking any deficiencies in shooting technique or stiffness of the arrow.

The early archer employed the practical method of try it and see what happens. And soon he would have discovered a favorite arrow, one that just happened to have the correct properties to make it fly straight, or straighter than the others. He would have hit what he was shooting at more often with it than with any of the others. And knowing that it could easily become lost or broken he would have tried to duplicate it exactly by finding and making others just like it. But try as he might he could never make them all the same and there would always have been one or two that were the favorites. And then somewhere along the way he would have discovered that by attaching crude fletching in the form of vanes or feathers to steer the shaft it could be made to fly straighter, farther. Equally important, the fletched shafts now all flew more nearly alike than they would before without fletching.

Straightness and stiffness, though still important, were no longer as crucial or as critical, and in the choice of arrow shafts the archer now had much greater latitude than before. With that innovation the three basic ingredients of a good arrow were in place: *a straight shaft; the proper stiffness; and fletching of some sort attached to the rear of the shaft.*

Early arrows would undoubtedly have made use of shafts that grew naturally straight or almost so. Hollow canes or reeds would have been good for this purpose and would have minimized the amount of fabrication necessary to make a finished arrow. In addition they would have been light for their stiffness which would cause them to fly faster. Sharpening one end for a crude point and cutting a shallow notch in the other to fashion a nock for the string would have been adequate for small game close up. Feathers or vanes of stiff leaves for fletching would have been attached by binding at both ends with thread or fine cord wound around the shaft. The shaft could have been strengthened at each end by wrapping a short section tightly with cord. For more durable shafts solid dowels would have been inserted and bound in both ends of the hollow shaft for cutting the nock and for sharpening or attaching a point. Stone points would have been tied in place with cord or leather thongs. Anyone boiling animal sinew would have discovered glue eventually, and glues would have been applied to reinforce and strengthen the fiber bindings on arrows.

Where canes or reeds did not suffice, arrow shafts would have been made out of the small stems or branches of bushes and shrubs. Ishi's favorite was witch hazel, but others such as birch, alder, willow, red osier dogwood, mock orange, Indian peach, red elderberry, serviceberry and juniper would all make suitable dowels for arrows. They could be scraped smooth and polished with a stone and then hardened and straightened by heating in a flame. When cutting round dowels out of square billets became commonplace it was discovered that certain woods carefully selected have the best properties for arrows. Norway pine was the preferred arrow material of English archers. Port Orford cedar grown along the Pacific Coast of Oregon became popular in this country and is one of the very best arrow woods found anywhere. It is hard and durable but light and will stay straight. Birch is strong and tough and can be straightened easily with the fingers by heating over a fire or hotplate. Many other woods have been tried including various types of pine and maple, Douglas fir, hemlock, larch, Sitka spruce and western red cedar. While all of these woods and many others can be used to make serviceable arrows no wood has been found to be superior to Port Orford cedar. A 1930's catalogue from the L. E. Stemmler Company lists arrows made of birch, Norway pine and Port Orford cedar, which by then had become the woods of choice in this country, birch for beginners and Norway pine and Port Orford cedar for the very best arrows.

*The central fact of arrow flight that determines everything else about its performance is that an arrow bends.* No matter how straight it is, when it is shot out of a bow it doesn't stay straight. The sudden impulse of the bowstring propelling the arrow forward causes the shaft to flex and oscillate. To understand the significance of that we need to think about what happens to the arrow as it leaves the bow.

It has long been noted that the arrow when drawn and aimed is not pointed along the center line of the bow held vertical but is pointed slightly off-line, to the left for a right-handed archer, due to the width of the bow at the handle or arrow shelf. The angle between the drawn arrow and the centerline of the bow is the distance the arrow is off-center divided by the length of the arrow. For a bow having a handle width of one to two inches shooting a 28 inch arrow this is an angle of about 0.018-0.036 radians, or 1-2 degrees. The archer compensates for this angle by aiming not along the center line of the bow but along the arrow itself at the spot to be hit. After the string is released however this angle gradually increases as the arrow moves forward until, at the point where the arrow finally leaves the string, the angle can be as large as 3-8 degrees depending on the brace height of the bow. Even if the arrow is aimed directly at the center of the target when fully drawn, it will be pointed to the left when the arrow leaves the bowstring. For every degree the arrow is pointed to the left it would fly two feet to the left of the aiming point at a distance of only forty yards. At one hundred yards it would fly five feet to the left and would miss a 48 inch target entirely. The exact size of the angle and the amount of deviation is not important. What is important is that the arrow does not follow the straight line along which it would be pointed when it leaves the string, but instead somehow manages to follow the line along which it was aimed at full draw. This effect has been termed the *archer's paradox* and its resolution was the subject of much speculation from early on.

Some early observers argued that the pressure of the arrow pushing against the side of the bow must cause the bow to move out of the way, allowing the arrow to fly unimpeded in the direction it is pointed at the time of release. Why the bow always moves precisely the correct amount independent of its mass, or inertia, seems not to have entered into consideration. Perhaps they would argue that the proper stiffness of the arrow for its weight is what determines the correct amount by which the bow moves during the time that the arrow takes to leave the string. Hence the need to choose arrows that all have the correct, and same, weight and stiffness for uniformity of flight. In that they are at least partially correct, though for the wrong reasons. If this argument were correct then the required stiffness of the arrow would depend on the mass weight of the bow as well as its draw weight. A stiffer arrow would be required to push a heavier more massive bow out of the way.

The great English archer, Horace A. Ford, whose best scores at the double York round became the standard of excellence for years and who thought very carefully and deeply about the techniques of shooting, offered a somewhat different argument. In his book *Archery: Its Theory and Practice* (London and Cheltenham, 1856; S.R. Publishers Ltd., 1971; Derrydale Press, 1992), he suggested that the pressure of the bow against the arrow *forward* of its center of mass deflects the arrow at first left, but then the bow pushing subsequently against the arrow *aft* of its center of mass deflects it back to the right and the two deflections in effect cancel each other out.

Neither of these explanations is correct. *The correct answer lies in the fact that the arrow does not stay straight, but bends under the force of the string and the resistance of pushing against the bow.* High speed photography has shown us what actually takes place.

When the string is released, the arrow pushes against the side of the bow under the sudden impulse of the string. As a result the arrow first bends in the middle toward the central plane of the bow limbs, while the front portion of the arrow bends away from the bow. Then as the arrow moves forward it oscillates back in the other direction bending in the middle away from the bow and in the front back toward the bow. But the front of the arrow has now moved past the bow and does not contact it. As a result the bent midsection of the arrow shaft clears the bow, in effect bending around it as the oscillating shaft moves forward. Then as the arrow leaves the string it oscillates in the middle back toward the center line of the bow. But now the midsection is past the bow and doesn't contact it, and the rear of the arrow, no longer constrained by the string, oscillates away from the bow and clears it without contact. Detailed pictures of this sequence were first taken by Paul Klopsteg and published in

*Archery Review* in December 1933 and January 1934, and were later included in the volume *Archery: The Technical Side* (Derrydale Press, 1992).

The arrow thus bends and oscillates as it moves forward, and if the frequency of oscillation is correctly chosen to match the acceleration and forward speed of the arrow, the portion of the shaft passing by the bow handle at any time is always bent away from the bow as it goes around it. The arrow snakes its way past the bow without contacting it beyond the initial contact and push.

The straight line around which the axis of the arrow oscillates, assuming the correct spine and no interference with the bow, is the line along which it was aimed at full draw before the string was released. The arrow bends around the bow but it does so along the original line of sight. *This is the real resolution of the archer's paradox.* Like all paradoxes there is no actual contradiction, just an apparent one that vanishes when the correct picture is finally understood. The arrow continues to oscillate around this line until the oscillations are gradually damped out by the friction of the shaft and fletching through the air and the internal friction of flexing the material of the arrow shaft. One of the practical functions of the fletching is to damp out these oscillations in a suitably short distance after the arrow clears the bow.

An arrow that leaves the bow at 200 feet per second has an average velocity closer to about 0.64 that value during the time it is being accelerated by the string. That means it takes about 0.018 second for a 28 inch arrow to clear the bow. In that time the arrow shaft should go through about one and a quarter complete oscillations to be correctly matched to the bow. The oscillation frequency is thus about 69 cycles per second. For an arrow velocity of 150 feet per second the time to clear the bow is about 0.024 second; so the oscillation frequency would be about 52 cycles per second. This is roughly the frequency range in which arrows shot from traditional bows should oscillate as they leave the bow. A shorter arrow traveling at the same speed will take less time to clear the bow and will have to oscillate faster; a longer arrow will have to oscillate slower. For arrow speeds of 150-200 feet per second and arrow lengths from 24-32 inches the frequency of oscillation ranges from about 45-80 oscillations per second.

It is tempting to think that this problem of interference between the arrow and the bow could be solved by simply cutting the riser section of the bow well past the center line of the limbs. An adjustable arrow rest that can be moved left and right would then allow the center of the shaft to be positioned along the exact center line of the bow with plenty of clearance for the fletching to pass the handle unobstructed. The arrow rest can be fashioned to flip out of the way of the arrow as it is propelled forward so as not to interfere with the flight of the arrow. An adjustable spring-loaded plunger mounted in the side of the handle could be added to absorb the initial push and any sideways motion of the arrow. What we are describing of course is precisely the arrangement employed on most high-performance target bows. Although this arrangement facilitates matching the arrow to the bow to achieve proper clearance and optimum arrow flight it does not in any way solve the basic problem, *which is that the arrow always bends under the impulse of the string.* Arrow shafts are unavoidably flexible and whether the bow is center-shot or not they will still bend under the accelerating force of the bowstring. There is no such thing as an infinitely stiff arrow or even one approaching that.

The better solution is to take advantage of the bending and oscillations to get the arrow past the bow without interference. *And that means matching the frequency of oscillation to the speed of the arrow and the time it takes the arrow to clear the bow.* The frequency of oscillation is to first order independent of the amplitude, or how far the arrow bends under the impulse of the string. But the amplitude is nevertheless important. It determines by how much the arrow clears the bow. We want the arrow to flex enough for the shaft and the fletching to freely clear the bow handle. This is especially true when using stiff vanes as fletching. Cutting the handle past center means that the arrow does not have to bend as far to give adequate clearance and for that reason is always a good idea. It also means that the frequency of oscillation does not have to be as closely matched to the arrow speed so there is greater latitude in choosing arrows that will match the bow.

We can estimate how much the arrow bends. When the arrow does not point along the center line of the bow the force exerted by the string is not directly along the arrow but at a slight angle to it. This results in part of the force acting perpendicular to the arrow. It is this perpendicular force that bends the arrow toward the plane of the bow when the string is released. The magnitude of this bending force is equal to twice the draw weight times the distance the front of the arrow is displaced from the center of the bow divided by the arrow length. The amount the arrow bends at the center is given by this force divided by the stiffness of the arrow. The important point here is that the more the shaft is displaced off-center the farther it bends under the force of the string so that the clearance stays always about the same.

For a 28 inch arrow shot one half inch off-center in a 55 pound bow the perpendicular force causing the arrow to bend is approximately 1.96 pounds. As we will see below, this is about the same as the weight used to bend the arrow when measuring the value of the spine. As a result the amplitude of oscillation is comparable to the spine of the shaft.

The frequency with which an arrow oscillates depends on its stiffness and its mass. *The stiffer the shaft the faster it oscillates.* A limber shaft oscillates more slowly because the elastic forces in the shaft material opposing the oscillations are weaker. As the stiffness increases, the elastic forces become greater and the oscillations speed up. It is the same principle that governs the motion of a spring. The stiffer the spring the faster it oscillates. On the other hand, *the greater the mass of the arrow the slower it oscillates.* The same elastic force will not accelerate a larger mass as rapidly as a smaller one. Similarly, hanging a larger mass on a stiff spring will slow the frequency of its oscillations.

We measure the stiffness of the shaft by the value of its spine. *The spine is the measured deflection, in inches, that results from hanging a 1.94 pound (880 gram) weight from the center of a bare shaft 29 inches long supported at two points 28 inches apart, i.e., half inch from each end.*

Here we have to be a bit careful. In common parlance the terms *spine* and *stiffness* are used interchangeably, which can be misleading since spine is defined so that it is *inversely* related to stiffness. The stiffer the shaft, the smaller the value of the spine. Note too that spine measurements are standardized to a 29 inch shaft. So the spine value does not tell us the actual stiffness of a shorter or longer shaft. We have to infer that from knowing how stiffness depends on length. Recommended spine values for draw weights of 80 pounds down to 20 pounds and for arrow lengths from 23 to 32 inches, range from about 0.25 to 1.70 inches for aluminum, carbon, and carbon-aluminum composite shafts from the major shaft manufacturer, just to give some idea of the range of values. *The actual stiffness of the shaft is the force causing it to bend divided by the value of the deflection*, and is measured in units of force, or weight, per unit of distance. In the case of standardized spine measurements the weight is always 1.94 pounds, and so we usually just specify the spine rather than converting it to stiffness. A *spine value* of one inch corresponds to a *stiffness* of 1.94 pounds per inch.

*The oscillation frequency squared is directly proportional to the stiffness of the shaft and inversely proportional to the arrow mass.* But stiffness is inversely proportional to spine. So the oscillation frequency squared is inversely proportional to the spine times the mass of the arrow. To maintain the oscillation frequency constant we have to keep the product of arrow mass and spine constant.

For a given length arrow the oscillation frequency that matches the arrow shaft to the bow depends directly on the arrow velocity. Arrow velocity in turn depends on the square root of the draw weight. As a result the correct spine value depends inversely on the draw weight. *Now we have reduced the entire problem to its simplest form.* Given a particular draw weight and arrow length we can in principle look up the spine value (of the corresponding 29 inch shaft) that will match that draw weight so that the arrow flies correctly and clears the bow without interference. That is what a spine table provides: it recommends shaft(s) of a given type and spine that will match a particular draw weight and arrow length.

In practice the situation is a bit more complicated. Most spine tables recommend spine values and shafts that match an *interval* of draw weights, usually in five pound increments, e.g., 45-50, 50-55, and so forth. The reason for this is the variation among bows, even of the same draw weight, in the time it takes the arrow to clear the bow—related to arrow velocity—which in turn is related not just to draw weight but also to the effective mass of the bow limbs and the mass of the arrow. In any range of draw weights there will be a broad range of values for the effective mass of the limbs. Even bows of the same draw weight can exhibit a wide variation in effective mass. The spine tables are attempting to cover this spread in effective mass and the corresponding spread in arrow velocity and oscillation frequency. For instance, a 50 pound bow with an effective mass of 200 grains will shoot a 400 grain arrow at the same velocity as a 55 pound bow having an effective mass of 260 grains, or a 60 pound bow with an effective mass of 320 grains; so the same shaft might fly correctly out of all three bows. These values represent the kinds of variations that one finds in traditional bows. Taking into account all forms of traditional bows, including wooden self bows, the variations are even larger than those we have chosen as examples.

In addition, shafts of different weights but the same spine may all match the same bow. The lightest arrow will have the highest oscillation frequency but also the highest speed and may clear the bow the same as a heavier arrow that has a lower speed and oscillation frequency. That is why the spine tables list a number of shafts of different masses all having about the same spine for each arrow length and draw weight interval. Again the effective mass of the bow is a complicating factor here. The oscillation frequency depends inversely on the square root of arrow mass. But arrow velocity depends inversely on the square root of the combined arrow mass *plus* the effective mass of the limbs. As a result, decreasing the arrow weight increases the oscillation frequency more than it increases arrow speed. As a result lighter shafts will require slightly higher spine values (less stiffness) to match the same bow. But to first order it is only the spine of a shaft, not its weight, that is required to match it to a given draw weight and arrow length.

The spine table that I am examining as I write gives a number of shaft recommendations and corresponding spine values for 29 inch arrows for the same 50-55 pound range of draw weights. These shafts vary in spine from about 0.4 inch to 0.47 inch. They also vary in weight from 350 grains down to about 200 grains. These shaft weights correspond to minimum arrow weights ranging from a little more than 300 grains to over 450 grains. About ten percent of this variation in spine can be accounted for by the ten percent spread in draw weight. The rest of the spine variation takes into account the spread in arrow velocity due to arrow mass and variations in the effective mass of bows of the same draw weight.

From what we have said, we would expect that doubling the draw weight would decrease the spine value by a factor of two. Looking in a spine table, however, shows that to be only approximately true. For one thing, the velocity of the arrow as it leaves the bow does not depend only on the square root of the draw weight. The velocity also depends inversely on the square root of the combined arrow mass plus the effective mass of the bow limbs. If doubling the draw weight also increased the effective mass by making the bow limbs heavier, then the arrow velocity would not go up by the square root of the draw weight but by a lesser amount. Then the required spine value would also change by less than a factor of two, which is what we actually observe in published spine tables.

A complete analysis shows that the stiffness of a shaft depends on its length, diameter, and elastic modulus, and in the case of hollow shafts, on its wall thickness. The elastic modulus is a property of the material out of which the shaft is made. Once the material is chosen the elastic modulus is fixed. One usually finds it expressed not as the elastic modulus but as the ultimate tensile strength of the material; but the two are directly related. The exact way that stiffness depends on each of these properties is complicated, though it can be fairly easily calculated. In fact the numbers in the spine charts can all be generated by direct calculations, given the material properties, the shaft diameter and the wall thickness. Without going into any details of the computations we can summarize some of the more important results.

A longer shaft will bend more for a given force than a shorter one of the same kind and hence has less stiffness and greater spine. Spine therefore is proportional to length. Increasing the elastic modulus of the shaft material makes it stiffer and decreases its spine. Likewise increasing the wall thickness of a hollow shaft makes it stiffer. And the stiffness of a hollow shaft depends on the *cube* or third power of its diameter. Combining all of these factors we can state that *the stiffness of a shaft is proportional to the product of its modulus, wall thickness and the cube of its diameter, and inversely proportional to its length*. If the shaft is solid instead of hollow then we replace the cube of its diameter times the wall thickness by the fourth power of its diameter. This would be the case for instance with wooden shafts. Using these relationships the spine values for the shafts listed in a spine table can all be calculated. The values in the tables are however measured.

One of the simplest ways to alter the oscillation frequency of an arrow is to change its mass by changing the weight of the point. The oscillation frequency depends on the ratio of the stiffness to the arrow mass. If the shaft is too stiff then increasing the arrow mass can decrease this ratio and lower the frequency. The net result of a heavier point is to make the shaft behave as if it were less stiff and had a larger spine value. Similarly, reducing the weight of the point can make a shaft that is too limber act as if it were stiffer and increase its oscillation frequency. Experimenting with the weight of the arrow point can sometimes be crucial in successfully tuning a target bow to match the flight of the arrows. The same shafts that work well with one weight point may not fly right with points that are heavier or lighter. Hunting points can be significantly heavier than target and field points and consequently can require stiffer shafts to fly the same as target or field arrows shot with the same bow. Quantitatively, a given fractional change in the arrow weight is roughly equivalent to the same fractional change in spine. Going from 100 grain hunting points to 125 grain points on 450 grain arrows is equivalent to about a 5 percent increase in spine or decrease in stiffness. The simple way to remember this is that the product of spine and arrow mass has to stay roughly the same to keep the oscillation frequency constant.

At first glance it might seem as if increasing the weight of the point to decrease the oscillation frequency would not work since the heavier point also reduces arrow velocity which in turn calls for an even lower oscillation frequency. But the oscillation frequency decreases faster with increasing arrow weight than the velocity does. This is because the velocity depends on the sum of arrow weight and effective mass of the bow, and the effective mass does not change as we change the arrow mass.

A word of caution about spine tables. They are largely empirical in nature. Not only does the choice of shaft depend on spine and such things as the effective mass of the bow and the weight of the point, fletching and nock, it also depends on the shooting style and manner of release. *The recommendations shown in a spine table represent starting values only.* Quite often one has to deviate considerably from the tables, going up or down in draw weight or arrow length to find the proper shaft and spine for your particular set up and shooting style. For years there have been complaints from acquaintances that the popular spine charts of the major aluminum shaft manufacturer consistently recommend spine values that are too low (shafts that are too stiff) for most traditional hunting bows. Whatever the merits of such complaints, they illustrate that the spine recommendations in the charts are *only recommendations.* They may err on the conservative side by recommending shafts that are too stiff, in the interest of safety or for some other bias. Or they may simply overestimate the arrow velocity (which amounts to underestimating the effective mass of the limbs) or underestimate how far off-center the arrow is being shot in many traditional bows. But they come with no guarantees. It is up to the archer to learn how to use them for his particular bow and setup.

The only way to be certain about the correct spine is to shoot the same shafts with and without fletching to determine whether, at distances of a few feet to a few yards, they fly to the same point of impact; then at the same distances shoot the fletched shafts through a thin sheet of paper to determine that they leave a round hole with the fletching neither to the left or right of center as they pass through the paper. If the end of the arrow goes through the paper to the right of center it generally indicates an arrow that is too stiff. If the fletching is to the left it usually means the arrow is too limber. But it is also possible to change the shape of the hole left and right just by changing some element of shooting form, particularly the forward force of the bow arm and shoulder and the amount of back tension and backward motion during the release. Shooting through a sheet of paper can be an important check on cleanness of release and other elements of form. If the fletching tears the paper above or below center, the nocking position on the string can be lowered or raised to correct the arrow flight, depending on whether the fletching is high or low. High and low fletching can also mean changes in the pressure of the fingers on the string, pulling too much with the bottom or top fingers in particular.

The purpose of fletching is to steer the arrow and keep it flying straight.

A related purpose is to make all of the arrows fly the same. Once an arrow leaves the string it is a ballistic body and travels in response to the location of its *center of mass* and *center of pressure*. In the absence of air resistance the center of mass moves in a vertical plane under the influence of gravity. The arrow moves as if all its mass were concentrated at the center of mass. In addition, it can also rotate about its center of mass. With no friction, these two motions—*translation* of the center of mass and *rotation* about the center of mass—would be independent and one would have no effect on the other.

Let us imagine a bare shaft exactly balanced at the midpoint, which is then the location of its center of mass. If the arrow tries to rotate about its center, air resistance pushing on the front half of the shaft promotes the rotation but an equal resistance pushing on the rear half opposes it. As a result the center of air pressure on the shaft is also located at the midpoint of the arrow. If however the center of mass is located forward of the middle, then when the shaft tries to rotate there is more of the shaft behind the point of rotation than in front of it and the greater air resistance opposing the motion keeps the shaft flying straight. The center of pressure in this case is located behind the center of mass. *This is the basic condition required for stability.* The greater the distance between the two the more inherently stable the flight. If instead, the center of mass is behind the center of pressure, then any attempt by the shaft to rotate around its center of mass is assisted by the net air resistance and the arrow deviates from a straight path and quickly veers right or left.

Bare shafts balanced in front of center can be made to fly straight if they are not subjected to very large oscillations or other deviations in flight. However there are more subtle effects of friction and motion through the air not taken into account in the simplified picture presented above which can also lead to unstable flight for a bare shaft. To counter all of these effects we attach fletching to the shaft. One of the primary aims is to shift the center of pressure well back without having to appreciably affect the location of the center of mass. The fletching adds a little mass to the rear of the shaft which is generally more than compensated by the weight of the point. Even with fletching the center of mass is typically still well forward of the middle. But now since the air resistance of the rear of the shaft is increased, the center of pressure is shifted to the rear. The greatly increased air resistance at the rear of the shaft strongly opposes any rotation around either a vertical or horizontal axis through the center of mass. The first kind of rotation is termed fishtailing, or *yaw*; the second is porpoising, or *pitch*. Fletching is intended to control or eliminate both.

To further stabilize the arrow we give it spin, or rotational momentum, around its longitudinal axis of motion. The faster a body spins the greater the force, or torque, required to produce any change in its angular momentum. That applies to the *rate* of spin as well as the *direction* of rotation. In the absence of torque a spinning body maintains both the rate at which it is spinning and the direction of its axis of rotation. In the presence of outside forces the greater the angular momentum of the spinning body (the faster it spins) the harder it is to effect any change in its motion. With arrows spin comes more or less for free. We attach fletching in the form of vanes or feathers along the axis of the shaft. We cannot put them on straight enough to prevent the arrow from spinning even if we tried. So we don't try. Instead we purposely attach them all offset at the same slight angle to the axis so that the shaft will rotate and acquire a certain rate of spin as it moves through the air. The advantage of fletching does not come for free however. The greater the angle of offset the more frontal area the fletching presents to air resistance and the greater the friction slowing the flight of the arrow. Smaller fletching can be angled more for the same amount of friction.

The use of fletching is guided by loose rules of thumb. There is no simple formula for the size or shape of fletching required. The basic rule is to use no more than it takes to do the job but to err on the side of too much rather than too little when unsure. What matters far more than the shape of the fletching is just the total area. The larger the area the greater the force damping out any oscillations. And the faster the damping response too. Shape mainly influences the noise made by the fletching as it flies through the air. Fletching that has its maximum area at the rear or is cut more nearly square at the rear can make more noise than fletching tapered at both ends, so-called parabolic fletching. Minimizing noise can be important in hunting arrows. Three vanes are more stable than two. With two it is easy enough to picture a direction in which an oscillation would not be as strongly damped as in another direction, possibly leading to unstable or erratic behavior. Arrows with only two vanes or with uneven fletching on one side of the shaft will often fly with a corkscrew motion. That becomes less likely with three vanes. More than four vanes are probably unnecessary in any situation, although five and even six have been used. The more vanes the smaller they can be. More, smaller vanes are more effective than fewer larger ones.

The size of the fletching should be no larger than necessary. Any additional size just adds friction, degrades the trajectory, and makes aiming more difficult, especially when shooting without a sight or when the exact distance to the target is unknown. The greater the side area of the shaft and the arrowhead the larger the fletching needed. A broadhead point presents a much greater area than a field or target point and has the effect of shifting the center of pressure forward. The area of the fletching on a hunting arrow should always be greater than the area of the broadhead so that the hunting point produces only a negligible shift forward in the position of the center of pressure. Otherwise hunting arrows may not fly the same with broadheads as they do with field or target points. Heavier arrows also require larger fletching. A heavier arrow has more energy and momentum which, especially the latter, make it harder to steer. For all of these reasons hunting arrows generally require larger fletching than do target or field arrows.

Hunting arrows should have enough fletching to damp out the oscillations of the arrow a short distance after it has left the bow, certainly within a few yards and closer than any distance at which you anticipate shooting. You can determine this easily enough by shooting through a thin sheet of paper and examining the shape of the hole. Fletching any larger is unnecessary and only slows the arrow. A lot of archers prefer fletching attached to the shaft along a helical spiral to impart faster spin and greater stability, especially on hunting arrows. But an arrow spins fast enough to stabilize even with straight fletching. And helical fletching creates a lot more drag. It looks cool, but it wastes energy and momentum and decreases penetration. The size of the fletching will depend to some extent on how cleanly the arrow leaves the bow which in turn depends on the archer's form and on the cleanness of the release. To guard against the kind of mistakes in technique that commonly occur under the adverse shooting conditions encountered in hunting, the fletching on hunting arrows should not be marginally small. There is no way to determine all of this but to give it a try and see what happens. For hunting arrows it is important to try them with broadhead points. Arrows that behave perfectly well with field or target points might not fly well at all with broadheads. Also it is very important that broadheads be put on the shaft straight. The plane of the blades should lie along the center line of the shaft. An out-of-line broadhead acts like a deviation in the straightness of the arrow, and as it rotates it causes the trajectory to wobble and the air resistance to be greater. The arrow will not fly as straight and will drop more.

The fletching on target arrows should be reduced as long as they are still flying well. This is especially important at the longer distances. The less the arrow slows down the quicker it gets to the target and the less time there is for something to happen to it on the way. It drops less under the influence of gravity and the trajectory is flatter, leading to a smaller dispersion of arrows at the target. The distance an arrow drops due to gravity depends on the *square* of the travel time, so shaving off a little time with less drag and higher velocity can be significant. Also it has less time to drift with the wind so that windage corrections are smaller. At 70 meters, or 77 yards, the difference between an average arrow speed of 180 feet per second and 160 feet per second is almost 0.2 second, or a little more than 2 feet of drift in a 10 mile per hour crosswind. The faster arrow also drops almost seven feet less due to gravity. However be sure to try your target arrows in the wind to make certain they have enough fletching.

Almost everywhere that archery was practiced feathers were the fletching material of choice. The primary flight feathers from a bird's wing have a natural airfoil shape that produces spin even if they are placed on the arrow shaft straight. Left wing and right wing feathers curve in opposite directions, so all of the fletching on an arrow should come from the same wing. It is never a good idea to mix left and right wing fletching. Feathers from either wing should be angled on the shaft to produce spin in the same direction as the airfoil shape of the feather. Right wing feathers should angle to the right. Feathers are still the fletching of choice with a lot of traditional archers. They are more pliant and forgiving than plastic vanes and other stiffer materials. If they touch the bow, which ideally they should not, they are less likely to deflect the arrow and disturb its flight. The disadvantage of feathers is that they are fragile and quickly become worn. Plus they are not waterproof and become limp and bedraggled in the rain, a particular nuisance for hunting. So they have to be coated with some kind of waterproofing, usually by dipping or spraying, and even then they often still get wet if exposed long enough.

Plastic vanes have largely replaced feathers as fletching among target archers. The plastic vanes are far more durable and can be made more precisely the same size and shape. They also have a more constant coefficient of friction through the air. They are made out of several different kinds of material. Some are soft and flexible, others are stiff and rigid. Plastic vanes have also become popular with bowhunters because they last forever and are unaffected by rain or snow and other adverse conditions. There are however some drawbacks to them. The soft, flexible ones tend to eventually warp and develop ripples or waves along the edges after long enough exposure to the sun, or as a result of being bent or distorted by continued contact with something. They will take a permanent set after a while. Leaving them bunched up in a quiver for a long time can distort them. The stiff rigid vanes hold their shape better. These changes in shape probably don't make that much difference, for hunting, but they do introduce differences in the fletching from arrow to arrow which potentially can introduce slight differences in the way they fly. It is just one more unnecessary variation to have to be concerned about. And vanes are far less pliable and less forgiving than feathers if the fletching brushes the arrow rest or side of the bow. It is especially difficult to get plastic vanes to fly well out of a bow that is not center-shot or when shooting off an arrow shelf instead of an elevated rest. The solution when all else fails is to try feathers. The way to be sure is to shoot the same arrows with and without vanes to see if they fly the same in both cases. If not then switch to feathers and compare them to the unfletched shafts. It could always be that the fletching is not the cause of any differences.

The fletching on flight arrows should be reduced to an absolute minimum. Any area greater than the absolute smallest size required to stabilize the arrow so that it comes out of the bow cleanly and flies straight and in the forward direction represents unnecessary drag that will decrease velocity and reduce the distance the arrow goes before falling back to earth. We are talking here about vanes half-inch long and quarter-inch high, something in that neighborhood. Rigid vanes that will not be distorted by air resistance or acceleration are probably best.

Although some traditional archers still prefer to shoot wooden arrows, especially for hunting and field archery, wooden shafts have been completely replaced by other materials for target archery and for almost any form of shooting where greater precision or higher scores are the primary objective. To see why, we have to think about what we are looking for in an arrow shaft material.

As we said earlier, the primary fact of an arrow that determines everything else is that it bends. We want a shaft stiff enough to withstand bending. We also want it light to achieve higher velocity. Combining the two, *what we want is a shaft with the greatest elastic stiffness per unit weight.* So we examine specifically the ratio of the elastic modulus to the density of the shaft material. For solid shafts, wood is about the best naturally occurring arrow material based on this criterion. It is light yet strong. Also good are stiff canes and reeds that grow hollow. No surprise. That is exactly what Stone Age archers quickly discovered.

We mentioned earlier that among all of the woods used for arrows Port Orford cedar from the Pacific Northwest of the United States has been found to be among the best, although many other kinds of wood will make serviceable arrows. Port Orford cedar grows in a very limited area, primarily in one small region along the Oregon coast, and concern about its continued availability has led to studies of the suitability of other woods available in greater supply. A number of woods have been tested and found to be suitable, but none surpasses Port Orford cedar in straightness and strength per unit weight. If you are going to shoot wooden arrows look for top quality Port Orford cedar shafts. They are still readily available. Buy them in large quantities already graded for spine and weight and then further grade and separate them into groups of more closely matched spine and weight. Even after all of that they will still be less expensive than aluminum or carbon composite shafts.

For solid shafts wood is better than even the lightest metals like aluminum. Wood is also superior to solid shafts made of fiberglass, even though fiberglass has the larger elastic modulus, because wood is so much lighter than fiberglass. For a period of time hollow fiberglass shafts that took advantage of its higher modulus while reducing overall weight became popular, for field and hunting arrows in particular, but were eventually displaced by the greater popularity, uniformity, and durability of aluminum shafts. Very strong aluminum alloys in the form of thin-walled tubing have a higher ratio of elastic modulus to weight per unit length than solid shafts of wood or hollow shafts of fiberglass, and for performance as well as precision and uniformity make superior arrows. These alloys have very high elastic modulus and ultimate tensile strength and are extremely hard and resistant to permanent deformation. They will stay straight through all kinds of abuse, but when they do bend they are too tough and brittle to straighten very successfully. Recently, hollow shafts made of graphite or carbon composites have become popular as target, field, and hunting arrows. These shafts rival in elastic properties and weight, as well as precision and uniformity, the very best aluminum alloy shafts. They are however not as durable and tough as aluminum. They are far more fragile and fracture more easily. More recently, shafts that combine carbon composites with aluminum alloy cores have resulted in equally good elastic properties with even lower shaft weights and higher arrow speeds. These shafts are especially well suited to target archery where their significantly higher cost is not such a prohibitive disadvantage.

They can also be shaped, because of the way they are fabricated, to have a diameter that varies along the length of the shaft. A lighter shaft that has the same stiffness can be made by barreling the shaft, that is, by making the diameter larger in the middle and tapering toward each end. The idea is to put more of the elastic material in the middle of the shaft where it bends the most, to increase its resistance to bending, and less nearer the ends where it can be made thinner and lighter. Barreled shafts were long ago recognized as having the advantage of lighter weight, and consequently higher velocity, for the same stiffness. Horace Ford mentions their reputation for "rapid flight" but doesn't recommend them. He was concerned about the mistaken effect that the changing diameter would have on the angle between the arrow and the center line of the bow, and the subsequent motion of the arrow following the release, a concern that grew out of his misunderstanding of the archer's paradox described earlier.

Hollow shafts, whether made of aluminum, fiberglass, or carbon composites have inserts glued in both ends for attaching the point and the nock. Some aluminum shafts have swaged tapered ends for gluing on the nock. Solid shafts of wood have a taper cut on each end for aligning and attaching the nock and the point.

Nocks can be fabricated of plastic or metal in various sizes and shapes, although almost all nocks now are plastic. Plastic has the advantage of light weight and low cost though metal is more durable. Even plastic nocks are sufficiently durable to exceed the average life expectancy of an arrow. However they can break, and it is always wise to check the condition of the nock before shooting as a broken nock can result in a dry-fire and a broken bow. Target and field points are machined out of metal, usually mild steel. They are generally tapered inside and slip over the tapered end of a wooden shaft for alignment and attachment, or glue directly into the end of a hollow shaft, or have a threaded shank that screws into an insert in the end of a hollow shaft. Broadheads are made of blades and ferrules welded or riveted together. They too have a threaded shank for screwing into an insert, or a ferrule tapered inside for gluing over the end of a wooden shaft or over an insert in a hollow shaft.

Now that we have one good arrow just the way we want it, we want to go about making sure all of the others are identical to it, so that any variations in trajectory from shot to shot have as little to do with differences between arrows as possible. The key variables of interest here are *weight, spine, straightness, and variations in material properties along the length* of the shaft.

Variations in length, diameter, and concentricity (or roundness of the shaft), as well as variations in wall thickness, show up as variations in weight and spine. We want all of the shafts to be the same length and to have the same diameter and wall thickness everywhere along the shaft. And we want them to be as straight as possible. Variations in elastic modulus or tensile strength show up as variations in spine. All of these variables are controlled by the precision achievable in fabricating and annealing the shafts and cutting them to a specified length. There is the issue of how well the diameter, wall thickness, and straightness of an individual shaft can be controlled during manufacture and the related issue of how well each can be controlled from shaft to shaft. These are generally but not always the same. Variations in material properties are determined by the manufacturing process in the case of synthetic materials or by nature in the case of wood. Manufacturers usually provide information on spine, weight, shaft diameter, wall thickness, tensile strength, and the like.

In addition to the weight of the shafts we must also control the weight of all the components that go to make a completed arrow. Points, nocks, fletching, even the quantity of glue should all weigh the same on every arrow. Some of these are controlled by manufacturing of the components, others by the care with which the arrows are assembled. What we as archers hope is that all of these variables have been controlled to the point where the only differences between individual shafts that matter to us are *weight, spine, straightness,* and *uniformity of material properties.* These are the variables that we can directly relate to the performance of the shaft as an arrow.

Weight and spine together determine the oscillation frequency of the arrow, which determines how it behaves dynamically as it leaves the bow. If every arrow does not oscillate the same way and with the same amplitude, even if they all clear the bow cleanly, they will encounter different amounts of air resistance, lose speed differently, and consequently not all fly the same. A difference in spine also means a difference in how much one arrow bends compared to another when the string is released and that has the effect of a comparable difference in straightness.

Differences in mass also produce differences in arrow speed. A lighter arrow has a higher velocity, clears the bow faster, spends less time reaching the target and has a flatter trajectory. A given fractional change in mass produces a fractional change in velocity half as large. A one percent change in mass causes a half percent change in arrow speed. Actually that's not quite right.

It is the change in the *combined* arrow mass and effective mass of the bow that is important. A given fractional change in arrow mass produces a smaller fractional change in the combined mass of arrow and effective mass of the bow limbs. A one percent, or 5 grain, change in the mass of a 500 grain arrow shot in a bow having an effective mass of 250 grains amounts to only a two-thirds percent change in the combined mass. Variations in arrow mass have less effect on arrow velocity with increasing effective mass. However, using the fractional change in the mass of the arrow alone *overestimates* the effect on arrow velocity and is the safer estimate. The actual effect will then always be smaller than the estimate.

A variation in straightness amounts to a variation in the direction of flight of the arrow. A bent arrow also presents a slightly different frontal area to wind resistance and thus loses more speed than a perfectly straight one. A significant bend changes the effectiveness of the fletching in steering it. In the next chapter we will give some quantitative estimates of how variations in weight, spine, and straightness might actually affect the dispersion of arrows at the target and compare those variations to what is actually encountered with various kinds of shafts.

When we do, we will find that the present technology for making arrow shafts has already advanced beyond the ability of any archer to shoot as well as the capabilities of arrows currently available. The very best aluminum alloy, carbon, and composite shafts are capable of better intrinsic accuracy than any archer is able to consistently attain. Only when one sees extremely tight groups bunched in the ten-ring at seventy or ninety meters is one seeing something approaching the ultimate accuracy and consistency of which, in practical terms, the shafts are capable. When the next shot strays, be assured it is not the fault of the arrow.

The exception, of course, is wooden shafts. There are several problems with wood that have to be overcome. The most notable is the inconsistency of material properties. These are determined by nature in the way the tree grew, not by any process of manufacturing. Selecting only the best, most-uniform, close-grained billets, then controlling the precision of diameter, concentricity, and straightness during the cutting and processing of the dowels can all help, but nothing can be done to overcome the natural variations in material properties inherent in the wood. The only thing that can be done is to start with a supplier who has a solid reputation of making quality dowels for arrows, then buy them in large enough quantities graded for weight, spine, and straightness and re-sort them yourself to even tighter standards, especially for spine and weight. We will have more to say about the kind of limits that make sense in the next chapter. Pay attention especially to spine. The dowels should all be cut the same way relative to the direction of the grain. And then the orientation in which they are spined should be marked and the nock oriented perpendicular to that direction. I know that some recommend orienting the nock always in the same direction with respect to the grain. But if it were me I would rotate each shaft in the spine tester and mark the direction in which they showed the least variation in spine and then orient the nock perpendicular to that direction. This way one can also select wooden shafts that will shoot as well as the archer's capabilities.

But what to do with all of the ones that fall outside that range? Make them up into knock-around, throw-away arrows. Archery is supposed to be fun, and the more arrows you have to shoot and can afford to loose and risk breaking the more fun you can have. Use them when warming up or for trying trick shots or aerial shots. Shoot them away through the woods or across an open meadow in a moment of spontaneous exuberance for the sheer delight at watching them fly. Take them along in the field for stump shooting and other shots that are too abusive for better, more expensive shafts. Make them up into completed arrows and then sort them by actually shooting them. You may find sizable groups that all fly about the same, something the spine tester and grain scale couldn't tell you, something that you can only discover by shooting them. Take them duck hunting or pheasant hunting or squirrel hunting or rabbit hunting. Even dove hunting. And shoot them with abandon. You won't be able to hit anything anyway.

What we learn from all of this is that the arrow is a lot more important than the bow. Paraphrasing the Seminole Tommy's philosophy of archery, any old bow will shoot straight but not any old arrow will. We can pick up almost any bow and shoot it well enough after a while. The top archers can figure out how to shoot one bow as well as another. I have seen some that I am convinced could string a broom handle and still beat you. David Hughes was certainly like that. So was Ed Rhode. And so are most of them. But the same is not true of arrows. They must not only fit the bow, they must all be alike. And no archer, regardless of how well he knows how to shoot, can shoot well with just any old arrows. The bow may be the instrument that we shoot. It is what we actually hold in our hands and feel pulling and pushing against our muscles, whose recoil we experience on release. We may admire its graceful curves and appealing symmetries, its cast and stability. The musical twang of its string may touch a chord deep within us somewhere. But without arrows it is nothing, just a bent stick. And without proper attention paid to the arrows it is capable of nothing.

The arrow is the true symbol of excellence in archery.

# The Ideal vs. Real Arrows

*The notion of an ideal arrow brings out once again the kind of tradeoffs we make in traditional archery.*

*A*ny attempt to think about what constitutes the ideal arrow depends very much on what is in the eye of the beholder. What you might think of as the ideal arrow depends on what you intend to do with it. We will assume at the outset that it is perfect in every other way. Yet what one attribute separates it from all the others and makes it the ideal? For the target archer it is clearly speed, the arrow with the highest velocity, the one that gets to the target quickest. The ideal arrow is the one that spends the least amount of time being buffeted and blown about by the wind and pulled downward by the force of gravity. For the hunting archer, speed, though important, is of no consequence if upon reaching the target the arrow is unable to penetrate it. It might as well not have gotten there as quickly, or even at all. So penetration, up to a point, triumphs over speed. And here we confront the dilemma that is at the heart of traditional archery. What is ideal for one purpose may be contrary to another. Still, these opposing aims allow us to think of real arrows in terms of these simple ideals.

For any bow, the lightest arrow is always the fastest. Arrow velocity just keeps on going up as we make the arrow lighter and lighter, until the arrow weight reaches zero. For the target archer then, the ideal arrow is massless, just as we found earlier that the ideal bow limbs were massless, and for the same reason—higher arrow speed in each case. But just as there are no massless limbs, there is no such thing as a massless arrow. Yet the concept points out a theoretical limit to the cast of any bow: the speed with which it would shoot a massless arrow. And *that speed is set by the effective mass of the bow limbs.* Looking back at the formula for arrow velocity (formula 4) in the chapter on measuring performance (chapter 5), we see that if the arrow mass is zero then the velocity depends only on the stored energy and the effective mass of the bow limbs. The square of the velocity is equal to twice the stored energy divided by the effective mass of the bow. This is the theoretical limit to how fast the bow can shoot any arrow, even one with no mass. Even though this theoretical velocity is not a practical possibility it is nevertheless interesting as an ideal limit to what is possible. It is also an ideal toward which to strive.

Notice that if the effective mass of the bow limbs were zero, corresponding to the ideal bow, then arrow velocity would keep on going up as the mass of the arrow decreased. In that case the theoretical maximum velocity would have no upper limit, and a lighter and lighter arrow would just keep going faster and faster. This is one of the main reasons why the concept of effective mass is so fundamental to understanding how a bow works. The effective mass of the bow poses an upper limit to arrow velocity no matter how light the arrow. The lower the effective mass of the bow the greater the arrow speed.

As an example, a 50 pound bow drawn 20 inches typically stores at least 42 foot-pounds of energy. If this bow has an effective mass of 200 grains, a value representative of fairly efficient traditional bows, then the theoretical upper limit to velocity is 307 feet per second, significantly higher than anything ever actually attained. This is a limit that can never be surpassed, except by redesigning the bow to lower its effective mass. It is likewise a limit that can never be achieved in practice. But we can assess the *practical limits* to what is possible by thinking not of a massless "ideal" arrow but an arrow of the least possible mass that is practical. Given the present technology the lowest shaft weights that still have spine values compatible with a 50 pound bow are about 6-7 grains per inch or 168-196 grains for a 28 inch shaft. Allowing for the weight of inserts and point, nock and fletching, we can conceive of an arrow weighing somewhat less than 300 grains as a practical lower limit. Combining that value with the 200 grain effective mass of the bow limbs gives a total mass of 500 grains and an arrow velocity of about 194 feet per second. Even if we shave off another 50 grains somewhere, either from the arrow or the effective mass of the bow, the velocity only goes up to 204 feet per second. And that is about it as far as a practical limit is concerned. We aren't ever going to do a lot better than that.

Even if you argue that we are being conservative here in our assumptions (I would argue that we are only being realistic) and we use more optimistic assumptions instead, the final result is much the same. A 50 pound bow might store as much as 48 foot-pounds of energy at a draw length of 20 inches. Assuming a combined effective mass and arrow mass of only 450 grains the velocity is still only 219 feet per second. Not many traditional bows will ever do that well.

Of course we can increase the draw weight, but when we do that the effective mass of the limbs goes up also and so does the mass of the arrow that will be stiff enough to match the higher draw weight, so the resulting gains in arrow velocity are modest. And now we are talking about a bow that most archers cannot shoot as accurately as they could one of a lighter draw weight. Reducing the effective mass of the limbs to the lowest value possible means making them thinner and more recurved and hence less stable, also not conducive to accuracy. More revealing might be to examine the practical velocity limits for a lower draw weight.

If we reduce the draw weight to 40 pounds and a stored energy of 37 foot-pounds, then sticking with an effective mass of 200 grains the theoretical limit to velocity is 288 feet per second. The lowest shaft weight that gives the required spine is once again in the 6-7 grains per inch range so the practical lower limit to arrow mass is still not much below 300 grains. The combined arrow mass and effective mass of the limbs is 500 grains giving a velocity of 182 feet per second. If we shave off another 50 grains from the arrow mass and effective mass combined, the velocity only goes up to 192 feet per second.

The point is that the practical limit to arrow speed doesn't really change that much, either up or down, no matter what we do. It is always considerably below the theoretical limit of what is possible for a massless arrow, even with the lightest shafts that modern materials technology has achieved. The ideal arrow for speed is one with no mass. In practice, the ideal arrow for greatest speed is always the one with the least mass. The *practical limit* at present toward that ideal is only a little less than 300 grains. It seems unlikely that it would ever go much below 250 grains for bows of draw weights above 40 pounds.

We should point out that we are excluding flight bows and arrows from consideration here. But it is interesting to look at the theoretical maximum velocity for these high performance bows as well. For a draw weight of 65 pounds and a draw length of 18 inches the bow can store about 50 foot-pounds of energy. With an effective mass as low as 100 grains the theoretical maximum velocity for 50 foot-pounds and an arrow of zero mass would be an astonishing 473 feet per second. An actual flight arrow of only 125 grains would have an actual speed of 316 feet per second. An effective mass and arrow mass combined of 200 grains would bring the speed up to 335 feet per second. Reducing the arrow mass and the effective mass of the limbs to these levels is the key to shooting greater distances.

While the lightest possible arrow may represent the practical ideal for achieving higher arrow speeds, it is the very opposite of what is needed for penetration. The theoretical ideal for maximum penetration is an arrow not with the smallest possible mass but one with infinite mass. In target archery penetration is unimportant. Even though a heavier arrow reaches the target with more kinetic energy and momentum, it doesn't really matter. Even the lightest arrow will still have adequate energy and momentum to stick in the target. All that is necessary is to mark where the point of the arrow hit the target face.

But arrow mass is paramount for penetration. The reason is that a heavier arrow always leaves the bow with more energy and momentum than a lighter one. The theoretical upper limit to the kinetic energy of the arrow is the total energy stored in the bow limbs at full draw. The stored energy is shared between the arrow and the bow in proportion to the mass of each compared to the their combined mass. The fraction imparted to the arrow is the ratio of the arrow mass to the combined arrow mass and effective mass of the limbs. This ratio is the quantity we earlier termed the energy efficiency of the bow. Looking back at the formula for efficiency (formula 3, chapter 5) we see that efficiency keeps on increasing as we increase the mass of the arrow. The theoretical maximum efficiency is 1.0, or 100 percent, which occurs ideally for an infinite arrow mass; or, in more practical terms, when the effective mass of the limbs becomes insignificant compared to the much larger arrow mass.

The theoretical upper limit to the momentum the bow can impart to an arrow is just equal to the square root of twice the arrow mass times the stored energy. The fraction of this theoretical maximum that is actually imparted to the arrow is the *square root of the energy efficiency*, which is always greater than the energy efficiency. That's just the way numbers work. The square root of a fraction is always larger than the fraction itself. As a result the momentum imparted to the arrow keeps on increasing as we make the arrow mass larger and larger. The theoretical maximum corresponds to an infinite arrow mass.

Either way the ideal arrow for penetration is one with infinite mass. Of course we are no closer to achieving that ideal than we are to attaining a massless arrow. The heavier the arrow the slower its speed leaving the bow. As its mass increases, its velocity approaches zero. The practical implications are obvious. We quickly reach a point where the trajectory of a very heavy arrow is totally impractical. In addition, the oscillation frequency must match the time it takes the arrow to clear the bow. The slower arrow takes longer to clear the bow, which means that it must oscillate slower and slower. The increasing mass would slow the oscillations so long as the heavier arrow did not become too stiff. At any rate we again have an ideal which is unachievable but in terms of which we can think about a more practical limit.

As with the target archer, the practical limit has to be approached from the standpoint of trajectory. What is the minimum arrow speed we are willing to accept? And that in turn depends on how far we are going to try to shoot. Even if we limit ourselves to a distance of 20 yards, a speed of 140-150 feet per second seems like a not unreasonable answer. I personally would not accept a speed any lower than that. In the first place there is no reason to. An arrow velocity at least that high is attainable with almost any decent traditional bow of moderate draw weight and reasonable weight hunting arrows, no matter what the limb design. A 50 pound bow drawn 20 inches will typically store about 42 foot-pounds of energy. Even with an effective mass as high as 400 grains, which is a value representative of the least efficient limbs, such a bow will still shoot a moderately heavy 450 grain arrow at a velocity of 149 feet per second. With only a slightly more efficient design having an effective mass of 300 grains we can achieve 143 feet per second with a 40 pound bow storing 32 foot-pounds of energy and 450 grain arrows.

An average velocity of 140-150 feet per second translates into about 0.4 second for an arrow to travel twenty yards. In that time the arrow will drop about 2.5 feet, or 30 inches, due to the effect of gravity. So it has to be pointed that far above the intended point of impact to hit the target. If we extend the range to 40 yards the time of flight goes to 0.8 second and the arrow drops 10 feet. For my money that is about the extent of any successful shooting at unknown distances without a fixed sight. I would not hesitate to shoot 20 yards at that arrow speed. But I don't believe anyone could consistently shoot well at much more than 40 yards with an arrow speed that slow using a point-and-shoot or other indirect method of aiming.

So what does a minimum acceptable velocity of 140-150 feet per second translate into, in terms of arrow mass? What is the practical upper limit of arrow mass to achieve maximum arrow penetration? Let's start with a draw weight of 50 pounds. That weight is within reach of the majority of bowhunters. At a draw length of 20 inches assume the bow stores 42 foot-pounds of energy. Some straight-limbed bows may not do quite this well but some recurve bows will do better than this. We may as well also assume a fairly efficient limb design, one with an effective mass of 200 grains. We can do better than that but at the same time many traditional bows do not do that well. Such a bow will shoot 760 grain arrows at a velocity of 140 feet per second and 636 grain arrows at a speed of 150 feet per second. We can already see that these arrow weights are considerably greater than those commonly used even by bowhunters, unless we take into account a few individuals who hunt big game in Africa or elsewhere and know to use heavier arrows for better penetration.

What do these weights become for a 40 pound bow storing 34 foot-pounds of energy? Staying with an effective limb mass of 200 grains we find that 577 grain arrows will shoot 140 feet per second and 477 grain arrows will shoot 150 feet per second. For a 60 pound bow storing about 50 foot-pounds of energy and an effective mass of 250 grains the comparable numbers are 893 grains at 140 feet per second and 746 grains at 150 feet per second.

This is more than enough information to suggest that a practical upper limit to arrow mass is about 500 grains for draw weights as low as 40 pounds and about 750 grains or more for draw weights 50 pounds and above. For weights greater than that it becomes a problem just to fabricate arrows that heavy and get them to fly properly. For that reason we have excluded draw weights above 60 pounds from our example even though some bowhunters use bows heavier than that. Of course still heavier draw weights would shoot arrows even heavier than these at speeds of 140-150 feet per second or more. As long as we keep the arrow weight below these values we have adopted a compromise that gives acceptable arrow flight at practical hunting distances while obtaining good penetration.

We can also look at the energy and momentum that result from these arrow weights. For a 500 grain arrow shot in a bow with an effective mass of 200 grains the energy efficiency is 0.71 so that 71 percent of the stored energy is actually imparted to the arrow, a very good value. The corresponding fraction for momentum is the square root of that, or 0.84, so that the arrow obtains 84 percent of the theoretical maximum momentum. For a 750 grain arrow and an effective mass of 200 grains the energy efficiency is 0.79 and the corresponding fraction of the maximum momentum is 0.89. These are extremely high values for both.

So we have narrowed the practical limits to how closely we can approach the ideal for arrow speed on the one hand and for penetration on the other. The ideal for speed is an arrow with no mass. The best we can really do in a practical sense is a little less than 300 grains, possibly as low as 250 grains, with the exception of special flight arrows where we can go down to about half that value by keeping them short to make them stiff enough. The ideal for penetration is an arrow with infinite mass, but practical considerations of trajectory and draw weight lead us to a realistic limit of 500 to about 750 grains. Somewhere between the ideal mass values of *zero* and *infinity* real arrows live in the narrow practical range from about 250 grains to somewhere between two or three times that number. We have made the point more than once that all traditional bows regardless of design and draw weight operate in a rather narrow range of energy efficiency and arrow velocity. Now we see that roughly the same is also true of arrows.

# Should You Change Arrows?

*Will changing to better arrows improve your shooting?*
*When are better arrows more than good enough?*

*I*s the archer who decides to shoot wooden arrows instead of aluminum or carbon composites at an inherent disadvantage when it comes to accuracy? What about the archer who chooses a less expensive aluminum shaft and settles for an alloy that has slightly greater variation in straightness? Should you always opt to buy the most uniform and precise—and the most expensive—shafts available, or would a less expensive one fly just as well, or well enough? Would shooting a better arrow than the ones you are currently using improve your shooting and your scores?

Every archer faces these kinds of questions when deciding which arrows to shoot. The bias is always in the direction of better and more uniform shafts. The rule of thumb most often seen and heard is to choose the most expensive arrows that your budget allows. It may interest you to learn that this kind of advice quite often makes absolutely no sense, budget aside. The problem is that many, if not most, of us already shoot shafts capable of greater accuracy and smaller dispersion than our skill in shooting can achieve. It is a matter of when *better* becomes *good enough.*

With arrows, better means the ability to achieve tighter groups. Since the same fletching can be used on any kind of shaft, we will assume that the accuracy of the arrow depends primarily on the properties of the shaft and that variations in the type or uniformity of the fletching are less important. From our conclusions we will find that assumption may not be warranted in every case. The main characteristics of the shaft that affect arrow flight are its straightness, its spine or stiffness, its weight, and the uniformity of these properties along the length of the shaft. Uniformity shows up mainly in the distribution of weight, which affects the point at which the arrow balances and which could possibly affect spine. We could also include other properties, notably the roundness or concentricity of the shaft, but that is already taken into account by the straightness and spine.

How straight does an arrow have to be? The answer depends on what is good enough. Suppose we arbitrarily adopt as our criterion that we want our arrows to group inside a nine inch circle at ninety meters. This is an exceptionally stringent requirement and few archers ever shoot well enough to achieve it, even with perfect arrows that have no variation in any of their properties. A difference in trajectory of nine inches at ninety meters is an angular dispersion of 0.0025 radians, or 0.146 degrees. If this amount of angular dispersion results from an error in controlling the direction the arrow is pointing, due to a deviation in the straightness of the arrow, it amounts to a difference of 0.076 inch in an arrow length of 30 inches. In other words, the straightness of a 30 inch shaft can vary by as much as ± 0.038 inch, or ± 38 mils, from one end to the other, and still be straight enough to group inside a nine inch circle at ninety meters. Compare this value to the straightness of ± 0.003 inch for XX75 shafts, or ± 0.001 inch for X7 shafts quoted by the major aluminum shaft manufacturer. By comparison, the difference between XX75 and X7 shafts is completely insignificant, even irrelevant.

The straightness values quoted by the manufacturer amount to a dispersion of about 1/4 inch and 3/4 inch at 90 meters for the two kinds of shafts. The archer who pays more for the straighter shaft will get what he pays for, but the difference will certainly not affect how well he is shooting unless perhaps he shoots these arrows out of a machine, and even then the difference in the size of the groups will be relatively insignificant. Most of us are already shooting arrows that are straight enough for the level of skill that even the best archers ever attain. Even wooden arrows can be made straight to much better than ± 38 mils, or can be selected or straightened to that degree with enough care and attention. A deviation of 38 mils is slightly more than 1/32 inch, and by placing the shaft on a flat surface it is easy enough to see a deviation in straightness smaller than that.

A bent shaft presents an increased frontal area to air resistance. This is potentially an important effect in determining how rapidly the arrow slows down, which in turn can affect its trajectory and its dispersion. A deviation in straightness as large as 76 mils will increase the frontal area of a 5/16 inch shaft by about thirty percent, from 0.077 square inch to 0.100 square inch. A deviation in straightness as small as ±3 mils will change the frontal area by only about two percent. A change that small is certainly insignificant. Whether a change as large as thirty percent is significant will depend on the size and type of fletching and how much the fletching contributes to the overall air resistance. If the resistance of the fletching dominates, as it usually does except perhaps in the case of very small target vanes, the increase in the frontal area of the bent shaft may be unimportant. This would be the case with most hunting arrows which have larger fletching. Where the frontal area of the fletching dominates, variations in the area of the fletching may be far more important than any small variations in the straightness of the shaft. At the same time variations in straightness cause changes in the frontal area presented by the fletching. This is another reason to keep the fletching on target arrows no larger than necessary to assure stable arrow flight. Wooden arrows may begin to lose ground to aluminum shafts at this point; but keep in mind that the dispersion limit we have adopted is fairly extreme and much too stringent for the degree of accuracy required in hunting, where most wooden shafts are likely to be used. Once again the difference between a straightness of ± 0.003 inch for XX75 shafts and ± 0.001 inch for X7 aluminum shafts is totally insignificant.

If there is as much as even a two mile per hour crosswind, and even if the arrow is traveling as fast as 180 feet per second, then the arrow will fly inclined at an angle of about one degree to the forward direction due to the sideways effect of the wind on the arrow. In this case the frontal area of a 5/16 inch arrow shaft is increased from 0.077 square inch to about 0.23 square inch, and a 76 mil variation in straightness is a completely negligible effect on the resistance of the arrow. In this case also the frontal area of the fletching becomes much greater and further swamps any effect of shaft straightness on air resistance. So if shooting in any wind, which is most often the case, straightness better than 76 mils will not improve arrow dispersion.

The force of the string pushing on the arrow causes it to bend as it leaves the bow. Two arrows that have the same stiffness, or spine, will bend the same amount and fly in the same direction. If one bends more (or less) than the other, then because the nock end of the arrow is attached to the string the difference in bending will constitute an angular dispersion between the direction of the two shafts. As before, a dispersion of nine inches at ninety meters, or 0.146 degrees, corresponds to a difference of 0.076 inch in the bending of a 30 inch shaft. This means that we also have to limit the variation in stiffness to no more than 0.076 inch. It is easy enough to select arrows that differ in spine by no more than this amount (a little more than 1/16 inch) at a deflection of much less than one inch for example. Using a spine tester with a rotating pointer, where the pivot point is located 1/10 the length of the pointer from one end (which means that the other end of the pointer will move ten times the deflection of the arrow), one can readily measure differences in deflection much less than 1/16 inch. This restriction on the variation in spine is not a very demanding requirement from the standpoint of measurement and is one that can be met by wooden shafts as well as by any grade of aluminum shafts. Yet it is still sufficient to limit the dispersion due to variations in spine alone to no more than nine inches at ninety meters.

Variations in arrow weight introduce variations in initial velocity. A lighter arrow will leave the bow with a higher initial velocity. Once the arrow is free of the bow differences in weight have no additional effect on the trajectory since all bodies fall at the same rate independent of weight. But two arrows aimed at the same point and having slightly different initial velocities will follow different trajectories. The arrow with the greater velocity will spend less time getting to the target and will not have time to fall as far as the slower arrow. The result is a dispersion caused by gravity due to differences in speed. The faster arrow will also have less time to drift in any crosswind. The result again will be a dispersion caused by the wind due to differences in speed.

It turns out that a one percent change in the *combined* mass of the arrow and the effective mass of the bow limbs produces a one half percent change in initial arrow velocity. The effective mass is fixed by the design of the bow and is constant. A one percent change in the arrow mass by itself will produce less than a one percent change in the combined mass. Ignoring the effective mass and using the change in the arrow mass as the change in the combined mass will therefore overestimate the change in arrow velocity. Even so this amounts to a difference in velocity of only one foot per second at an arrow velocity of 200 feet per second. It is entirely unrealistic to expect variations in arrow velocity to ever be less than this amount. It is unrealistic to expect them to be even this small, due to normal variations in the archer's shooting form. This variation in arrow velocity corresponds to a dispersion at ninety meters of four inches for an arrow velocity of 200 feet per second; and a dispersion of seven inches for an arrow velocity of 150 feet per second. Both of these values are within our limit of nine inches. But a one percent variation in arrow weight is a fairly stringent requirement. It means only a five grain variation in an arrow weight of 500 grains. Wooden shafts can be selected to this standard but usually are not, and here we encounter a requirement where aluminum has a distinct edge over wood. Even so, there is no practical advantage in choosing the most expensive aluminum shafts available. Wooden shafts that don't conform to this tighter weight restriction can always be re-sorted into smaller groups that do. Wooden shafts are rarely used for target archery anymore and the practical variation in weight should be judged against the less stringent requirements of the kinds of shots taken in hunting and field archery.

A variation of two percent in arrow weight produces less than a one percent variation in arrow velocity, or two feet per second at a velocity of 200 feet per second. A variation of that size produces a dispersion at ninety meters of about eight inches at an arrow velocity of 200 feet per second and about fifteen inches at a velocity of 150 feet per second. Although the latter value exceeds our limit of nine inches, it is still not unreasonable and is entirely acceptable for the accuracy that most archers are able to attain. It is more than adequate for the shorter ranges encountered in hunting, where most wooden arrows are going to be used. Shafts matched to within 10 grains at 500 grains satisfy this requirement. At fifty yards even a variation as large as two percent in arrow velocity produces less than nine inches of dispersion for an arrow traveling 150 feet per second or faster, which is more than adequate for most shots taken when hunting. This corresponds to a four percent variation in arrow weight, or 20 grains for an arrow weight of 500 grains.

Keep in mind that we have to control the weight of the finished arrow to these limits, not just the shaft. We also have to control variations in the weight of the point, nock, any shaft inserts, and the fletching and glue to the same stringent limits.

The dispersion caused by wind drift due to variations in arrow speed and time of flight depends on how fast the wind is blowing. But for most shooting conditions the dispersion caused by the wind will be less than that caused by gravity. At ninety meters a one percent variation in arrow speed at 175 feet per second leads to a variation in the flight time of the arrow of less than 0.02 seconds. This variation in flight time gives only a six inch dispersion caused by the wind even for a wind speed of twenty miles per hour. The dispersion due to *variations* in wind speed is likely to be much larger. In other words you are far more likely to miss due to *changes* in the wind speed, and direction, than you are due to any variations in arrow speed. When the wind is blowing changes in wind speed are generally much greater than variations in arrow speed.

Another way to get a handle on the importance of weight variations may be to compare it to changes caused by variations in draw length. If the distance the bow is drawn changes, so does the energy stored by the bow limbs and the force imparted to the arrow, which in turn causes a variation in the initial arrow velocity. It turns out that a given fractional change in draw length produces roughly the same fractional variation in arrow velocity. This means that a fractional change in draw length produces twice the variation in arrow velocity as the same fractional change in arrow weight. In other words, a one percent change in draw length, which amounts to about 1/4 inch in a typical draw length, is roughly equivalent to a two percent variation in arrow weight. It is reasonable that the archer will be able to consistently achieve the same draw length to within one percent. With a clicker or some sort of draw-check, one can do even better. On the other hand, it does not make much sense to control arrow weight to any greater precision than one is able to control draw length.

At this point we see that it is more important to control variations in arrow weight than either straightness or spine. At the practical limits to which we usually control weight it still has a significant effect on arrow speed and trajectory. Weight is what the bow directly propels, and it should vary by no more than one or two percent.

The remaining characteristic left to consider is uniformity of the shaft along its length, in particular uniformity of weight, since to fly the same all of the arrows should balance close to the same point. Here again this is not a very severe restriction and one that wooden shafts as well as aluminum should have no trouble meeting. A one percent variation in the balance point corresponds to a variation of 1/3 inch for a 30 inch shaft, or about one diameter of the typical arrow shaft. This degree of balance can be easily achieved and can be adjusted by small changes in the weight of the point so long as these changes fall within the allowed weight variations.

We have not considered a number of other properties, like concentricity or roundness of the shaft. Variations in roundness should be detected as variations in the measurement of the straightness of the shaft as it is rotated, and also as variations in stiffness as the shaft is rotated in the spine tester. What is not so easy to assess is the effect that variations in the elastic modulus or stiffness of a shaft along its length have on its flight. This is one property where aluminum and graphite composites either separately or combined have a decided advantage over wooden shafts. It is not obvious exactly what flight characteristic would be most affected by variations in stiffness along the length of the shaft but its oscillations leaving the bow definitely would be. How to assess the degree to which, and whether, that would introduce any significant dispersion in the flight is not so clear. We could attribute a confidence or peace of mind effect to any such variations and say that in that measure all aluminum or graphite composites are decidedly superior to wood.

That brings to mind the possible psychological effect of shooting the best shafts that money can buy, whether they actually fly truer or not. The confidence of the archer is an intangible, impossible to assess but equally hard to dismiss or overlook. The confidence that comes from shooting better arrows, or more importantly, any lack of confidence that results from shooting arrows not as good as the best available might just make the difference in performance, especially under the pressure of competition shooting.

What about other reasons to change arrows? We have tacitly been assuming up to this point that the motivation for changing arrows is to achieve tighter groups by better controlling straightness, spine, weight, and uniformity of these properties along the length of the shaft. So we have tacitly been assuming that we are comparing arrows of different kinds that are ostensibly the same in all of these properties, except for how well each is controlled. But there may be other motivations for changing arrows. We have ruled out any advantage in straighter shafts over what can be easily achieved with less than the best shafts available. The value of spine is fixed by the draw weight and speed of the bow so that short of changing bows we cannot change spine by very much. But we might want to consider changing arrows simply to change the arrow weight. And there could be two very good reasons for doing that.

The first is to achieve greater arrow speed in target archery. The faster the arrow flies the less time it takes to reach the target and the less time there is for wind and gravity to affect its flight. Arrow velocity depends inversely on the square root of the combined arrow mass and effective mass of the bow limbs. For an effective mass of 200 grains changing the arrow mass from 400 grains to 300 grains leads to about a 10 percent increase in arrow speed and a 10 percent decrease in flight time. That in turn produces a 10 percent decrease in drift due to wind and a 20 percent decrease in the distance the arrow falls due to gravity during its trajectory. All of these are in the direction of smaller arrow dispersion at the target and constitute real reasons to shoot lighter target arrows.

The second is to achieve greater arrow penetration for hunting arrows. Arrow penetration increases with increasing kinetic energy and momentum of the arrow. The fraction of the energy stored by the bow that is actually imparted to the arrow increases with increasing arrow mass and is given by the energy efficiency of the bow, which is just the ratio of the arrow mass to the total combined arrow mass and effective mass of the bow limbs. The fraction of the total momentum imparted to the arrow is also given by the energy efficiency. If we shoot 400 grain hunting arrows in a fairly efficient bow with an effective mass of 200 grains the energy efficiency is the ratio of 400 to 600, or 0.67. If we change to 500 grain arrows this value improves to the ratio of 500 to 700, or 0.71. This change is in the direction to improve arrow penetration. But at the same time the increase in arrow weight will result in a decrease in arrow speed. For a bow with an effective mass of 200 grains going from 400 to 500 grain arrows will decrease arrow speed about 8 percent.

Should you change arrows then? As long as you are already shooting arrows that meet the general requirements that we have outlined, there is absolutely nothing to be gained by going to so-called "better" arrows. They may in fact be better, in terms of precision and uniformity, but the point is that they are beyond what is already good enough. In particular, if your present shafts are straight to within ± 0.010 inch or better, are matched in spine to the same precision, and are matched in weight to one or two percent, then don't expect to see any improvement in your shooting as a result of switching to more uniform, and more expensive, arrows. The size of your groups is already being controlled by your skill and your shooting form, and not by any variations in your arrows. You might however still obtain an advantage by switching to lighter target arrows for greater speed, or heavier hunting arrows for greater penetration. The latter improvement in penetration will have to weighed against the effects of lower speeds resulting from the heavier arrow mass.

# Shooting

*The basic elements of good form are all well understood and easy enough to describe, but can be far more difficult to acquire and master, or to maintain and hold on to.*

*N*othing so easy to do is quite so difficult to do well as shooting a bow. At the highest levels of mastery it is all done by the proper feel, some of it very delicate, and has to be assimilated, retained and reproduced by *muscle memory*. Trying to tell someone else how to shoot well or learning how to do it yourself by reading about it or from someone else is just as difficult. After all, how does anyone describe *feel* so that someone reading about it or hearing about it gets the same feel themselves from just the description. It is easy enough to describe how one conceives and thinks about the correct feeling involved in the various steps of shooting a bow; but the description is not the same thing as the actual feeling and that can only be learned by eventually discovering it for yourself. And it has to be first discovered, often quite accidentally, then recognized, and finally reinforced by continuous repetition, all the while managing to do it correctly without developing any bad habits for long enough to acquire and retain the necessary muscle memory. Not an easy task, either for the teacher or the student.

In addition, the proper feel that leads to consistent shooting at the highest levels seems to be actually different for different archers. Talk to any number of really good archers and chances are they will each describe the feeling they get when they are *really on* in quite different ways. They will even differ in what part of their form they choose to single out as the most important to talk about. One will focus on the bow arm and shoulder, another on pulling with the back, another on the anchor, another on tempo and rhythm, one on the release, another on the follow through or pulling smoothly through the clicker, another on aiming, the list goes on and on. Each of these you can be sure represents a personal discovery that each one has made somewhere along the way, but none of them alone is sufficient unto itself and all of them, plus more, represent things that each archer has to struggle with and master at some point. But that's probably the good news. It means that there are multiple pathways to the correct technique of shooting a bow, and multiple ways of doing it well. The task, and the trick, is to discover your own path within the overall framework consisting of the essential elements of good form.

People have been at this problem for a long time. The first systematic study and description that we are aware of dates back to a work by Roger Ascham (*Toxophilus; the School of Shooting, in Two Books*, The Simon Archery Foundation, Manchester Museum, The University, Manchester, England, 1985; Derrydale Press, 1992) published in 1544 and presented to King Henry VIII of England. Ascham was an advisor to the king and tutor of later-to-be Queen Elizabeth I. The title is from the Greek words for bow (toxon) and love (philo).

*Toxophilus* has the distinction of being not only the first work on shooting the bow but also the first scholarly work written in English instead of Latin. Book I is a rambling justification and defense of archery, which was in the process of being supplanted by firearms as weapons of war. Henry VIII has always been one of my heroes because at one point he banned the playing of golf from the realm saying that it was beginning to interfere with the practice of archery. Book II is an analysis of the steps involved in proper shooting. There Ascham breaks down good shooting into, "*Standing, knocking (sic), drawing, holding, loosing, whereby cometh fair shooting...*" Ever since, those have become the essential steps in terms of which shooting technique has been presented and discussed. It is still a delight to read what Ascham wrote about shooting and about the archer's equipment if only to witness the accumulated wisdom of English archery up to that time. The book is full of advice that is timeless and still worth heeding today. After all archery is an ancient craft and though technology and fashions change, some things, such as the elements of good form, never do.

The next landmark work is by Horace A. Ford (*Archery: Its Theory and Practice*, London and Cheltenham, 1856; S.R. Publishers Ltd, 1971; Derrydale Press, 1992). Ford was the British Grand National Archery Champion and

Holder of the Champion's Medal a record twelve years, eleven of them in succession, beginning in 1849. His best single and double York round scores, shot at distances of 100, 80, and 60 yards became the standard of excellence and were seldom surpassed by anyone shooting comparable equipment. There can be little doubt that within the context of the sport at the time there has never been a more disciplined and more accomplished or dominant archer. In addition he was a keen observer and clear thinker concerning the techniques of shooting. Ford's little book should be read by every serious student of shooting, if for no other reason than his advice on never fully stopping the draw prior to the release. There is also a lot of good information on English longbows and arrows, and the archer's paradox and aiming. Ford breaks down shooting into *standing, drawing, aiming, holding* and *loosing*, and has chapters dealing with each topic, adding a chapter on aiming to the list originally given by Ascham.

Ironically, there is suspicion that Horace Ford later developed serious shooting problems of his own, and, if so, almost certainly the affliction that goes by the name target panic or premature release. After his incredible run as champion he distanced himself from archery and stopped shooting altogether, telling a close friend that he sorrowfully regretted spending so much time at archery. Some have argued that his commitment to his religious convictions and the time he devoted to religious causes was the reason. But he also returned journals and newsletters sent to him by interested parties in the United States during the early growth of target archery in this country, across the front of which had been scribbled "archery is an odious sport," quite easily the bitter sentiment of someone brought low from such a pinnacle by the ravages of target panic. At least one more-recent national and world archery champion went from shooting record breaking FITA scores to mediocrity virtually overnight due to the same shooting problem, to eventually give it up and leave the sport. We will discuss this common shooting affliction in detail later.

Before getting into the individual steps involved in shooting we will begin with some general comments.

*Something has to always trigger the shot. Or more correctly, something has to trigger the release.* In the sequence of shooting there has to be something analogous to pulling the trigger on a gun. One might expect that aiming should trigger the shot. That the correct aiming picture should be the final step that triggers the release. And in the beginning that will be the case for most archers. But repeated triggering on visual cues alone can lead to the serious problem known as target panic or premature release which we will discuss in more depth later. The trouble is that if the bow is just drawn and aimed with no clear trigger in mind, the archer ends up trying to achieve and hold the correct aim which is never quite good enough to trigger the release. The result is that either the archer is able to aim and hold the bow aimed but then freezes up and can't trigger the release; or the attempt itself to achieve the correct aiming picture ends up prematurely triggering the shot. Hence the names target panic and premature release to describe this condition. As we will see the solution is some step that triggers the release in conjunction with, but separate from, the act of aiming.

*The bow is shot with the back, not with the arms.* There comes a point in the draw when the pull is transferred from the arm muscles to the back muscles so that the arms and shoulders can relax and settle into a stable position at full draw. If you do not master this step you will never be able to shoot consistently, even though you may at times shoot fairly well for a few arrows. Nothing reduces the size of groups more dramatically than this single step. And nothing is more likely to produce an erratic arrow that is not part of any group than failure to complete it. It is very difficult to shoot consistently using primarily your arms and pectoral muscles, requiring a strength and a precision of "hand-eye coordination" that is almost impossible to achieve and maintain for very long. The better you do at it the more likely you are to throw the very next arrow completely away, usually by flinching or jerking the bow arm or drawing arm during the release.

*It is also impossible to shoot consistently using a static release*, although here again you may occasionally shoot a few arrows well this way. A static release means stopping or relaxing the backward pull on the string prior to the release. The release should come while the string is still being drawn or at least while the pulling effort is maintained or is increasing. The string may appear to be at rest but the back tension generating the pull should be still increasing, not static or decreasing. Once you relax the backward pull prior to releasing the string then any number of bad things can happen before the shot gets away and none of them are any longer under your direct control. And the longer the pause after losing tension before the release is actually made, the bigger and worse the effect usually gets. The act of triggering the shot usually involves increasing or maintaining back tension in some fashion.

In spite of the conventional wisdom quoted above, a few archers have been able to shoot fairly well with a static release, although none of them have accounted for the current level of record breaking scores. I have seen several good archers who shot this way, occasionally with impressive results. At close distances of twenty yards or less they are often unbeatable. Quite a few bowhunters shoot this way without ever using the back at all. Where you find them out is at longer distances where, even when they are otherwise shooting well, they will consistently miss low. This occurs when they let down more than at other times. It is almost impossible to control.

*One of the little ironies of shooting a bow is that you can't learn how to do it right without first doing it wrong.* Or if you are fortunate enough to do everything right at the beginning, you will eventually reach a point where you don't, or can't, seem to do it right anymore. That is the time when you are finally able to learn something new. The secret is to recognize when you are doing something wrong and not keep doing it over and over until it becomes an ingrained habit that is hard to break. Every archer should experiment with different ways of doing almost everything in the execution of a shot, from whether to roll the elbow of the bow arm down or up, where to locate the rear aiming point, whether to use a square, open, or closed stance, whether to use low, medium, or high wrist for the bow hand, whether to keep the bow shoulder low or let it ride back and up, whether to come to full draw before starting to aim or arrive at full draw with the bow already aimed, and how to actually trigger the release after aiming, to list some of the more apparent ones. Don't copy someone else's form, unless it happens to also feel right and work well for you. Develop your own form instead. And constantly experiment with it to determine how changes affect where the arrow goes. That will be your key to correcting shooting mistakes when they occur.

*Tempo is very important.* But there is a fundamental difference between just shooting fast, and consciously increasing the tempo at which you execute the deliberate steps in the act of shooting. If after a while you find yourself unable to slow the tempo and make yourself shoot slowly and deliberately, then you are just shooting fast and learning a lot of bad habits in the process. The pace of executing the shot should always remain under your control. It is possible to learn to shoot faster without letting your form come apart at the seams and have all sorts of bad habits creep in. But you have to work at it. Never shoot all of your practice shots fast. Slow the tempo some of the time and check each step of the process for conformity to the form you have developed and are trying to maintain. Then learn to speed up the process without leaving out or skipping any of the individual steps. *Never leave out the step of aiming, including the step of checking the aim before triggering the shot.* There are a lot of very good target archers who shoot fast, but they still shoot deliberately, merely at an increased tempo, and they still check the aim before releasing. If you cannot check and change the aim before releasing, and you are not already using a clicker, chances are you will soon have to, to overcome a case of premature release.

A tempo too slow is also bad. It leads just as surely to freezing or snap shooting, which are two more names for target panic, as does shooting too fast. *There is no perfect aim.* When the sight bead or the sight picture has settled down to small excursions about the intended impact point, then go ahead and trigger the shot. Perfection here isn't possible, and it isn't necessary either. And trying to achieve it isn't desirable. What counts is that the sight bead or aiming picture is making acceptably small excursions before triggering the release. The group size will be determined by the size of those excursions if all other parts of the shot have been executed correctly. By trying to achieve perfection you set up a vicious feedback loop. Trying to get the aim perfect prolongs the shot and tires the muscles, making it harder to aim, requiring longer and further tiring the muscles, until finally you are forced to release before you are ready. This quickly becomes a habit and eventually leads to target panic. Never allow yourself to get in that rut.

These are some general considerations to keep in mind as we discuss each of the individual components of the archer's form.

The correct stance is the first step in shooting. The best stance to start with is a square stance with the archer facing perpendicular to the direction of the shot and the feet parallel about shoulder width apart. The knees should not be locked since that restricts blood flow and leads to fatigue and shaking. Instead the legs should be straight but relaxed and very slightly flexed at the knees. One should have a feeling of stability and control of the body with the legs and feet. The hips should be allowed to relax and roll down and forward where they should sit comfortably. This in turn slightly arches the lower back and promotes pulling with the back muscles. In this position the muscles of the lower abdomen can be tensed to hold the upper torso still. This posture gives a very stable stance and helps reduce muscle tremors and shaking of the bow arm and shoulder. If you do it correctly, without forcing it, it is also effortless and very comfortable.

A square stance works well for most archers. Opening the stance slightly by moving the front foot back slightly and turning it, usually no more than 45 degrees, to partially face toward the target helps many shooters get their back more into the shot. It is easier to feel the tension in the back muscles at full draw in this stance. One has to be careful however to maintain the front of the chest pointing perpendicular to the line of sight. This means swiveling the hips slightly clockwise with respect to the direction of the legs. If you are pulling correctly with the back muscles this happens more or less automatically and naturally. The face and eyes should in any case be turned toward the target to give a clear unobstructed sight picture. Many shooters find an open stance more stable than the square stance. Having the body turned partially toward the target brings the leg muscles more into play in controlling both backward and forward as well as sideways motions. The feet can be slightly closer together in an open stance with no loss of stability. This stance is also better on uneven terrain where the archer has to lean toward or away from the target to keep the upper body perpendicular to the direction of aim. In an open stance it is easier to develop a feeling that the feet have a grip on the earth to hold the body still.

The opposite modification of the square stance is a closed stance in which the rear foot is moved back slightly and turned partially away from the target. This has the effect of rotating the body slightly clockwise and away from the direction toward the target. A closed stance helps some shooters get the bow arm and shoulder more in line with the arrow and brings both shoulders into better alignment parallel to the direction of the arrow, giving a very compact form that tends to stay in line through the release and follow through. However it causes more of the draw weight to be supported by the bow arm and shoulder, and less by the back, and can result in a loss of back tension, in addition to making it more difficult to feel the back muscles and bring them into play. The better alignment of the shoulders brings the string closer to the bow arm and can lead to clearance problems, especially if the bow arm elbow is rolled up instead of down and under. And there is more of a tendency with a closed stance to have the bow shoulder cave in towards the arrow or to lose control of the bow shoulder during the release, especially with a heavier draw weight. It is not a good stance for shooting a hunting bow unless you are suddenly caught off guard and have to take a quick shot from this position. Then you might want to know how to do it.

Another important part of the stance is the placement of the hand on the bow. The bow should rest against the pad of the thumb between the thumb and the palm, with the bow vertical and the palm inclined about forty-five degrees to the horizontal; or forty-five degrees to the plane of the bow and string if you shoot with the bow canted. The fingers should be open, or if closed only loosely in contact with the grip. A tight grip transfers to the bow any torque exerted by the hand and wrist and can deflect the shot. A good way to insure against this is to keep the hand open and loosely curl the fingers toward the palm with the fingers not touching the bow, which is supported entirely on the pad of the thumb. Of course, if shooting a hunting bow you probably want to keep the fingers lightly curled around the grip to prevent having the bow come out of your hand. It can happen. It is usually best to use a bow sling to prevent dropping the bow if it does happen.

There are three basic positions to adopt for the wrist: low, medium, or high. Low wrist means letting the wrist relax and completely collapse so that the palm is as vertical and far back as it can go and more or less perpendicular to the bow arm, with the heel of the hand pushing directly against the bow. The exact position of the palm will depend somewhat on the shape of the grip. The ideal grip for low wrist is one that is round or oval and nearly flat or only slightly dished, the kind found on the English longbow. The strength of this position is that the wrist is already collapsed as far as it can and so cannot collapse further during the shot. The main pressure of the bow hand on the grip is transmitted through the heel of the hand which means the center of pressure is lower on the bow handle. That requires the bow be tillered so that the bottom limb bends less than the upper by a greater amount than with a medium or high wrist position.

A medium wrist position has the wrist directly in line with the forearm so that the pressure of the hand on the bow is transmitted through the center of the thumb pad and the web between the thumb and forefinger. This is perhaps the most natural wrist position, especially with a shaped or contoured grip, and the one that gives the most control over the bow at full draw. It is the position that most archers just naturally adopt without thinking about it. And it is the one that requires the least amount of conscious thought while shooting. Its only drawback is the need to guard against the wrist collapsing. For this wrist position the shape of the bow grip is very important. It should be contoured to match the natural shape of the hand with the wrist in the correct position. Then the bow handle becomes the guide to proper hand placement to help prevent the wrist from collapsing during the shot.

The high wrist position turns the wrist and bow hand down and supports the force of the bow entirely against the webbing between the thumb and forefinger. It minimizes contact of the hand with the bow and reduces the transmission of torque to the bow. This is the least stable position and requires strong wrists and hands for sustained shooting. Yet it has been used by some extremely good archers over the years.

The position of the wrist affects what we do with the bow arm. Low wrist works best with an inert bow arm rigidly straight with the elbow locked and the shoulder carried low. The bow arm is controlled primarily by pushing it strongly toward the target. High wrist works best with the elbow locked and the shoulder up and slightly back. The bow arm is controlled principally by the muscles in the shoulder. Medium wrist calls for the shoulder to be in an intermediate position slightly back and the arm and elbow straight but not as rigidly extended. The bow arm is controlled by the arm and shoulder muscles combined.

The only thing to say about nocking the arrow is to do it the same way every time. Don't do it absently or without thinking. Make it a definite step in the execution of the shot. Do it at the same point each time and in exactly the same fashion. And think about what you are doing while you do it. Personally I think it should come after setting up the stance, not before. You may want to adjust your stance after the arrow is nocked, but it should be nocked only after you have taken your stance. By then you are concentrating on the execution of the shot and nocking is done as deliberately and consistently as every other step. Always check to make sure the arrow is placed correctly on the string and is on the arrow rest or shelf and not riding on top of the cushion plunger or somewhere else it should not be. Then make another quick visual check at the start of the draw to verify that the arrow is still properly nocked and in place. This check should also extend to the stance and posture as you begin to draw the bow. Naturally these comments apply less to bow hunting where the arrow may be carried nocked for long periods of time. But even there one should always check the position of the arrow on the string and on the shelf or arrow rest before drawing the bow.

There are two ways of drawing the bow. The first is to fully extend the bow arm and set the arm and shoulder into place, pulling the string back only as far as required to comfortably hold the bow extended; then, after checking to make certain that everything is correct, the string is pulled smoothly the rest of the way to the rear anchor. It is a two-step process. There is a pause after the bow arm is extended and the bow is in place. This gives time to check the position of the bow hand and the elbow and shoulder of the bow arm, as well as the position of the hand, elbow and shoulder of the drawing arm. This check is both visual and by feel. Everything should feel right and the visual check should verify what that correct feeling looks like. It also gives time to check the position of the head and whether the head is turned to fully face the target. The fingers of the drawing hand should be perpendicular to the string with the string no farther forward than the first joint. Many archers prefer to place the string farther back, midway between the first and second joints, for a more secure-feeling grip. You should think of the fingers as a rigid hook that fits over the string and pulls it back. What is no good is having the string so near the finger tips that it feels like you are about to lose your grip. That produces a tendency to grab at the string, rolling the arrow off the rest and tensing the muscles of the drawing hand, making it harder to relax the hand for a clean release. Except for the muscles that hold the fingers bent into a hook, the hand and arm should be relaxed. The elbow should be up in line with the arrow or slightly above it and the drawing hand should be carried at least as high as the rear aiming position.

The alternative method is to bring the bow up while simultaneously extending the bow arm and drawing the string to the rear anchor in a single, smooth, continuous motion. When the bow arm reaches its full extension the bow should be in position, either vertical or canted, and the string should be at full draw with the bow already close to being correctly aimed. This is the method preferred by most bowhunters and those using an indirect or point-and-shoot method of aiming since it is the most natural to drawing and swinging the bow into position on target. It is also faster to execute, and it is easier to pull a heavier bow this way. The first method however is the most systematic and deliberate and is preferred by most target archers and even some bowhunters. When using the continuous draw there is no pause during which to get the bow arm and shoulder into the correct position. They either have to end up in the right position automatically or there has to be a pause at that point to check and correct their position. Pausing at the end of the draw to correct elements of form is a good way to relax and lose back tension and develop a static release. Either way can be made to work well and can be made consistent with regular practice. For taking quick shots at moving game the continuous method preferred by most bowhunters is the obvious choice.

Whether to roll the elbow under and away from the string or let it turn upward is a matter of preference and individual anatomy. Rolling it under gives better string clearance and is usually recommended for that reason. Personally I cannot maintain the elbow rolled under with any consistency. For me the elbow joint just naturally comes to a position roughly vertical or turned slightly up. If I roll it under I have to be constantly thinking about it or it won't stay there. For some individuals the elbow is always up when fully extended and locked. Do whichever is more comfortable and automatic for you. The less you have to think about the better.

But a word of caution. *The bow arm should be straight*, which means fully extended. You can't be consistent shooting with a bent elbow in spite of the fact that you may shoot a few arrows well that way. I have tried it repeatedly. It is easy to get in the habit of bending the elbow ever so slightly because it gives the arm muscles a feeling of having better control over the position of the bow when aiming. But with the elbow bent you lose control over what the bow does when the string is released. And it becomes almost impossible to control whether it is bent exactly the same amount on every shot. When shooting a heavy bow this way the bow will inevitably creep backward while aiming, especially if you try to shoot slowly and deliberately. It becomes one more thing to have to be aware of and check. Even when I have managed to shoot well for a few ends with my elbow bent, my arrow groups invariably get much tighter when I switch back to a locked elbow. *Extend the arm fully and remove that variable from your form.* You don't actually have to rigidly lock the elbow to do that. You can shoot with a "soft" elbow so long as the bow arm is pushing the bow firmly forward at all times during the shot.

It is the bow arm that points the bow. And pointing the bow is fundamental to the act of aiming and keeping the bow aimed. So controlling the position of the bow arm is equally fundamental to shooting well. Under no condition should the arm be left free to flop about during the release. The position of the arm however should not be controlled by the arm muscles. The arm should remain relaxed. Otherwise tension in the arm can cause the bow to move off line at the release. The bow arm has to be always under the firm control of the back and shoulder muscles, which point it in a given direction when the arm muscles are relaxed. I have often had my arrow groups suddenly converge by the simple step of becoming aware of controlling the position of the bow arm with the muscles which surround and encage the shoulder. This is one of those instances of something that is learned more by feel than anything else. One you have experienced the proper feel you can instantly summon it up and go back to it. Until then you may have difficulty even understanding the difference between controlling the bow with the shoulder muscles instead of the arm muscles. It is nevertheless an important distinction.

By whichever method the bow is drawn the string is pulled back to the *rear anchor* position. The rear anchor is not the place on the face or head to which the hand is drawn for the purpose of aiming. That is the *rear aiming* position. The worst image you can have is that of drawing the hand back to a spot where it stops. Drawing the bow to the rear anchor should be a continuous motion, or rather a continuous process, that never quite fully stops until after the string is released and the follow through is complete. *The rear anchor is a position of the drawing arm and shoulder that allows the entire draw weight of the bow to be transferred to the back and shoulder muscles, allowing the arms to relax.* The string has to be pulled far enough to get the back muscles involved in drawing and holding the bow. There is a definite point at which all the force is transferred from the arms to the back and you should be able to feel that transition taking place. It should start to occur well before you reach the rear anchor and should be complete once the rear anchor position is reached. It helps to think of the forearm as an inert extension, to the end of which the fingers are attached as a hook and which is drawn back using the muscles of the back, especially those that pull the shoulder blades together, to move the elbow rearward. At some point the back muscles should be doing all of the pulling. The position where that transition is complete is the rear anchor. At the rear anchor the elbow should be far enough back that the forearm and elbow are in line with the arrow, viewed from both the rear and the side. If the elbow is still sticking far out to the side it probably means that you have not drawn all the way to the rear anchor. Both shoulders should be in line with the arms and parallel to the line of sight to the target, which is also the proper alignment for greatest stability. Pulling correctly all the way to the rear anchor is totally a matter of feel.

To determine your correct rear anchor position draw the bow without regard to where the aiming position of the drawing hand should be. Just pull the hand back until you feel the transfer of all the force to your back muscles. Do this a number of times until you can recognize the feeling and the point at which it occurs each time. This should be an extremely comfortable and stable position since it allows you to relax your arms and hold the bow drawn with the more powerful back muscles. If you are not overbowed it should be accompanied by a feeling that you could hold the bow drawn that way indefinitely. For me it is the sensation of having the back muscles cocked and ready to fire. It is almost like placing the string over a rear hook to take some of the force off the muscles. Although the tension in the back muscles has actually increased and should continue undiminished until after the release, there is a feeling overall of relaxation since the back muscles are more powerful than those of the arms. The sensation of holding the bow drawn this way is one of drawing the shoulder blades together. That is also the proper sensation for triggering the release.

After drawing to the rear anchor the hand has to contact the rear aiming position. This fixes the rear of the arrow always in the same place relative to the line of sight for the purpose of aiming. The rear aiming position is usually somewhere beneath the chin or along the bottom of the jaw for target archers and those shooting with a sight; or at the corner of the mouth or somewhere higher on the face for those who use point of aim or gap sighting, or what I prefer to call point-and-shoot aiming. These latter methods of aiming are often lumped together and termed "instinctive" but that term is very misleading. Instinctive aiming implies the absence of any conscious method of aiming except to simply focus on the point to be hit while drawing the bow and releasing. Beyond a distance of a very few yards, I have never seen anyone who could do this very well, certainly not well enough to stick with it as the primary method of aiming.

What actually happens in practice is that you become aware of where the end of the arrow is pointing, termed the point of aim, in the peripheral visual field and make corrections accordingly. If the arrows are going low you compensate by raising the point at which the end of the arrow is aimed, which becomes the new point of aim. Gap aiming works much the same way except one gauges the size of the visual gap between the end of the arrow and the intended spot to be hit and then adjusts the gap on subsequent shots according to whether the arrow flies high or low. A third slightly different method is to picture in your mind the trajectory in your field of view along which the arrow is going to fly from the bow to the target and then launch the arrow along that path. This is the essence of the "become the arrow" method of aiming. The estimate of the trajectory is changed on subsequent shots according to whether the arrow went high or low. With constant repetition one can learn what the correct point of aim, or size of the gap, or trajectory should be according to a visual estimate of the distance to the target.

None of these methods of aiming is purely instinctive. All of them rely on conscious corrections learned from experience. I prefer to call these and other indirect methods simply point-and-shoot aiming. For point-and-shoot methods, the rear aiming position should be as close to the eye as practical without distorting the vision, certainly no lower than the corner of the mouth, so that one is looking as closely along the arrow itself as possible. The shape of the face and comfort of the drawing hand will determine the exact rear aiming position for point-and-shoot aiming. No matter which aiming method is used, the drawing hand should always be at the same rear position on every shot for consistency and reproducibility in aiming.

Varying the rear position of the drawing hand also varies the draw length, which has the effect of varying the energy stored in the bow and the velocity imparted to the arrow. There are two principal effects to be concerned with here. The first is that a large enough change in draw weight can render the spine of the arrow incorrect for achieving the proper oscillation frequency that allows the arrow to clear the bow without interference. Fortunately, unless the spine value chosen is right on the edge of what works, it would require a relatively large variation in draw length to get the oscillation frequency out of synch. For a bow in the 30-60 pound range a one inch change in the draw length produces no more than a 2-3 pound variation in draw weight, which should be within the variations allowed for a given spine. And controlling the draw length to one inch is easy enough without any draw-check, other than the archer's ability to come to the same rear anchor and aiming position on each shot.

The second effect is the variation in arrow velocity caused by varying the draw length. A given fractional change in draw length will produce roughly the same fractional change in arrow velocity and time of flight. With a draw-check device like a clicker, the draw length can be controlled easily to within better than 1/16 inch, which is a fractional change of only 0.3 percent in a 20 inch draw length. We will assume for the moment that the only dispersion is the *difference* in how much the arrow drops due to variations in arrow speed. It is that difference that we want to keep as small as nine inches at ninety meters. Let's see how large the dispersion will be for a 0.3 percent variation in arrow speed and flight time. An arrow traveling 175 feet per second takes a little less than 2 seconds to go ninety meters. To be conservative and allow for wind resistance and slightly slower speeds, let's assume a full 2 seconds. A 0.3 percent variation in 2 seconds is 0.006 seconds and that amount of variation in flight time gives about a 4.5 inch variation in how far the arrow drops during its flight, which is well within our goal of nine inches. In fact we can allow the draw length to change by as much as 1/8 inch before the dispersion becomes as large as nine inches.

Consistently controlling draw length this closely without the use of a draw-check device is probably at the limit of what it may be reasonable to expect even from good archers. That may well be one of the main reasons that the highest 90 meter FITA scores have all been shot using a clicker, though I personally think it has as much to do with being able to consistently aim with the aid of a clicker.

A couple of things to notice. The greater the speed the quicker the arrow gets to the target and the less it drops during its trajectory, leading to a smaller dispersion for the same percentage variation in arrow speed, something that we have pointed out before. Unfortunately we can't increase arrow speed by much, but we can prevent it from being any lower. The same 0.01 second or so variation in flight time will produce only a 2-4 inch dispersion for variations as large as 10-20 miles per hour in the speed of a cross wind. In a wind steadier than that, wind dispersion will be a secondary effect. The target archer's greatest enemy is not the wind but gravity. You can play the wind or wait for a lull in the breeze, but gravity never goes away.

Now comes the trickier and more difficult part of shooting. *Something has to trigger the shot.* Something has to signal the brain that it is time to release the string. This is the step in the sequence that is not on the list of Ascham or Ford or anyone else until much more recent times. Ford got further than Ascham by adding aiming to the list. *But aiming and triggering the shot are, or should be, separate acts.* And when we don't keep them separate we create a situation that leads to erratic shooting. Triggering the shot is the most fundamental and important step of all, on which the success of all the other steps depends. You can do everything else flawlessly up to the point of triggering the release and still make a perfectly terrible shot if it is not initiated in the right way.

We aim the bow visually. If we also use visual cues to trigger the release, then we set up a dangerous conflict in which the brain tries to act at counter purposes. It tries to achieve the perfect aim visually while also trying to trigger the shot whenever the visual picture is close enough. Now since the aim can never be perfect the brain is faced with conflicting objectives. And the release is always triggered as a result of an internal compromise. The harder we try to improve the aim the more we have to suppress the desire to release. But by suppressing the release, the longer we have to hold and the harder we make it to achieve the perfect aim. We want to release at the exact instant the visual picture is perfect, which lasts for shorter and shorter intervals the harder we try to achieve it and the more precise we try to make it. So we begin to compromise and try to release just as the visual picture *approaches* perfection.

This is called *shooting on the move* and the habit of doing it is the universal precursor to the affliction referred to as target panic. Even shooting on the move we still try to approach as close to perfection as possible. What happens is that *eventually the motion of the sight picture towards perfection becomes the trigger for the shot*. If the sight bead or the aiming picture hangs up at any point and we try to force it toward perfection, that in itself ends up triggering the release by one part of the brain, even though another part is not ready. We begin releasing earlier and earlier until finally any motion toward the correct visual picture will spontaneously trigger the shot.

When this first happens to you chances are you will not be able to believe it. No matter how much you tell yourself that you are not going to release until you have achieved the correct visual picture, you will still release on the very attempt itself. So great is the internal disparity between what you tell yourself you are going to do and what the brain actually does that I have seen shooters look around them in utter disbelief to see if anyone noticed what they had done, even though no one could possibly know without being inside their minds. It seems that your mind is no longer under your control and in one sense that is correct. The mind is under the control of a habituated behavior.

The way out of this problem, or better still to prevent it in the first place, is to separate aiming from triggering the shot. We have to aim the bow visually. *So we need some other way of initiating the release.* The trigger has to come in conjunction with aiming, that is, *during aiming*, but not as part of it. A clicker does just that. The arrow is placed under a thin strip of metal mounted to the side of the bow. Then the bow is drawn and aimed. The shot is triggered separately by the sound, or feel, of the metal strip slapping against the bow when the tip of the arrow is slowly pulled through the clicker. During the entire process we continue to hold the bow aimed as well as we can. The shot comes as a surprise and not as a conscious effort to shoot when the sight picture is perfect, although most of the best clicker shooters can consciously make the clicker go off when they want it to. The highest scores ever shot have been achieved using a clicker. It is hard to argue against the success of this way of shooting.

No matter what else you may think about the clicker and its place in traditional archery, it is irrefutable that it makes aiming possible without triggering the shot and that its use can cure even the most intransigent cases of target panic. The success of the clicker is our key to how we should go about triggering the release. We have to have some way other than visual.

The correct way is by slightly increasing tension in the back muscles once the visual aim has settled down into its smallest excursions about the desired image. The key is not to attempt holding the perfect visual image but only one that never wanders too far off. We are not interested in eliminating all deviations, only in achieving the smallest deviations that are sustainable. Then while maintaining that visual picture we trigger the shot by increasing back tension and drawing the shoulder blades together with the back muscles, even pulling the arrow farther back in the process as if pulling it through a clicker. So long as the aiming picture is describing small excursions about perfection it doesn't matter what the exact picture is at the instant the release occurs. The size of the arrow groups will reflect the small size of the aiming variations.

*Mentally we have to think beyond aiming.* There has to be a further step that takes the process beyond achieving the correct aim. That way anything that occurs while setting up the correct aim will not become a trigger for the release. If you would prefer, we can think of aiming itself as a two-step process. The first step is setting up the correct visual picture. The second step is to trigger the release by increasing back tension. Notice that if you don't already have tension in the back it is not possible to increase it. The back muscles must already be involved in pulling the bow prior to aiming. It will be too late to establish the proper back tension after aiming. At that point the attempt will only disturb the aim and we will have to start all over again. Equally crucial is not to lose back tension while aiming. If you have achieved the correct rear anchor that establishes the proper back tension, then you will be able to maintain it less consciously and with much less effort. Once you have the back muscles "fully cocked" it becomes easier to hold them that way. And it also becomes much easier, practically effortless, to increase back tension slightly to trigger the shot.

The release itself is easy. You don't have to really "do" anything. You just simply quit holding the string. A lot of nonsense has been written about the release. Someone complains that their release is off or that it is not as smooth as it should be, or that they are plucking the string or flinching when releasing, or that the fingers hang up and won't come off the string, or some other similar complaint. The implication is always that the release is some active process involving something that you have to consciously do with your fingers to get them smoothly off the string without disturbing the motion of the arrow. Nothing could be further from the case. *All that is required is to quit holding the string.* When the release occurs correctly it happens so fast and so effortlessly that it will seem as if nothing at all happened with your fingers and that the string just simply went right through them. You will not be conscious of having done anything. And you won't feel a thing. One key to whether you are releasing correctly is whether your fingers get sore and blistered. If they do it is more than likely because they are not relaxed during the release.

The usual complaints about the release are not about the release at all. They are about having the muscles of the hand and arm tense at the instant of release so that you can't simply let go of the string and quit holding it. There are generally two causes. The first is failing to set the string back far enough on the fingers, preferably behind the first joint, to give the feeling of a secure hold on the string. As a result the muscles in the back of the hand and the forearm are tensed in an effort to grab at the string and secure a better grip, or one that at least feels more secure. The solution is simple. Take a deeper hook on the string, placing it behind the first joint, even midway between the first and second joints. And bend the fingers more at the beginning and keep them bent. Don't let them straighten during the draw. Think of your bent fingers as an inert hook pulling the string. The more secure feeling that results will allow you to be able to relax the hand and arm, and the fingers will come off the string easily. How far back you place the string on the fingers should have absolutely no effect on how effortlessly they come off the string.

The other cause which is much more fundamental and serious is the failure to use the back muscles properly in drawing and holding the bow. Most complaints about the release result from using the arms to pull the bow instead of the back. The rear anchor position is never fully attained so the drawing arm never fully relaxes and transfers all of the force to the back. The arm and wrist muscles stay tense making it virtually impossible to instantly relax the hand and let go of the string. When the back is being used correctly the arms can relax to the point that only the muscles keeping the fingers bent are under any tension. The release is then only a matter of relaxing the fingers. The release is instantaneous even with the string as far back as the second joint. If you are experiencing what seems to be a rough release, change your grip to a deeper hook on the string and get your back into it more so that you can relax your arms. One of these two things will fix the problem.

With the proper back tension, the follow-through becomes automatic. A slight increase in back tension triggers the release, and once the string is released the drawing elbow and shoulder should move rearward. Nothing else much should happen. The bow arm should stay pointed roughly where it was although it will seem to jump slightly forward and to the side. The eyes should remain focused on the target and should pick up the flight of the arrow only peripherally. The drawing hand should be perfectly relaxed and should come to rest beside the neck or rear of the jaw. The extent of the motion backward is unimportant. It is only important that whatever motion there is be rearward and not forward. It is not necessary that the hand fly abruptly backwards and end up resting on top of the shoulder. Often that is merely an indication of pulling with the arm instead of the back. I have seen very good archers for which the rearward motion upon release was practically imperceptible, yet it was still there. The whole posture should be one of relaxation without the loss of any control. The only remnant of tension should be in the back muscles but they too should be relaxing.

The description we have given thus far is for the most part that used in target archery. How do we modify any of this for the archer who does not stand straight and erect but leans forward slightly at the waist, angles his head and cants the bow rather than holding it vertical? That describes the stance of many, if not most, bowhunters and field archers who use point-and-shoot aiming instead of a sight. The principle change involves posture. Leaning forward at the waist makes it more difficult to get your back into action pulling the bow and makes it harder to feel and maintain back tension. There is a tendency to pull more with the arm and the muscles at the top of the shoulder. Consequently the force pulling the bow never gets completely transferred to the back muscles and the arms do not relax but stay tense. This tendency is exacerbated by drawing all the way to the rear anchor in one step while extending the bow arm in one smooth continuous motion, which is likewise the method employed by most point-and-shoot archers. *When drawing this way it is essential that you never completely stop the draw*. If you do you will instantly lose back tension. The tendency to lose back tension is also exaggerated by a heavy draw weight. If you are overbowed the draw weight may simply overwhelm the back muscles and they are never able to settle into position.

A slightly more open stance makes it easier to get the back muscles into action and makes it easier to feel and maintain back tension. Even if you adopt the stance of leaning at the waist and even if you speed up the tempo of shooting it is still essential that you settle into the rear anchor position and transfer the force from the arms to the back in order to relax the arms and have a consistent release.

Canting the bow does not in itself cause any particular problem. Leaning at the waist and canting the bow makes it natural to angle the head slightly. It is essential that the rear aiming position put the eye right above the arrow so that the eye is looking along the arrow and not at an angle to it. The positions of the head and rear aiming point have to be adjusted to keep the arrow directly beneath the eye. Otherwise the arrow will go to the left or the right of where the eye is looking. And all of this has to be done the same on each shot. Being conscious of looking along the arrow is the visual check of whether your stance is consistent on each shot. After a while it becomes automatic and you will be able to feel instantly whether you have set up the stance correctly.

Even with a leaning stance and canted bow it is still preferable I believe— although I go back and forth on this point in my own shooting—to draw the bow by first extending the bow arm and positioning the arm and shoulder and then draw to the rear anchor, instead of doing it all in one motion. Drawing in this two-step fashion has the effect of separating the act of pointing the bow and controlling the bow arm from the act of drawing the bow. That separates aiming from drawing the bow. The draw can continue smoothly, separate from aiming. There needs to be no pause in drawing the bow to the rear anchor in order to check the bow arm; the draw can continue smoothly, uninterrupted, even while the aim is corrected and the release is triggered. There is no pause to interrupt the back tension or cause the archer to relax and let down. In my view this produces a more consistent form.

Should you shoot with a glove or a tab? The conventional wisdom is that a tab gives a more sensitive feel and a smoother release. There is also the criticism that a glove or finger stalls like those made of hard cardigan leather develop a crease and that the string will hang up in the crease or be deflected sideways in coming out of it during the release. I am not sure I believe any of those things, or much else that has been said about the virtue of tabs over gloves, or vice versa. I don't want to feel the string. If I did I would shoot without any finger protection. The only feeling I want from the string is a dull pressure evenly distributed against my bent fingers. The more I feel the string the more it hurts, and nothing makes it more difficult to complete the execution of the shot smoothly and consistently than the anticipation of sharp pain when the string is released. Those shooters using a mechanical release or even a hand-held non mechanical release don't feel the string and they shoot just fine. The concern about the crease in the glove doesn't make any sense at all. What about the groove or ledge that holds the string drawn with the non mechanical release? If the string will release effortlessly from the fingers even when it is placed as far back as the second joint, which it certainly will—witness the number of top archers who shoot that way—then a slight groove or crease in the surface of the finger stalls is not going to make any difference whatsoever, except perhaps in the mind of the shooter.

The key to a clean, crisp release is to have the draw weight supported by the back muscles, and the wrist and forearm relaxed, so that all that is required to release the string is to simply relax the fingers. The string will be away so suddenly and cleanly that it will seem to have gone right through your fingers. If you try to release with your arms and wrist tense then you will find it difficult to get a clean release no matter what kind of finger protection you use. I suppose in that case there might be some slight advantage to a tab, but it would certainly be the wrong remedy to the problem. In short, either a tab or a glove will work fine. I prefer the greater convenience and protection of cardigan leather finger stalls when I am shooting a hunting bow, but I have used both even then. The glove gives more protection, is faster to use and leaves the hand freer to do other things.

What about mechanical releases? It is difficult to justify them as part of traditional archery. They have no real place in the history and development of the sport. But more important they seem to be outside the spirit of keeping traditional archery focused on the athletic ability of the archer and not on always using more and more gadgetry to solve the archer's shooting problems. There can be no doubt whatsoever that releasing the string from a single point rather than from three fingers takes some of the variables out of the process. And there is no doubt that a mechanical release cleanly separates aiming from triggering the release and can be an effective remedy for target panic. The problem with including them is that it opens the door to any other mechanical technology that comes along as the remedy to the physical limitations of the archer. And their inclusion almost automatically creates another separate category of shooters which further splinters the sport. It is a path down which there will eventually be no traditional archery.

The same criticisms cannot be said of hand-held non mechanical releases. They can be traced back to devices like the thumb rings used by Turkish archers in shooting their laminated recurve bows. They are very much a part of archery traditions. They too are an effective way to separate the act of aiming from the act of triggering the shot. They are far less convenient and more difficult to use than a mechanical release but so much the better. There was a period in the 1970's when non mechanical releases were in common use for shooting traditional recurve bows in target and field archery. They are tricky to use and have absolutely no place in hunting. It is also not clear that in the hands of the best shooters they give any inherent advantage over a finger shooter. Perfect scores indoors have been shot both ways.

It is worth emphasizing again that all of the shooting techniques discussed above have to be acquired and assimilated by feel. And they are executed by feel also. You have to experience and learn for yourself how it feels in your muscles and your mind to be doing each step correctly. And the only sure evidence of doing it correctly means having the arrows group consistently. It really doesn't matter so much where they group so long as they are grouping somewhere. The group can always be moved around and made to end up in the intended spot later. But first you have to gain enough proficiency that you can begin to acquire a feel for doing each step correctly, without in the process developing a lot of bad habits that inhibit your progress and become difficult to overcome later. It can be tricky. It is one of the reasons why shooting a bow can be so simple in principle and yet so difficult to do well.

Descriptions can help, but there is no short cut around developing your own feel for each part of the process. The proper feel will be very much your own and not necessarily the same as anyone else's. The best you can do is read a description of how to execute each step and then try to imagine for yourself, based on all your past experience performing physical tasks, what it is going to feel like to perform that step. But in the final analysis you really only begin to learn it by doing it over and over until it becomes embedded in your muscle memory.

Most of what you learn will quickly begin to feel like second nature and will soon become automatic to the point where you do not have to consciously think about it anymore, except to stop and check periodically to make certain that you are still doing it the same each time. That leaves you free to concentrate on the less automatic parts of the shot. *And not every step in the execution of a good archery shot is equally important for every shooter.* Every archer should learn which steps have the greatest impact on their own success and focus attention on those. It helps to simplify the execution of the shot to the most important steps and to picture the execution of the shot beforehand in terms of those crucial steps. Then all of the other parts that have become fixed in the muscle memory and are more or less automatic do not have to clutter one's mental picture of executing the shot.

For me it starts with being conscious of controlling the bow arm; having the arm straight and fully extended, and being aware of having the bow arm under the active control of the muscles that cage the shoulder. When I don't consciously feel that control in the shoulder muscles funny things happen to my bow arm when I release, and my arrow groups open up. I check the position of the bow arm and hand, as well as the conscious feeling of control, during the slight pause in drawing the string. After that they stay the same and I do not think of them again until I am aiming and then I become conscious again of the shoulder muscles controlling the movements of the bow arm. That conscious feeling of control prevents the sight picture from freezing up at any point. The second check point is the placement of my fingers on the string and being aware of having them bent far enough to give a sure grip, and keeping them bent and not letting them straighten out during the draw. Part of the feel here is that of having the correct muscles in the hand tense but keeping the rest of the hand and wrist relaxed. When I don't have that feel then I experience trouble relaxing my fingers to trigger the release. The last check is coming fully to the rear anchor position and transferring the force from my arms to the back muscles before I begin aiming. This is done entirely by feel. There is the feeling of relaxation in the arms and of confidence and security in holding the bow drawn. When I have the correct feel here I know the shot is going to be good even when other elements of my form are not perfect.

Finally there is aiming, aiming, aiming. Aiming is the key to good shooting, the *sine qua non*. You can make a lot of mistakes in the other parts of your form but if you have the bow aimed correctly when the release is triggered then the arrow is going to end up somewhere in the vicinity of the right spot, even if the bow arm is not fully under control and the release is ragged and you don't follow through all the way. Sometimes it is hard to miss if you can just keep the bow aimed. And virtually impossible not to when you don't.

After taking my stance and nocking the arrow and seating my hand on the grip, and before drawing the bow, I mentally picture the execution of the shot in terms of these few steps. The other elements of form I pretty much execute unconsciously from muscle memory except when practicing each individually to check that I am still doing them the same way each time. After the shot, as part of the follow through, I quickly go over in my mind my impressions of how well I executed each of these steps, plus I visually check where my bow arm and drawing hand ended up for anything that tells me about the execution of the shot. I go through this sequence on each shot. I have reduced the process of picturing the shot beforehand down to its simplest form in these few essential steps. Every archer who isn't just shooting mindlessly has to go through something like this process and will generate his own mental roadmap of how he conceives and executes the shot. For each person it will be different, but it is essential to have some simpler way of mentally picturing the shot.

Finally, there are right ways and wrong ways to practice. You have to always be on your guard not to acquire bad habits. Never practice to the point of fatigue, boredom, or indifference. When you aren't learning anything stop and go do something else. Constantly experiment. Don't just keep doing something the same old way. Occasionally try something new and see what happens. Keep learning. And pay attention. Build up a mental catalog of which elements in your form make arrows fly left, right, high, and low. That way you can more quickly identify mistakes and make corrections if you begin to experience problems. The really good shooters can get in trouble and, even under pressure, get out of trouble in just a few arrows. It isn't how long you practice but how well. In each session pick out one or two things to concentrate on and give them extra attention. You will generally be the most receptive and learn the most when you are most enjoying yourself. If practicing becomes a chore take a break. Go shoot a round for the sheer joy of it. After all, that is why we choose traditional archery. Because it is fun.

# Target Panic!

*Understanding what it is and what can cause it is fundamental to knowing what to do about it and how to go about curing it.*

*Y*ou pull the bow back with a death grip on the string, determined not to shoot until you are ready. The previous attempts have all ended in failure, and this time you are determined not to release the string until you have completed aiming. With the bow fully drawn you squeeze the string tightly and force the sight bead into the center of the target, only to find that it refuses to settle down and stay there but wanders off and gets hung up outside of the bull's-eye. When you attempt to force it back into the center, you unintentionally release the string before you are ready and in the process throw the arrow to the left or some other direction. The release is not clean and crisp but hesitating and grasping. Embarrassed, you look around to see if anyone noticed. "Why did I shoot?" you wonder to yourself, "I wasn't ready yet." And then you repeat the same frustrating experience, again and again, always with the same result.

The condition goes by many names and takes many forms, but they are all the same basic phenomenon. It is called target panic, freezing, snap shooting, and premature release (and like the other kind of premature release it leads to the same feelings of shame and inadequacy). It will eventually afflict every archer at some time that shoots long enough and often enough. It is an equal opportunity malady, affecting sight shooters and point-and-shoot aimers alike, those shooting the very highest scores as well as those shooting the lowest, plus everyone in between. Once encountered it is never completely mastered and is always in danger of coming back.

Some of the best shooters in the world have been reduced to quitting the sport in frustration and bitterness over being unable to cope with it. It is likely what led the great English archer Horace Ford to give up archery altogether and refer to it afterwards as an "odious sport." It drove national and world target archery champion Ray Rogers from the ranks of world-class archers virtually overnight. The author watched NFAA freestyle champion Ed Rhode struggle with it day after day while winning the national championship. If you have ever noticed a shooter jerk and flinch slightly while aiming, or worse, almost release the string but grab at it and stop short, you have witnessed an archer who could be only a few arrows away from developing a full-blown case. The more competitive-minded the shooter the more likely he is to fall prey. Jack Whitt, formerly business manager of Ben Pearson Archery, who for several years wrote a shooting column for one of the national archery magazines and was himself a competitive archer and golfer, likened it to the putting problem in golf referred to as the "yips." It is the reason more archers miss what they are shooting at than any other cause. Because of it many archers never really aim before they shoot. Most who shoot fast do so because they can no longer do otherwise. An archer afflicted with this condition will often deny the problem more adamantly than an alcoholic denies being addicted. And everyone who says they haven't encountered it is either lying or just hasn't shot enough. It is the archer's central problem.

What causes this bizarre behavior? What could be so difficult about getting the bow aimed properly before releasing the string? *The condition develops quite naturally, little by little, as a result of using visual cues to trigger the release.*

The archer is under the strain of holding the bow drawn. There is a natural tendency to want to release the string and relieve the muscle tension. Any difficulty in getting the bow aimed as precisely as the archer wants, prolongs the strain and heightens the mounting mental desire to go ahead and get it over with and release the string. Coupled with this, the ideal sight picture the archer is striving for can never be completely achieved, and even when it is, it cannot be maintained for more than a fleeting instant at a time. One part of the brain wants to release the string before the sight picture drifts off and another part wants to make the sight picture even more perfect and precise. Little by little the archer begins to release the string slightly before the desired sight picture is achieved, or slightly after and before it can be achieved again. Instead of the shot being triggered by the perfect sight picture, it is triggered slightly in advance, *in anticipation* of the correct sight picture. This behavior becomes reinforced over an increasing number of shots, until eventually releasing too soon becomes a habit, a conditioned reflex. The condition producing the release reflex is not the desired one, but the anticipation of it. This can all happen so gradually and so insidiously that the archer realizes it only after it has become a well-entrenched part of his conditioned behavior. Like Pavlov's dogs salivating at the sound of a bell in anticipation of food, the archer becomes conditioned to release the string in anticipation of achieving the correct aim.

For many archers this is the furthest extent to which the condition develops. These archers can bring the bow to full draw and hold it drawn without releasing so long as they aren't attempting to complete the act of aiming, but the instant they try to do so the release is triggered. For this kind of shooter the sight picture can be close to correct, maddeningly close. What usually happens is that it gets hung up at some point as one tries to close in on the correct image. For a sight shooter that means the sight pin will come to rest somewhere right outside the bulls-eye, usually at the same place each time. But if you attempt to readjust the sight to make that place the correct position for the sight pin, then it will begin to hang up somewhere else. You will no longer be able to make the sight pin stop and stay at the new aiming point even though it is no longer the center of the bulls-eye. For a point of aim shooter the end of the arrow will come to rest near, but not on, the desired spot. For someone using gap aiming the bow hand will move toward the correct location in one's peripheral vision but will stop short of going all the way there or will go there but not stay there. In each case the sight picture becomes frozen at the wrong place, hence the term "freezing" as a description of the problem. Any attempt after that to force the correct sight picture triggers the release.

This type of shooter can draw the bow, aim it and hold it aimed indefinitely without any problem, *so long as he knows in advance he has no intention of actually shooting*. But that is only because in his mind the act of aiming has now been completely severed from the act of releasing. There is no longer any intention of releasing the string, so the sight picture is separate from the desire to release. But let him even *begin* to think about releasing and he will do so instantly, ready or not. The author once shot right through a closed bedroom window while practicing aiming in front of a mirror, just by momentarily allowing himself to think about releasing. And therein lies an important clue about how to overcome this condition of releasing prematurely, to which we will return later.

Archers who develop this form of premature release develop various ways of trying to compensate for it in their shooting technique. The primary one is to shoot "on the move." The correct sight picture can be achieved momentarily, so long as you don't try to hold on to it for any length of time. The sight bead can be swept through the bulls-eye; it just can't be made to stop there and settle down. If the intention is to stop it there, the release is triggered by the attempt to move towards the bulls-eye. So the archer begins to shoot while sweeping through the correct sight picture, whether it is with a sight pin or point of aim or gap shooting or some other method. The bow never comes to rest fully in the process of aiming but moves past the desired sight picture one or more times before the release is made. One of the more consistent methods is to aim high initially and shoot as the bow is slowly lowered through the correct sight picture. It is usually easier to lower the bow through the correct sight picture than to try to raise it.

Shooting on the move is a form of *rhythm shooting*, and when the shooter is on, it can be unbeatable. It is a delicate matter of trying to coordinate getting the bow to the correct sight picture by the time the release is made. Sometimes one's timing is on and this works well. When it is off you tend to throw arrows all over the place. The problem with shooting on the move like this is that it becomes progressively more and more difficult to sweep through the correct sight picture *slowly*. The sight tends to hang up farther away from the center and has to be swept through the bulls-eye faster to do so at all without releasing. Then the timing becomes more difficult and the arrows more scattered. This type of shooting seldom produces good groups consistently, or for very long. However I once watched a very good target archer shoot a perfect American Round outdoors this way at a local tournament. The next month at the NFAA nationals he couldn't hit a thing.

Another form of compensation is to decide to shoot at the very first instant the correct sight picture is achieved after coming to full draw. This can work well for a while. But it tends to gradually speed up the completion of the shot. After a while it becomes increasingly difficult to keep from shooting immediately on coming to full draw and before achieving a stationary rear anchor and rear aiming point. You may achieve the correct sight picture and release on it this way. But the drawing hand is still moving, the bow arm and shoulder are not set and stationary, and the archer's form literally flies apart on the release, opening up the groups and scattering arrows.

Archers who compensate for premature release by shooting on the move learn to try all of these and other variations and to switch between them to find whichever one is working best at the moment. Any new approach to aiming can work well initially, for a few arrows, before it too leads to the conditioned reflex of releasing early.

As this conditioned reflex develops further, the archer comes to shoot a little bit earlier each time, progressively in advance of having the bow aimed. Finally any attempt at all to aim the bow at the end of the draw triggers the shot. In the most extreme cases the archer finds it impossible even to come to a complete stop at full draw, or even to reach full draw, before releasing the arrow, a behavior that leads to the term "snap shooting." These shooters attempt to have the bow aimed at the instant full draw is achieved and to release the string the moment the rear anchor is reached, before the sight picture has time to wander off and freeze at the wrong position. Usually it is the only way they can shoot even reasonably well. The problem is that there is not time to get the bow arm and shoulder and back tension all properly set before the arrow is released. The archer's form is still changing at the moment of release, and along with the challenge of trying to coordinate the release with aiming, now there is the added challenge of coordinating the motion of the bow hand, bow arm and shoulder, drawing arm and hand, and back muscles. Most archers who shoot fast like this do so because they can no longer keep themselves from doing it. They literally cannot draw the bow and hold it drawn without releasing, *unless they know beforehand that they have no intention of shooting at all*, and even then I would not want to stand in front of one of them. Shooting fast, even snap shooting, is perfectly all right and necessary at times in hunting, *so long as you shoot that way because you want to and not because you cannot prevent it*. Done too long though it can become a conditioned reflex that is increasingly hard to break. That is one of the reasons that not all of one's practicing should be done at a fast tempo. You should also practice slowing down the tempo to guard against the inability to do so when you want to.

What are the some of the contributing factors that lead to premature release? The main one is being *overbowed*, shooting a bow too heavy in draw weight. The harder it is to pull the bow to full draw the greater the compulsion to release the string before the aim has really settled down. If the draw weight is heavy enough, the archer may shake so badly that it is impossible to hold the bow steady and shooting on the move becomes unavoidable. And the draw weight may be too great for the back muscles to support it while relaxing the arms. The arms never get to relax and the release is not smooth and effortless. It only takes a little while shooting such a bow to develop a really bad case of premature release. Even if you are going to use a heavy bow for hunting it is better to do more of your routine practicing with a lighter draw weight that is well below the maximum you can handle and only tune-up with the stronger bow in shorter sessions. A bow whose mass is too heavy to hold still while aiming can produce the same effect. This is a danger when going overboard with the weight of external stabilizers added to the bow.

Trying to achieve ever greater precision of aim is also a contributor. The archer who is never satisfied but holds the bow drawn too long trying to refine the aim finds it more difficult the longer he holds and the more tired he becomes, until finally in desperation he releases on the incorrect sight picture. Stung by that he tries even harder the next time and the next, always with the same result. The habit of premature release tends to be more prevalent for this reason with sight shooters than with those who use point-and-shoot aiming. A bow sight with a very fine sight pin allows greater precision in aiming than the end of the arrow used in point of aim shooting or the peripheral vision sight picture used in other methods of indirect aiming. Switching to a coarser pin, or focusing on the pin rather than the target so that the target is slightly blurred can sometimes help. A fine pin is also harder to see and can slow down the process of aiming. Purposely keeping the bow moving slightly around the correct sight picture so that the sight picture never becomes static or freezes on the incorrect image is another way to keep the aim less precise. I have seen good shooters who never stop moving the bow while aiming. Shooting at longer distances where the smaller image of the bulls-eye makes it more difficult to aim will exacerbate the habit of releasing prematurely. So will any other kind of shooting problem which leads the archer to miss consistently and have less confidence in aiming. This tendency is what led originally to the name "target panic" for this problem.

So what can we do to prevent it? The remedy is simple in principle, though not always in practice. We suggested the basic idea earlier. *The root cause of premature release is using visual cues to trigger the shot. To cure it we have to separate the act of aiming from the associated act of releasing the string. Aiming of course has to be visual. So we must find some other way to trigger the release that is not visual, or at least not totally visual.* There can be any number of ways of accomplishing this.

The most foolproof solution for the target archer shooting with fingers is to use a clicker. This is the real use to which the clicker was immediately put after its invention originally as a draw-check device. Typically it consists of a thin strip of spring steel mounted against the sight window of the bow. The bow is drawn and aimed with the point of the arrow beneath the clicker. While holding the bow aimed, the arrow is slowly pulled through the clicker. The release is not made in response to the sight picture but in response to the sound (or the feel) of the clicker snapping against the side of the bow as the point of the arrow comes through it. *The fact that the clicker instantly cures the problem of premature release is proof positive that we understand the root cause.* In fact, any similar scheme for releasing in response to a different cue than the strictly visual cue of aiming will work the same way.

A number of other schemes have been proposed from time to time for triggering the release independently of aiming, without requiring a mechanical device like the clicker. One suggestion is to draw the hand to the corner of the mouth for aiming and trigger the release by making contact between one of the drawing fingers and a tooth in the upper jaw. The upper jaw instead of the lower because the position of the upper jaw with respect to the eye is fixed and can't be opened or closed like the lower jaw. Another is to draw the hand beneath the chin and trigger the release by increasing the pressure of the string against the front of the chin. If you happen to be shooting hunting arrows you could trigger the release by drawing until you feel the back of the broadhead touch the top finger of your bow hand. This of course requires a bow handle that allows the arrow point to contact the hand, and many don't. Another suggestion is to draw until the string touches the eyebrow or some other point on the face. There are all sorts of possible variations of the same idea. I have tried all of these schemes and others like them and for me none of them works especially well. They all try to replace the precision and certainty of the clicker going off with some other event that is imprecise and physically ambiguous. They all amount to pulling back until you let go, and if you can do that while aiming and drawing to the same point every time then you don't have a problem in the first place. None of these schemes works as well as triggering the release by deliberate back tension. And none of them will work without that step anyway.

The clicker itself is by no means a panacea. There are problems associated with it too. One has to learn to use it correctly which isn't easy. And that means adopting a shooting style that allows the arrow to be pulled through the clicker smoothly and consistently. The bow must be drawn so that the clicker is positioned near the tip and then slowly drawn farther while the bow is aimed, so that the arrow can be pulled through the clicker with only a slight extension of the draw. This is accomplished by tightening the back muscles that draw the shoulder blades together and move the drawing elbow rearward, while keeping the drawing arm relaxed. The secret to using a clicker is to be able to make it go off when you want it to and to be able to do it the same way each and every time. Otherwise the archer begins to anticipate the clicker and to release prematurely again, this time before the arrow is pulled through the clicker. What was once target panic now becomes a case of "clicker panic."

The other obvious drawback to the clicker is that it does not lend itself to use with hunting arrows, although clickers adapted to broadheads have been devised. They are mostly clumsy and unsuccessful and really have no place on a hunting bow.

For many shooters, using a clicker takes the enjoyment out of shooting. All aspects of form and technique become dictated by the clicker. Draw the bow too far and the clicker goes off before you are ready. Not far enough and it won't go off when you want it to. Taking your eyes off the target or the sight to look at the clicker destroys the concentration of aiming. The anticipation of the clicker going off gives some shooters the nervous shakes. Others shake because they cannot relax the arms and let the back muscles support the draw weight of the bow and still manage to pull the arrow through the clicker. The shooter has to be always conscious of the clicker. To use it consistently requires frequent practice. But if you can't shoot without releasing prematurely any other way, then the clicker restores the fun to shooting. That is why it has become so popular. Once you learn to use it there is always the nagging realization that you couldn't shoot without it. It cures the immediate problem but as long as you depend on it, it does not permanently alter the behavior that led the problem to occur in the first place. Yet if you learn to use it correctly and use it long enough you can then begin to shoot without it by simply going through the same motions that you use to aim and shoot with the clicker.

Even if we choose not to shoot with a clicker, *we can look upon it as indicating how to shoot in order to prevent the problem.* Aiming alone must not trigger the shot. *There has to be some conscious additional step that triggers the shot or in conjunction with aiming.*

The usual recommendation is to use back tension to trigger the shot. For some it is consciously pulling the drawing hand and elbow rearward with the back muscles after the sight picture is achieved. For some the shot is triggered by the *perception* of moving the elbow rearward even though to an observer no actual motion may be apparent. For others it is squeezing the shoulder blades together or tightening the middle and lower back muscles. Equally important is the act of pushing the bow forward with the bow arm while pulling rearward with the back and shoulder muscles. Nothing spoils the maintenance of back tension more than allowing the bow arm to collapse or creep backwards. The proper image is push-pull at the moment of release.

All of these methods have the unwanted effect of throwing the shot off if the motion is exaggerated or done suddenly. Perhaps a better way of thinking about it is to trigger the shot not by increasing back tension but by consciously continuing or maintaining it while aiming. It begins by drawing the bow far enough to allow the back muscles to come fully into play. As you reach the end of the draw you should be able to consciously feel the load being transferred from the arms to the back, and in particular to the muscles that you feel 'bunched up' in the middle of the back. Getting this feeling and not stopping the process of drawing the bow until you have it is the most important part of the entire process. This means keeping the elbow and the plane of the drawing arm horizontal or slightly above, in line with the arrow. The archer should have the sensation of the back muscles being "cocked" and under tension at full draw. At this stage the bow is held drawn by the back, not the arms. Then aim the bow, and while pushing the bow forward to maintain the aim become conscious of maintaining or increasing this back tension to trigger the shot.

Horace Ford described this whole process as being aware of never completely coming to a stop when drawing the bow and releasing. An observer may conclude that the arrow comes to rest at full draw. To the archer the sensation is one of continuing to push and pull the bow all the way up to, and on through, the point of release.

However you choose to accomplish it, this final step beyond aiming is the key to conquering and avoiding the problem of premature release.

# The Cardinal Sin

*Trying to shoot a bow too heavy in draw weight has been the downfall and ruin of more traditional archers than almost anything else. Here is why it makes no sense and why to avoid falling into that trap.*

Traditional archery has its own cardinal sin. And almost everyone who tries shooting a traditional bow succumbs eventually to its temptations. The archery term for it is *overbowed*, and that aptly describes it. It is the combined sin of pride and arrogance and envy and disdain, trying to shoot a bow whose draw weight is too much. It can be too much because of the detrimental effect it has on the archer's ability to shoot *that* particular bow. It can be too much because of the bad habits the archer develops that impair his ability to shoot *any* bow. Or it can be too much simply because it is more than is needed, *and more draw weight than is really necessary is always a bad idea.* It is the kind of hubris the shooting gods delight in punishing harshly. And they do it with a vengeance. The sport is practically set up to assure that every archer will eventually sin. And upon sinning there seems to be no going back, no easy road to redemption. For most who sin long enough the way back can be long, painful, and fraught with difficulties.

We are told that shooting a bow is at least partially a feat of strength. Homer's story the "Test of the Bow" in the *Odyssey* shows just how far back the image of the mighty archer and his powerful bow, beyond the strength of all but the most determined and heroic effort, can be traced in the human consciousness. If a bow half as strong will do, then surely one twice as strong will do that much better. Why settle for a weaker bow when a stronger one will shoot faster and harder? Didn't Howard Hill routinely shoot a 100 pound-pull bow? As a boy the author personally witnessed Ben Pearson shooting a 90 pound bow in exhibitions. Fred Bear reportedly shot a 65 pound bow in his mid-seventies. Can't anyone who works at it conscientiously do the same? And if you can, then why wouldn't you want to? The images go on and on. And so does the advice that one reads. If you are going to hunt elk or moose then a bow heavier than the one you have been using for deer is necessary. And there is the matter of personal pride in not wanting to admit that you really can't master the greater draw weight. Or the envy you are tempted to feel for anyone who can. Or the disdain that you have for the insipid advice to be more modest in your choice of bows. And the arrogance that all the bad habits that come from being overbowed won't happen to you.

And that is the real problem. Being overbowed almost invariably leads to bad shooting habits. Not only will you probably not shoot the heavier draw weight as well as a lighter one, but eventually you will not be able to shoot any bow well. The only exception might be someone who only shoots heavier draw weights very occasionally and then only for brief periods, in short, someone who doesn't do it often enough or long enough to get really good at it. But that isn't what usually happens Once you take on the task of shooting a draw weight greater than you can comfortably command, then the quality of your shooting falls off and you end up practicing longer and harder trying to get back to doing as well as you were before; all the while developing and reinforcing any number of bad habits that slowly become so ingrained in your form that finally you cannot keep yourself from doing them no matter how hard you try. The farther you go once you start down that path the more difficult it becomes to stop and get back to where you were before. More than one archer has simply given up in frustration and abandoned archery altogether.

The bad habits can take many forms. To be able to pull and hold the bow you have to use your arms and biceps and can't fully transfer the draw weight to your back muscles. Instead of completely relaxing your arms you keep them tensed at full draw. That leads to muscle tremors and the shakes, which aggravates the problem of getting the arrow aimed the way you want it before triggering the release. To hold the bow drawn more comfortably you let the shoulder of your bow arm cave in toward the arrow. The string begins to hit your arm on every shot. That and the pressure on your bow arm cause you to start bending your elbow slightly instead of keeping it perfectly straight or locked in place. As a result of struggling to hold the bow drawn you end up releasing before you are completely ready, usually while the bow is still moving toward the correct aiming picture. Releasing earlier and earlier in the aiming process gradually becomes a habit and soon you can't prevent it even when you try. Finally you can't even get the bow completely drawn before you release the string.

Suddenly you have developed a full-blown case of target panic or premature release or whatever name you choose to call it, and for you any semblance of good shooting is quickly becoming a thing of the past. In addition you have developed a sharp pain in your shoulder from the unnatural and awkward position it has to assume to draw the bow and hold it drawn, and the pain does not go away between practice sessions. Ironically, what usually goes through your mind is not that perhaps you should go to a lighter bow, but that if only you keep working at it and trying harder you can finally master the draw weight and get around all of these problems. By then it is usually too late. The only way back is to start completely over with a much lighter bow and relearn everything again from scratch. The longer you persist before taking that step the longer and more difficult becomes the path back to good shooting again.

So how can you tell if you are overbowed? One obvious indication is whether or not you are encountering any of the serious shooting problems mentioned above. But of course you don't want to have to wait that long to discover it. By then the damage is done. Instead there is a simple test. *The test is whether you can hold the bow drawn with just the back muscles that pull the shoulder blades together.* If you can comfortably draw the bow while transferring the draw weight completely to the back so that the arms at full draw are relaxed and the bow is being held back entirely, *and comfortably*, by the back muscles, with no sense of urgency to release the string, then you are not overbowed. If not, you probably are.

This test is very much a matter of feel. If you have never held a bow drawn with only the muscles of the back then you won't know what I'm talking about. It also probably means that you have never learned to use your back correctly. If you have, then you know that the shoulder blades squeezed together is like having a hook on which to hang the string at full draw, allowing you to completely relax your arms and shoulders except for those muscles which you can feel "bunched up" in the middle of the back. The only thing holding the bow drawn is the hook formed by the fingers of the drawing hand and the muscles drawing the shoulders together. Many archers never get to this point in executing a shot, especially those who pull heavy draw weights and those who shoot fast with little or no pause at full draw. Members of the latter group are in constant jeopardy of developing a case of premature release.

To check whether you are getting to this point bring the bow to full draw and settle into your normal rear anchor position. If you can now comfortably move the drawing hand back and forth by simply using the back muscles to move the drawing elbow backwards and forwards then you are in the correct rear anchor position. This is the position you want to achieve in order to test whether you are overbowed. If you can do this comfortably you are not overbowed.

Certainly a minimum amount of physical strength and conditioning is needed to shoot a bow at all. This is especially true of a bow strong enough to be used for hunting. In some instances a person may just not be physically able to handle any bow strong enough for the task, whether it is the demands of hunting or shooting the longer distances in target and field archery. But most often archers are overbowed unnecessarily by shooting a bow with more draw weight than is really needed.

To look at this problem, let us suppose that you have been shooting a 65 pound hunting bow. I have chosen that value because I believe it is at the upper limit of what most bowhunters attempt and I want to compare it to bows of 55 and 45 pound draw weights. I could just as easily have chosen 60, 50, and 40 pounds to compare. The final conclusions would not change. Assume that the bow is drawn a distance of 20 inches, corresponding to a 28 or 29 inch arrow and a brace height of 8 or 9 inches, stores about 54 foot-pounds of energy, and has an effective mass of 250 grains, all representative values. Assume also that we are going to shoot 400-450 grain hunting arrows, for the simple reason that I don't recommend going below that for adequate penetration. The bow we have chosen will shoot arrows of that weight 186-193 feet per second.

Now let's switch to a 55 pound bow of the same design. For the same draw length the stored energy will be about 46 foot-pounds. The 15 percent decrease in draw weight may translate into a reduction of about a third of that, or 5 percent, in the effective mass, to about 237 grains. This bow will shoot 400-450 grain arrows at 173-180 feet per second, still more than adequate and if the truth were known more than many bowhunters get out of the traditional bows they are currently shooting. A more efficient design having an effective mass of only 200 grains would shoot the same arrows 178-185 feet per second, almost the same speed as the 65 pound bow. But I would personally choose to put the decrease in effective mass into an equal increase in arrow weight and leave the arrow speed the same. That would be in the direction of better arrow penetration.

Finally a 45 pound bow of the same design and draw length storing at least 38 foot-pounds of energy and having an effective mass of 223 grains would shoot 400-450 grain arrows 159-165 feet per second. A more efficient design with an effective mass of 200 grains would shoot the same arrows 162-168 feet per second. Limbs this efficient are available among the bows being built by some bowyers.

The message is clear. It is really not necessary to shoot a draw weight over about 50 pounds no matter what kind of hunting you are going to do. Even 45 pounds is adequate for many purposes, and for the most efficient recurved or reflexed limbs a 40 pound draw weight is almost as good. Combine these values with the better accuracy most archers can achieve by reducing the draw weight and it makes no sense to be overbowed, even for hunting. You may have to try a lot of bows to find those that have the lightest and most efficient limbs and that have the shape force curve that stores the greatest amount of energy, but the payoff is well worth it. And that is the direction in which you should be looking to improve your shooting. The point is to be able to hit what you are shooting at.

Instead of looking at this as a problem of draw weight, it is probably better to look at it as a problem of efficiency. Instead of being satisfied with a bow that has an effective mass as large as 400 or even 300 grains, insist on a design that has an effective mass of no more than 200 grains, or even less.

These values are attainable by proper design. Then you won't have to shoot a 65 pound hunting bow. A draw weight somewhere between 45 and 55 pounds will be more than enough to give adequate arrow speed for hunting distances, even shooting 500 grain arrows, which will provide more than adequate penetration. The truth is that a 40 pound hunting bow will shoot hunting-weight arrows, 400 grains and above, fast enough for any animal as large as a deer if you can shoot well enough. The lighter draw weight will allow you to shoot better and be able to place the arrow where you want it. Arrow placement is far more important than draw weight in determining a successful outcome when hunting with a bow and arrow.

Instead of continuing to buy bows too heavy to shoot well, archers should instead exert pressure on bowyers to design and build more efficient limbs. After all, the buyer and shooter of bows is more in command of the technical directions of the sport, or should be, than the bowyers who sell bows only by supplying what archers are willing to purchase. That kind of pressure is one of the things that has been too long missing in traditional archery. Howard Hill, rest in peace.

Much the same thing is true of target bows, and here it may be even more instructive. If you have been shooting a 45 pound draw weight that stores as much as 38 foot-pounds and has an effective limb mass as low as 150 grains, then it will shoot 400 grain arrows at a speed of 176 feet per second and 300 grain arrows 195 feet per second. The same bow with a draw weight of 35 pounds storing as much as 30 foot-pounds of energy and with a slightly lower effective mass corresponding to the lower draw weight will shoot the same weight arrows at speeds of 158 and 175 feet per second. These arrow speeds differ by about 10 percent between the two bows. Based solely on arrow speed the heavier bow does not offer any commanding advantage. It is possible to shave a few more grains off the arrow weight to improve both of these numbers. The advantages of a lighter draw weight are potentially even greater in target archery since the only objective is higher scores. The easier it is to pull the bow and hold it drawn the more likely the archer will be able to aim and trigger the release correctly and so avoid the kind of serious shooting problems associated with increasing draw weight.

The smart archer will resist the temptations of traditional archery's cardinal sin and think more modestly, and more intelligently, about the problem of draw weight. By all means, if you opt for a heavier bow, start low and then carefully and slowly work your way up. Stop whenever you become convinced by the evidence before your eyes that you are becoming overbowed.

# A Primer on Limb Design

*Analyzing and understanding the design of a bow limb
requires only a few analytical tools and some simple basic
principles of what we are trying to achieve.*

*M*ost of the traditional bows built and sold today were designed by a
process of trial and error based on long experience. I have visited a
number of bowyers, from individuals making only a few bows per
year to larger companies making many hundreds of bows per year. When
asked about the origin and specifications of their designs they invariably trundle
out the old notebooks in which are carefully recorded the final dimensions
and measurements of the most successful versions of each experimental
design. Some of these designs have been in existence, several in continuous
production, over a period of forty or fifty years, largely unchanged. Others are
off-shoots of designs that extend back even farther. In many cases the exact
origin of the design has been lost in the old records or survives only in the
successive memories of the bowyers still building them. Very few if any of
these designs were arrived at by any sort of formal analysis. There is absolutely
nothing wrong with that. Many of the designs that have resulted from trial
and error are excellent and achieve high levels of efficiency and performance
and durability. There is also nothing very surprising about it either. Designing
a bow limb analytically is a complicated affair involving a large number of
parameters all of which have to be adjusted simultaneously. Even with the
best analytical approach any final design is still an approximation in which
there are numerous trade-offs among the various parameters, depending on
the judgment of the bowyer and what he is trying to achieve. Designing a bow
limb is still partly science and partly art.

There is the choice of the shape of the limb, whether it is to be straight
or curved and whether it is to be reflexed or deflexed. There is also the cross-
sectional shape and whether it is to be a self limb or a composite laminated

limb. If it is to be laminated then there are the dimensions of the width and thickness of the laminates and how each should taper from the riser to the limb tip, along with the thickness of the fiberglass. There is also the length of the limb and the radius of curvature all along its length. And all of these parameters have to combine in such a way that the limb bends in the shape desired and gives the desired draw weight at the correct draw length. Finally there is the requirement that the resulting limb be stable and that it have adequate margins of safety against breaking. The combined problems of geometry and physics can be formidable.

Given that there is an existing design to serve as a starting point, an empirical trial and error approach makes perfect sense. Why else would you start any other way? That is how most of the present designs evolved, as gradual changes in previous bows that had been found to work reasonably well. A lot of bowyers who start out primarily just wanting to try their hand at making a few bows begin this way. They simply take an existing design whose performance they like and copy it, or combine what they think are the best features of two or more designs, changing the final version a bit as they go to improve it and incorporate their own ideas. It's a perfectly good way to get started. None of the existing limb designs that have been around for a while are proprietary.

You can always evaluate an existing design and determine the margin of safety without any fancy analysis by simply overdrawing it to see where the limb finally fails. A limb that is ultra-safe always has room for improvement to reduce its effective mass and make it faster, by doing things like shortening the length and making it thinner, reflexing and recurving it more, tapering the thickness of the laminations faster from the limb root to the tip, and tapering the width more toward the tip. The overall length of the bow can be adjusted by the length of the handle section once you have the limb designed the way you want it. All of these things can be pursued to the point where the margin of safety has been reduced to a reasonable level or until the limb starts to twist and become unstable. At that point you have reached a practical compromise between limb speed and performance on the one hand and stability and reliability on the other. The program of limb development outlined in these few steps is a reasonable way to proceed. Most bowyers, large and small, operate as a practical matter in much this fashion.

But with so many individual parameters to adjust, it becomes time consuming and expensive to change them one at a time to find out what will happen in each case. To proceed more effectively it is helpful to have some idea in advance how the individual parameters are related to one another and what effect changing one of them will have on the others and on the performance of the limb. And for that a quantitative method of analysis can be helpful. It can also be useful in providing design insights that are not at all obvious or easy to discover any other way. We want to present here just enough of an introduction to such an analytical approach to give the reader a feeling for what exactly is involved. Without designing an actual limb we want to at least indicate how to go about it and what the *guiding principles* are.

When a bow limb bends, the elastic material in the front of the limb is compressed and that in the back is stretched. The front portion of the limb is under compression and the back portion is under tension. At the boundary between the two is a thin neutral zone which is largely stress free. We measure the amount of compression or tension at any point by the *strain*, which is just the local fractional change in volume of the material. The farther the material from the neutral zone the greater the strain. The limb material resists being compressed or stretched; the material being compressed pushes against the bending force and the material being stretched pulls against it. The greater the elastic modulus and the farther the material from the neutral zone, the greater its resistance to bending. This resistance is what gives the limb its property of stiffness. We term these forces of resistance the *internal bending moment* of the limb. To hold the limb bent there has to be an equal and opposite *external bending moment* provided by the force required to draw the bow. The bending of the limb then is governed by the equality of these two bending moments, which for a limb having a rectangular cross section is expressed by equation (5):

$$\frac{x\,F\sin\phi}{\cos\theta} = \frac{E_0\,w\,t^3}{6\,r} + \frac{E_g\,w\,t^3}{6\,r}\left[\left(1+\frac{2\,d}{t}\right)^3 - 1\right]$$

The term on the left side of equation (5) is the bending moment supplied by the force $F$ drawing the bow. The quantities on the left side of the equation are shown in figure 4. Figure 4 is drawn for a recurved limb, but the geometry shown applies to any limb regardless of its shape. The string makes the half angle $\theta$ with the arrow; $\varphi$ is the angle that the string makes with the straight-line distance $x$ from the limb tip to any point on the limb.

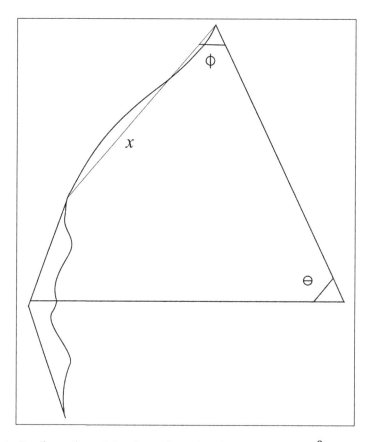

**Figure 4. Configuration of the drawn bow showing parameters x, $\theta$, and $\varphi$ used in analyzing limb design.**

The first term on the right side of the equation is the internal bending moment due to the elastic properties of the wood. The second term on the right is the bending moment due to the elastic properties of the fiberglass on the front and back of the limb. $E_o$ is the elastic modulus of the wood and $E_g$ is the elastic modulus of the fiberglass. Note that these two terms have the same form except for the extra factor in brackets in the second term, which results from the layer of fiberglass on the front and back of the limb. The other quantities are the width $w$ and thickness $t$ of the wood, the thickness $d$ of the fiberglass on the front and back, and the radius of curvature $r$, all measured at the point designated by $x$ on the limb. This equation applies at each point along the limb, but the variables can assume different values at each point. For example, the width, thickness, and radius of curvature may, and generally do, vary along the length of the limb.

*Equation (5) constitutes the first of the design principles we have to obey. This equation has to be satisfied at every point along the limb.*

First however we need to point out a basic limitation of equation (5). It assumes that a stress-free limb is straight. As the radius of curvature increases without limit, both of the terms on the right side of the equation go to zero, corresponding to a limb with no internal stress. But an infinite radius of curvature means that the limb is not bent, or in other words is straight. Equation (5) therefore describes a limb that is straight in the unstressed, or unstrung, position. All of the internal stress in the limb is described by the radius of curvature of the limb bending toward the string. This is not the case for a reflexed or recurved limb, which is not straight but is curved away from the string in the unstrung condition. In that case the radius of curvature of the drawn bow does not correctly measure the total internal stresses of the limb. Such a limb is glued together with a built-in radius of curvature away from the string. The laminations are curved before gluing and then are glued together with that curvature frozen in. This built-in curvature has to be straightened before the limb can take on a curvature toward the string. A reflexed or recurved limb therefore has *greater* internal stresses when strung and drawn than those described by equation (5). We will add these extra stresses in later.

Figure 5 illustrates the way we can measure the radius of curvature at any point along the limb using the sides of a right angle. We place one side of the right angle perpendicular to the surface of the limb at the point along its length where we want to determine the radius of curvature. The other side then intersects the curve of the limb some distance away. We measure the distances *a* and *b* shown in figure 5 where the sides of the right angle intersect the center of the limb. Then the radius of curvature is given by the expression:

$$r = \frac{b^2 + a^2}{2\,a}$$

We can make *a* any length we want. The shorter it is the closer *b* will intersect the limb to the point of intersection by *a* and the shorter the length over which we obtain the average radius of curvature.

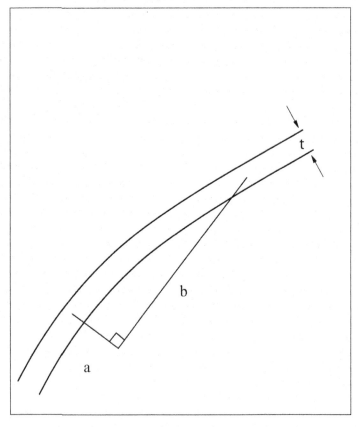

**Figure 5. Section of a bow limb of thickness *t* illustrating the measured distances *a* and *b* by which the radius of curvature is calculated**

Notice that there is nothing in equation (5) that limits how far we can draw the bow. The draw length doesn't enter the equation explicitly anywhere. However the draw length enters implicitly through the radius of curvature. The farther the bow is drawn the more the limb is bent and the smaller the radius of curvature. But the more the limb is bent the greater the internal stresses of compression and tension. For every elastic material there is a level of stress called the ultimate tensile strength beyond which the material will fracture. The ultimate tensile strength divided by the elastic modulus gives the maximum strain or deformation that the material can sustain before it fails. The strain in turn is related to the radius of curvature and the thickness of the limb material.

*The second of our design principles is to always keep the strain in the limb safely below the fracture limit.*

Let $\varepsilon$ represent the strain of the limb material. Then for a laminated limb with wooden laminations of total thickness $t$, fiberglass of thickness $d$ on the front and back, and radius of curvature $r$, the maximum strain in the wood is given by

$$\varepsilon = \frac{t}{2\,r}$$

and the maximum strain in the fiberglass is given by

$$\varepsilon = \frac{t + 2\,d}{2\,r}$$

Note that these two expressions become the same if we set $d = 0$ in the second expression. In that case the limb just becomes a wooden self limb of thickness $t$ and radius of curvature $r$.

In each case we have to keep the value of $\varepsilon$ below the fracture limit by limiting the thickness of the wood and fiberglass and by keeping the radius of curvature sufficiently large, that is, by restricting how sharply the limb bends. For the hardwoods typically used as laminations in bow limbs the elastic modulus is somewhere around 1,500,000 lbs./in.$^2$ (pounds per square inch). The tensile strength is about one percent or so of the elastic modulus, so the strain at which the material fractures is on the order of 0.01. The maximum strain in the wood has to stay below 0.01, or one percent. For the fiberglass commonly used on bow limbs the elastic modulus is around 6,000,000 lbs./in.$^2$. The tensile strength is about 170,000 lbs./in.$^2$ and so the tensile fracture strain is about 0.028, or 2.8 percent. The compression strength is around 90,000 lbs./in.$^2$ and the compression fracture limit is about 0.015, or 1.5 percent. These are the percentages by which one can change the volume of the materially locally by stretching or compressing it before it fractures. We have to keep the maximum strain in the fiberglass below these levels. Notice that the compression strength of fiberglass is not as high as the tensile strength, so a compression fracture on the face of the bow is the most likely failure mode.

What looks at first hand to be a fairly messy expression in equation (5) can in fact be reduced to something much less formidable with a little thought. *We are only interested in the condition of the limb when the bow is at full draw.* So the force $F$ represents the draw weight of the bow. The angle $\theta$ is a constant of the geometry, fixed by the length of the bow and the draw length. For bows of intermediate length the string makes an angle somewhere in the vicinity of 90 degrees at full draw so $\theta$ is approximately 45 degrees or so, and $\cos \theta$ then is about 0.707. The angle $\varphi$ changes slowly as $x$ goes from zero to its maximum value. For a straight limb at full draw the angle $\varphi$ slowly decreases as $x$ increases. For a recurved limb $\varphi$ increases at first near the limb tip then beyond a certain point in the recurved section slowly decreases as $x$ increases. At any rate the changes in $\varphi$ are not large and to a first approximation we can treat sin $\varphi$ as a constant. At full draw $\varphi$ is roughly 90 degrees for many limbs and we will take sin $\varphi$ to be approximately 1. This leaves $x$ as the only significant variable on the left side of equation (5). The left side of the equation reduces to a constant (for the sake of illustration we will take it to be roughly $1/0.7 = 1.4$) times the product $xF$ of the draw weight and the distance from the limb tip to each point along the limb.

The product $xF$ assumes its largest value at the limb root where $x$ is largest. So the applied external bending moment is always greatest at the base of the limb. That in turn means the right side of the equation will have its largest value at the root of the limb, so that is where the internal bending moment will be greatest. We can choose the values of the width and the thickness of the wood and fiberglass, and then the radius of curvature is fixed by the right side of the equation. But as we saw above we have to choose them so that the strain in the wood stays below about 0.01 and in the fiberglass below about 0.02. That means we have to restrict the radius of curvature to stay above a certain value determined by the thickness of the wood and fiberglass. At the same time the width and thickness of the limb have to be large enough to generate the draw weight. The draw weight goes up fastest with increasing thickness. So what we usually do is choose the thickness large enough to give the desired draw weight and then make the limb long enough (the radius of curvature large enough) to keep the strain below the fracture limit. We have to trade off these values to achieve both of our first two design principles.

To see how this works let's assume some actual values. Suppose we are designing a 50 pound bow with an 18 inch limb. Then the left side of equation (5) yields a value of 1260 (50 x 18 x 1.4). The right side of the equation must also equal this value. Suppose we want $w$ = 1.75 in., $t$ = 0.18 in. and $d$ = 0.040 in. at the limb root (we are free to choose limb width, wood thickness, and fiberglass thickness). Then using the values of $E_o$ and $E_g$ given previously, the right side of equation (5) yields a value of about 18.1 in. for the radius of curvature at the limb root. The maximum strain is 0.005 in the wood and 0.007 in the fiberglass, well below the fracture limit in each case. So this limb obeys both of our first two design principles by a generous safety margin at the limb root. That means it can be still further optimized to lower its mass and make it more efficient.

We can move in this direction by making the limb thinner and shorter. Let's reduce the thickness of the wood to 0.12 in. and the length of the limb to 16 in. Then the left side of the equation becomes 1120 and the right side of the equation yields a value of 15.1 in. for the radius of curvature. The strain in the wood reduces to 0.004 (the wood is thinner now) and in the fiberglass the strain stays at 0.007, again both safe values. Whether this radius of curvature at the limb root is small enough (whether the limb bends enough at the root) to achieve the desired draw length depends on how much the rest of the limb bends and the total length of the bow, which are yet to be determined. If the rest of the limb did not bend at all, as an extreme example, then to achieve the desired draw length we might have to make the bow (riser section) longer than desired; or the radius of curvature at the limb root might become so small that the strain there would exceed the fracture limit; or the draw weight might become too large. What happens at each point along the limb affects what happens at every other point. This is because the shape of the whole limb and the length of the riser section together determine the draw length. At any rate these numeral examples indicate how the equation is used in practice at each point along the limb.

To get a better feeling for the right side of the equation we can investigate what happens if we set $d = 0$, which amounts to leaving the fiberglass off the front and back of the limb so that we are dealing with a plain wooden limb. With $d = 0$ the second term on the right side of the equation becomes zero, as it should, since this term arises solely from the bending moment in the fiberglass, and we are left with only the first term. This simplified version of the equation tells us how a self limb bends. The product of draw weight and distance from the tip, on the left side of the equation, is proportional to the width of the limb and the cube of the thickness on the right side and inversely proportional to the radius of curvature. This means that a fractional change in the limb width produces the same fractional change in draw weight. But a fractional change in the limb thickness produces a fractional change in draw weight three times as large. A ten percent decrease in the thickness produces a thirty percent decrease in draw weight.

When the thickness of the fiberglass is not zero we can compare the relative sizes of the two terms on the right side of equation (5). They differ only by $E_o$ and $E_g$ and by the factor in brackets in the second term. The value of $E_g$ is typically 3-4 times that of $E_o$. The value of the factor in brackets varies from less than 3 at the limb root to almost 6 at the limb tip for draw weights in the 50 pound range. Combining these values we see that the magnitude of the first term on the right is only about 5-10 percent that of the second term. The wood contributes only about 10 percent of the total bending moment at the limb root and only about 5 percent at the tip. For purposes of rough estimates we may choose to ignore the contribution of the wood to the bending moment and just use the second term, corresponding to the bending moment of the fiberglass. We can multiply the second term by 1.1, if we wish, to approximate the contribution of the wood to the total bending moment.

*The third of our design principles is to have the limb bend so that the maximum stress is the same everywhere along its length.*

If the stress is lower somewhere it means that portion of the limb is not working as hard as the rest and represents excess mass which contributes unnecessarily to the effective mass and lowers the efficiency of the limb. To keep the maximum stress everywhere the same the maximum strain should be the same everywhere, which in turn means that we want the radius of curvature to be as nearly constant along the limb as can be arranged. A straight bow ideally should bend along the arc of a circle. As we move toward the tip of the limb, the value of *x* on the left side of the equation decreases toward zero. The quantity on the right side of the equation has to decrease also. But if we want the radius of curvature to stay constant then our only freedom is to decrease the product of the limb width and the cube of the thickness from the limb root toward the tip.

One way to do this is by making the limb width proportional to its distance from the tip. Then as the distance from the tip decreases the limb width decreases in the same proportion. However we can't decrease the width all the way to zero at the tip for obvious reasons. In addition, long before the width reaches zero the limb will become unstable and prone to twist, especially if it is reflexed or recurved. We have to leave the limb wide enough near the end to keep it from twisting. Another approach is to decrease the thickness of the limb toward the tip. Again we can't decrease the thickness all the way to zero. We have to maintain a certain minimum thickness at the tip. *An analysis shows that the optimum rate at which to taper the thickness is one third the ratio of the thickness at the limb root to the limb length.* That translates into a rate of taper between 0.002-0.003 inch per inch for most cases. Near the end of the limb the distance from the tip decreases much faster than the product of limb width and cube of the thickness, and as a result the radius of curvature increases near the tip of the limb. As a practical matter the end of the limb will not bend as much as the rest of the limb. The requirement of stability dictates it.

*The fourth design principle is to make the maximum stress as high as possible everywhere in the limb without exceeding the fracture limit anywhere.*

That means making the strain as large as possible since the stress is just the strain multiplied by the elastic modulus. Our goal is to reduce the effective mass of the limb by reducing the actual limb mass everywhere we can. We can obtain the same draw weight with less material by straining it closer to its fracture limit. Any material in the limb not stressed equally near the fracture limit represents excess mass that is not contributing to the stiffness of the limb. To reduce limb mass we want the limb to be as narrow as possible. But we are constrained by considerations of stability to keep the limb wide enough to prevent twisting and dynamic instabilities when the string is released. So there is a definite lower limit for the limb width. We also want the limb to be as thin as possible. But the draw weight depends on the cube of the limb thickness so when we reduce the thickness we reduce the draw weight even faster.

The only variables left are the limb length and radius of curvature. We can stress the limb more by bending it farther. If we shorten the bow by shortening the limbs, they have to bend more for the same draw length. We can shorten the limb and keep the bow the same length by increasing the length of the center section. Shorter limbs on the same length bow will bend farther for the same draw length. The average radius of curvature of the drawn limb will be smaller and the strain in the limb material will be higher. The problem is to get the limb to bend uniformly along its length. The external bending moment is greatest at the limb root. If the limbs become too short they bend too much near the limb root and not enough along the rest of the limb. Trying to remedy this problem by tapering the width or thickness leads back to problems of instability.

The only other way to bend the limb farther without shortening it is to reflex or recurve it. By gluing up the limb in a reflexed or recurved shape it has a built-in radius of curvature in its unstrung position and has to be strained just to bend it in the direction of straightening it, and then strained more to bend it far enough to string it. So the final radius of curvature of the strung or drawn bow does not correctly describe the total amount of strain or stress in the limb. It omits the additional strain required to straighten the original curved shape of the limb before it could be bent toward the string. Thus the terms on the right side of equation (5) *underestimate the total strain and the total internal bending moment of a reflexed or recurved limb.* Equation (5) has to be modified by adding in the additional bending moment due to the radius of curvature of the unstrung limb. The resulting equation is a bit more cumbersome, but *it illustrates how shaping the unstrung limb adds to the bending moment with no increase in limb mass, allowing limb mass to be decreased while maintaining the same draw weight.*

The *additional* bending moment in the wood is a term identical to the first term on the right side of equation (5), except with $r$ replaced by $r'$, *where $r'$ is the radius of curvature at each point along the unstrung limb.* Similarly the *additional* bending moment in the glass is a term identical to the second term on the right side of equation (5), with $r$ again replaced by $r'$. These two additional terms have to be added to the right side of the equation. The result is an equation identical to equation (5) except with $(1/r)$ replaced by $[(1/r') + (1/r)]$ in the two terms on the right side.

As an example of how we can take advantage of this increase in bending moment, suppose that the *unstrung* limb is curved away from the string at each point along its length with the same radius of curvature as that assumed by the fully drawn limb in the opposite direction. In that case the right side of equation (5) is *doubled* in magnitude over that of a straight limb, and consequently the draw weight of the bow is doubled too, with no increase in the thickness or width of the limb. This is a decided advantage, because now we can reduce the thickness of the limb and still achieve the same draw weight. Reducing the thickness by twenty percent reduces the draw weight by half, $(0.8)^3 = 0.5$. Thus by reflexing and recurving the limb we can attain the same draw weight with twenty percent less limb mass, which is in the direction of reducing the effective mass of the limb and increasing its energy and momentum efficiency. We make the limb more efficient simply by shaping the unstrung limb to be curved instead of straight. *This is the most effective way to increase the internal stress in the limb, and consequently the internal bending moment, without further shortening its length.*

The external bending moment supplied by the draw weight, the left side of equation (5), decreases as the distance from the tip of the limb decreases. Near the end of the limb the draw weight times the distance from the tip may not be large enough to straighten the recurved end of the limb and bend it toward the string. In that case we do not derive the full benefit of recurving the limb. In any part of the limb that stops bending, the internal bending moment does not increase since at that point the internal deformation or strain stops increasing. We can attempt to have the limb tip bend more by decreasing its width and thickness, but as we have already noted both of those options are limited by considerations of stability. It is better in this regard to reduce the thickness of the limb than the width. By recurving the limb tip less it will bend more before the internal bending moment becomes equal to the external bending moment.

For any portion of the limb that does not straighten completely from its curved unstrung shape and bend toward the string, then equation (5) as we modified it previously *overestimates* the internal bending moment. *For those portions of the limb* we have to modify equation (5) in a different way that reduces the bending moment resulting from the shape of the unstrung limb. The result is an equation identical to equation (5) except with $(1/r)$ replaced by $[(1/r') - (1/r)]$. The term containing $(1/r')$ represents the maximum additional bending moment that can occur from curving the unstrung limb, while the term containing $(1/r)$ *subtracts* the bending moment lost due to the fact that the curved limb does not completely straighten and bend toward the string. Here $r$ is still the curvature of the limb at full draw, but now in the direction *away* from the string, hence the minus sign. This form of the equation applies only to the curved portion of the unstrung limb that does not straighten completely and bend toward the string when the bow is fully drawn, and that usually means the end portion of the limb.

We can now combine all three of these expressions into a single equation. The result is equation (6):

$$\frac{x\,F\sin\varphi}{\cos\theta} = \frac{E_0\,w\,t^3}{6}\left(\frac{1}{r'}\pm\frac{1}{r}\right) + \frac{E_g\,w\,t^3}{6}\left(\frac{1}{r'}\pm\frac{1}{r}\right)\left[\left(1+\frac{2\,d}{t}\right)^3-1\right]$$

where $r'$ is the radius of curvature of the *unstrung limb* and $r$ is the radius of curvature of the *bent limb* at each point along the limb denoted by $x$. We use the *plus* sign at all points where the curvature of the fully drawn limb is *toward* the string and the *minus* sign where the limb curves *away* from the string. *Equation (6) then applies at each point along a limb of any shape and represents the complete design equation.* There are still some smaller effects not taken into account in equation (6), but it is close enough to guide us in the design of a limb.

Note that if we let $r'$ become infinite, corresponding to an unstrung limb that is *straight* rather than recurved or reflexed, then the terms containing $r'$ go to zero and equation (6) reduces to equation (5) just as it should. Note also that the two terms on the right side differ from one another only by the factors of $E_0$ and $E_g$ and by the final term in brackets involving the thickness of the fiberglass and the wood in the limb. As we discussed previously in connection with equation (5), the magnitude of the first term is normally no more than about ten percent that of the second term. The wood contributes only about ten percent of the total internal bending moment. In most cases we can ignore the first term and multiply the second term by 1.1 to approximate the contribution from the wood.

In this form equation (6) illustrates how we are able to make the right side, representing the internal bending moment of the limb, as large as we like so long as we do not exceed the fracture limit. We are completely free to choose the shape of the unstrung limb by the shape in which we glue the laminations together. We can make $r'$ as small as we wish by reflexing and recurving the limb to whatever degree we choose when we glue it together. The more we curve it away from the string, the smaller the value of $r'$ becomes at each point along the limb, and the larger the terms containing $r'$ on the right side of the equation become. In this fashion we can achieve a higher draw weight without increasing the width and thickness of the limb, thereby leaving the effective mass the same; or instead we can keep the draw weight the same while reducing the width and thickness to lower the effective mass of the limb and improve its efficiency. *Shaping the unstrung limb provides the traditional bowyer with additional design options and freedom and is his most effective design tool.*

It is often impossible to design the recurved end of a limb so that it completely straightens in order to take full advantage of the additional bending moment built into the unstrung limb. Unless the radius of curvature is large, corresponding to a more gradual degree of recurve, the limb usually becomes unstable before we get it thin enough to straighten and bend toward the string. But there is another design option. *We can purposely recurve the end of the limb so that it doesn't bend and in that way force the limb to bend more somewhere else.* The idea here is to keep the actual mass of the limb as low as possible to reduce its effective mass while still maintaining the desired draw weight. We especially want to reduce the mass of those parts of the limb that are moving the fastest when the arrow leaves the string, and that means the end of the limb. We can make the end thinner, and lighter, and at the same time keep it stiff enough not to bend and become unstable by recurving it more, making its built-in radius of curvature smaller. Since the end of the limb doesn't bend, it will have to bend farther down where the applied bending moment is greater. We can recurve that portion of the limb, while reducing its thickness, to bend so that the internal strain is closer to the fracture limit, thereby reducing its mass.

This kind of design strategy violates the principle of trying to achieve the same internal stress at all points along the limb, but it is in the direction of our other design principle of forcing those parts of the limb that do bend to be stressed as close to the fracture limit as is consistent with a safe design. Although the stress in the limb is not the same everywhere, the effective mass can be reduced in this way to make a faster more efficient limb. We purposely recurve the end of the limb to reduce the mass required to keep it from bending, and thereby force the limb to bend elsewhere with greater internal stresses, in order to make a more efficient limb. Thus we play off one of our design principles against another, which is what design compromises are all about.

We can use our freedom to shape the unstrung limb in whatever way we choose to take advantage of the relative strengths of the elastic materials in bow limbs and achieve other design innovations. As an example, the ultimate strength of both wood and fiberglass is greater in tension than in compression by almost a factor of two. That means that we can strain wood and fiberglass more in tension than in compression before they fracture. We would like to have a way to take advantage of that property in the design of the limb. Since we can strain the limb more in tension we should be able to design it to have less mass in tension than in compression. And that suggests a way to decrease the effective mass of the limb and make it faster and more efficient.

In one such scheme, we can glue fiberglass to the back of the limb with the limb recurved much farther than the final shape of the unstrung limb. Then with fiberglass glued to the recurved back, we bend the limb forward and glue fiberglass on the face of the limb. In this configuration the back of the limb is under tension, the amount depending on how far it was recurved when gluing fiberglass to the back and how far forward we bend it when gluing fiberglass to the front. When the completed limb is released it comes to an equilibrium shape somewhere intermediate between the two extremes. The back of the limb is held stressed under tension by the resulting tension in the fiberglass glued to the front of the limb. When the bow is fully drawn the back of the limb is strained, or stretched, more than the belly of the limb is compressed, taking advantage of the greater strength of wood and fiberglass in tension over compression. The fabrication of the limb requires an extra step since the fiberglass cannot be glued to the back and front of the limb at the same time.

This is an example of a pre-stressed limb, one that is already stressed before the bow is strung or drawn. In this case the back and belly of the limb are pre-stressed under tension. Pre-stressing in this manner allows the tension in the back of the fully drawn limb to be greater than the compression in the front of the limb. That way both the front and back of the limb can be stressed nearer their limit so that there is no excess material in the limb and the effective mass can be as small as possible for the desired draw weight. For a pre-stressed limb in which the stress levels in the fiberglass approach the fracture strength of the material, the corresponding stress levels in the wood can also be close to the ultimate fracture strength. We can minimize the strain in the wood by keeping it as thin as possible. For that reason a pre-stressed limb may have only a single lamination of wood rather than multiple laminations. Pre-stressed limbs are usually designed closer to the fracture limit than more conservative, less efficient, limbs. They are consequently more prone to failure and, being thinner, they are also less stable and require more exacting technique in shooting. They are also more prone to twisting after fabrication. For that reason they have never become very popular with bowyers who prefer a reputation for more reliable and more stable limb designs. Yet they possess the inherent advantage of greater arrow speed at lower draw weights.

Most of the questions routinely encountered in the design of traditional bows can be addressed and answered with nothing more than the few analytical tools and design principles presented in this brief introduction. As a way of illustrating a practical application we can outline how we might go about approaching an actual design.

It begins with selecting the length of the bow. Traditional bows range in length from very short bows of 48-52 inches used primarily for hunting, to 66-70 inches for longbows and recurve bows used for target archery. We can probably best characterize length according to type. Most recurve target bows are from 64-70 inches with the most popular lengths being 66-69 inches for arrows 27 inches or longer. English longbows are typically 68-70 inches long to keep the compressive stress in the thicker limb below the fracture limit. Longbows of the American flat bow design can be made shorter without danger of breaking and are found in lengths all the way from 56-69 inches or so. Recurve hunting bows range from 48-64 inches with the most popular lengths probably being 58-62 inches. These lengths are measured along the contour of the back of the bow. For straight bows that is the same as the distance from nock to nock. But for deflexed, reflexed, and recurve bows this length is greater than the distance from nock to nock. One can see from all of this that length is a complicated and confusing parameter for traditional bows and is not a particularly useful way to characterize them. Instead it makes more design sense to think about length in terms of the length of the limbs and the length of the handle section of the bow.

Any bow with limbs longer than necessary is a less than optimum design. And the limbs are longer than they need to be if they are stressed too far below the fracture limit. Limbs too lightly stressed will have a higher than necessary mass and will be less efficient in imparting kinetic energy and momentum to the arrow. They will be sluggish and have greater recoil or hand shock. An English longbow or a long, thick-limbed American flat bow will have these characteristics. They are simply not very efficient designs. That may be no reason not to choose them. They have other kinds of appeal; they are superb for rapid shooting at close distances or at moving targets. But one should realize at the outset that they will not shoot as efficiently as some other designs.

To increase the internal stress we can shorten the limbs or we can reflex and recurve them. At the same time we want them to be as thin as possible consistent with attaining the desired draw weight. All of these things reduce the mass of the limbs and make them faster. We can shorten the limbs and still maintain the bow length we desire by adjusting the length of the handle or riser section of the bow. The riser ideally should be inert; it should not bend. It has to be long enough to provide adequate space for the grip, usually five or six inches; and enough room for a sight window or a clear view of the arrow for aiming, another three or four inches; and it has to provide sufficient length to attach the limbs, an additional three or four inches on each end; but beyond that we can make it any length we want. The limbs can be made demountable or the limb root can be incorporated as an integral part of the riser.

The working part of the limb, the part beyond the riser fadeout or the limb root, that actually bends, does not need to be longer than 16-20 inches even for a highly recurved limb. The internal strain can be kept safely below the fracture limit for a limb shorter than that. Coupled with a 16 inch riser, limbs of this length could be used to make a short 48 inch bow. Combined with a 25 inch riser, limbs in this same range would make a bow 69 inches long, including the static part of the limb root. This then is the range of lengths with which we need to be concerned for designing an efficient limb. In particular, there is no need to consider limbs longer than this.

Next comes the choice of overall shape. We always have the option of making the limbs and the bow straight. A straight bow will generally have the most hand shock. Hand shock can be reduced by deflexing the limbs. Any loss of limb stress and limb speed that results can always be regained by also reflexing the limbs. There is really no good reason not to choose the deflexed-reflexed configuration, unless for some reason you just happen to want a perfectly straight bow. The result is a bow that is more comfortable and pleasant to shoot. The minimum amount by which the limbs should be reflexed is so that the limb tips and the back of the handle form a straight line. The limbs can be reflexed beyond this, but it doesn't make much sense to reflex them any less than to put the end of the limb back in line with the handle where it would have been if the limbs had never been deflexed. Many American flat bows are made in the deflexed-reflexed shape and most of them are not reflexed much beyond this point. A lot of them would benefit by being reflexed more. To stress the limb more we have the option of reflexing it farther, recurving it, shortening it, or any combination of these options. Few American flat bows are truly recurved but some are more highly reflexed and shortened to make faster more efficient limbs.

The amount by which to deflex the limbs seems to be somewhere around 15-20 degrees. That degree of deflex greatly reduces hand shock and yet is not so pronounced that the reduced limb stress cannot be easily recovered by reflexing and recurving the limb. The degree of limb deflex is determined by the shape of the riser. The more the limbs are deflexed at the riser the more they have to be reflexed or recurved to recover the lost stress. But the more they are reflexed and recurved then the thinner and narrower they have to be to get them to bend properly all along the limb, and the less stable they become. So the degree of deflex sets up a tradeoff with the amount of recurve and the limb stability.

Once the bow length and overall shape are decided we are ready to design the limb. We start by choosing whatever preliminary reflexed or recurved shape we wish for the unstrung limb. We do this by specifying the radius of curvature $r'$ away from the string at each point along the unstrung limb. The maximum external bending moment in equations (5) and (6), the left side of the equation, occurs where the limb first starts bending at the riser fadeout or root, since that is where the draw weight times the distance from the limb tip is greatest. So we have to make sure the limb root is thick enough to support the desired draw weight. It can be thicker than this but if it is any thinner then the internal bending moment will be too small to yield the desired draw weight.

We have already chosen the unstrung radius of curvature at the limb root. Next we need to estimate the radius of curvature at the limb root when the bow is fully drawn. *A workable first estimate is to assume that the limb bends uniformly along its entire length, make a full-scale drawing of the bow, and measure (or calculate) from the geometry what the radius of curvature would have to be to achieve the desired draw length.* For a straight-limbed bow with a short handle and limbs that bend in a circular arc, a good first approximation would be roughly the length of the arrow. For bows with longer handle sections and short recurved limbs the value would be less. Don't worry about trying to get this first estimate too exact. It will get refined in subsequent iterations of the design exercise. We also need to choose the limb width at the root. A value somewhere around 1.75 inches is generally a good starting point, less for thicker limbs and more for thinner ones. We also have to specify the fiberglass thickness and for most draw weights a thickness of 0.030-0.040 inch is sufficient.

Putting these values into equation (6) we can find the limb thickness that gives the desired draw weight $F$ for the straight line distance $x$ from the limb tip to the limb root. This value then determines the thickness of the limb everywhere else. If we taper the total thickness of the laminations by either 0.002 or 0.003 inch per inch from their thickness at the limb root, the thickness of the limb everywhere else is determined by its thickness at the base. We also have to specify how the limb width is going to decrease from the base of the limb to the tip. Here it is best to be conservative and maintain a very slow taper toward the tip. This can always be refined in later iterations of the first design.

Next we have to check that the maximum strain at the limb root does not exceed the fracture limit. We have to strain the reflexed limb to straighten it and then strain it further to bend it to the fully drawn position. We have to insure that the sum of these two strains does not exceed the fracture limit of around 0.01 in the wood and about 0.015 in the fiberglass. For this we use the formulas given earlier for calculating the maximum strain in the wood and in the fiberglass, with $(1/r)$ replaced by $[(1/r') + (1/r)]$ to combine the two strains, where $r'$ is the radius of curvature of the unstrung limb shape we have chosen, and $r$ is the estimated radius of curvature of the fully drawn limb.

Assuming that the fracture limit has not been exceeded at the limb root we next have to determine from equation (6) how the radius of curvature of the fully drawn limb actually varies along its length. This information gives us the final shape of the drawn limb. We know the limb thickness and the limb width everywhere and fiberglass thickness. We also know the radius of curvature $r'$ everywhere along the limb, since that is determined by our initial choice for the reflexed or recurved shape of the unstrung limb. Putting these values in equation (6) along with the desired draw weight we can find the radius of curvature $r$ of the fully drawn limb at each value of $x$ along its length. It is only necessary to do this every few inches along the limb to get an adequate picture of its shape. The more points at which we calculate $r$ the more detailed our knowledge of the final limb shape. At some point along the limb the reflexed or recurved shape may not completely straighten and bend toward the string, and to obtain a value of $r$ there and beyond we have to use the minus sign in the equation.

Having found the final radius of curvature at points along the limb, we check to make sure that the maximum strain at each of those points does not exceed the fracture limit in the wood or the fiberglass. This is the end of the first iteration in our design exercise.

We can start a second iteration by using the calculated values of the curvature to sketch a new shape for the drawn limb and from this second sketch obtain a much better estimate of the radius of curvature at the limb root. Using this new estimate we can go back through the entire procedure outlined above a second time to calculate new values for the radius of curvature at the same points along the limb. This second iteration should produce relatively smaller changes in the shape of the limb and the subsequent estimate of the radius of curvature at the limb root. We continue this process of iteration until the changes in the values of the curvature become sufficiently small. At this point we have a workable limb, though one that may still be far from optimum.

We can decide whether to modify our initial assumption about the shape of the unstrung limb, or we might even want to change the limb length or width, depending on what we found out as a result of the first set of iterations. If the limb is stressed too far below the fracture limit everywhere then we might want to shorten the limb or increase the amount of initial reflex or recurve. If at any point the maximum strain exceeds the fracture limit then we would want to decrease the degree of reflex or recurve or maybe even lengthen the limb. We can continue to go through this process, each time modifying the starting assumptions, until we converge on a satisfactory design.

A good starting point for the whole exercise is an already existing limb that comes at least close to the performance level the bowyer wishes to achieve. An existing design takes the guesswork out of choosing the initial values for the shape of the unstrung limb, the thickness of the wood laminations at the limb root and the width of the limb along its length and can reduce the number of iterations needed to converge on a final design.

Each complete set of design iterations should get us closer to an optimum limb. As even someone adept at mathematical computations can see, this process can be tedious and time consuming. (For someone so inclined, much of the work could be taken out of it by programming the actual computations on a hand-held calculator or a computer.) But it can also eliminate much of the guesswork and the trial and error from bow design and greatly reduce the number of limbs that have to be built and tested before an optimum design is found. Even if one does not actually use the analytical approach, a better understanding of it can focus the bowyer on the correct direction for improving an existing design. It can be especially helpful when trying to design as close to the failure limit as possible without breaking a lot of limbs in the process.

# The Upshot

*The upshot was originally the term for the final or concluding shot in an archery match. It has come to signify more broadly the outcome, the conclusion, or the final word.*

I learned to shoot while I was very young. Some of us afterwards are never able to put it completely aside. The muscles have a memory for the tug of a taut bowstring, the mind for the sight of a well-shot arrow quivering in the mark. The "witchery of archery," Maurice Thompson called it, and the lyrical passages of that little book are as alive in my memory now, after all these years, as they were then, when they became my first real literary experience. Saxton Pope believed the bow held a special affinity for those with English surnames, but the appeal is much more individual, and more universal, than he imagined.

I can scarcely recall a time before I became interested in archery. It seems to me now that I must have been born with this strange and compelling fascination, like some sort of ancient racial memory embedded in the nervous system. To those who would scoff I can only smile and confide in what I know in my own heart. Looking back, I have lived most of my life in the practice of archery, or its contemplation, as often in the contemplation as in the practice. The two have become fused in my mind until now they are one and the same, and archery is never long out of my thoughts.

As I write, my latest bow rests gleaming on a rack of elk antlers on the wall with its dark, waxed string draped smoothly across the polished grip and along the length of the gently recurved limbs. Its simple, elegant lines evoke a flood of memories that are all of any substance I have accumulated in this life, and hold out the promise of a future far less complex than the one I know is in store for me. One should write only of important things, but few things are ever more important or enduring than those of the heart from one's youth.

The bow has become a symbol in my life, a means of thinking back about it, of reliving the past, and a metaphor for understanding the present. Significance is to be found as often in the uncomplicated as in the profound, and life is best understood in terms of its simple physical and mental experiences. It is not a bow I see on the wall, but all the bows I have ever owned, and the arrows, broken now or lost and forgotten, all of the memorable shots and near-misses that once made are never forgotten, and all the dreams and hopes and ambitions, those realized and those more numerous which simply fell by the way never to be realized. It comes back to me at times in floods, and at others in broken bits and pieces, painfully now and then, with twinges of regret, and always with the same strange mixture of joy and sadness—joy at remembering what it was like at the time, tempered by the realization those days are over now and belong forever to the past. I have written these words many times before in my mind, and when I finally put them all together here at last, they will repay a debt I owe to those who experienced them with me, and who taught me, and to whom I long ago promised them.

As I sit here I can still feel the warm sunshine that was so much a part of my youth, and hear again the laughter, and the smooth hissing sound of long low feathers as a glinting cedar shaft arcs high upward in the morning light to descend again toward a mark which at that distance I had no right to hit, but did. I watch once more, transfixed, as the wild hog plows to a stop in the freshly rooted earth of the open meadow, its spine neatly severed, and then hear the whoops and shouts of my companions and the jubilation of the three of us as we rushed wildly to claim our prize. I was still fourteen at the time, my brother only twelve.

Periodically, I put aside the pages I have been writing and pick up the bow and string it and, nocking an arrow, pull it to full draw and hold it aimed until my muscles begin to quiver. The draw weight is only fifty-five pounds, but I must stay in shape to shoot it comfortably and with complete control. Besides, I have an even heavier bow in mind. I spend most of my practice time holding it drawn, aiming, since I learned long ago that aiming is what makes a good shot. The release and follow-through are automatic if everything else is right, and it is best not to think too much about it anyway. There is a lot of nonsense written about how to shoot a bow, some of it by people who shoot well enough but don't really understand why. It has taken me years to gradually sort it all out but I have learned at last what makes a good shot, even when I cannot bring myself to do it. After all this time my form is still a little off, and I realize now that it always will be.

As bows go, this latest one is a simple affair, yet complex. Even though the limbs are deflexed at the handle and recurved gracefully backward at the tips, it is still in spirit a longbow. All the others somehow are not really bows at all, but mechanical contrivances—with wheels and cables and pulleys, technological solutions to a non-problem, so characteristic of the times—by those who are not engaged in archery but who instead are embarked on the quest for perfection and mechanical efficiency, who are involved in the reinvention of the firearm and the wheel and all the other gadgets with which we have surrounded ourselves. These so-called compound bows are noisy, cumbersome contraptions that stand as mechanical monuments to the recapitulation of the industrial revolution, in an implement as ancient and as basic as the most primitive culture.

The limbs of my bow are made of maple, not as a single piece of wood but in the form of thin wide slats planed flat and smooth on a machine and tapered gradually from the handle to the tip, then sandwiched and glued together with an epoxy resin and bonded on the front and back to a thin layer of fiberglass. The resulting composite structure will support the compressive and tensile stresses of the fully drawn bow much better than wood alone and produces a faster limb, one that is lighter and more delicate for a given draw weight, so that less of the stored energy will be retained by the bow and more of it imparted to the arrow. Cut deep into the riser on the left side is a sight window and a crowned shelf for the arrow. The grip itself is contoured and shaped to conform to the hand, but it is otherwise straight and graceful and is smooth and polished for comfort. The limbs are coated with a hard, durable waterproof finish. The string is sixteen strands of dacron, which resists stretching, with formed loops at each end, wrapped on both ends and in the middle with dacron thread to protect against abrasion, then waxed with resin and beeswax and twisted to give the proper brace height. Two thin metal bands are swaged onto the string to mark the nocking point of the arrow. The arrows for this bow are wooden, Port Orford cedar, with plastic nocks and metal points and with real feathers for fletching.

Altogether, this bow is perhaps a far cry from anything that would have been possible before the advent of modern materials technology, especially in the quality of its construction, in its durability and ruggedness, and in the consistency of its performance. Yet for all that it is still not vastly superior to the best laminated and composite bows of the past. Both represent about the most that can be achieved in the way of speed and efficiency—with compromises for stability and durability—without resorting to the mechanical advantage of cams and pulleys.

Beyond that, the rest is up to the archer, the way it has always been, the way it always should remain. Archery is at core a contest, a feat of strength and skill pitting the coordination of hand and eye and the command of muscle against the task of drawing and shooting a bow properly, and it is not to be endlessly subverted by substituting for human frailty and limitations the artifacts of more and more technology. Let those who would demean it by forever simplifying the task adopt firearms instead; and if the noise is objectionable and the recoil too harsh, they can turn their creative efforts to the development of silencers and muzzle brakes and shock absorbers and be content in their separate pursuits.

When the arrow flies unerringly it is because of the archer, because arm and nerve were steady and the aim true, and not because the arrow velocity was a few feet per second higher or the draw weight a little less, or because the bow was center-shot or stabilized by hanging extra masses all over it. No, not for any of these reasons. None of those things makes that much difference anyway. Long before any of them, when English archers still shot by resting the arrow on top of the bow hand, Roger Ascham had correctly discerned the elements of good form. No one viewing Praxitiles' statue of the archer god Apollo can doubt that the early Greeks, too, admired and understood in the most modern sense the elements of proper form.

Far more important than improving the bow is anything that can be done to make the arrows all alike. Horace Ford's best scores have but seldom been equaled by modern archers shooting wooden arrows, though some undoubtedly could. But even here I would draw the line. Beyond a certain point, further improvements become meaningless except as their own justification and the ability of the archer remains the ultimate limitation. It is better to understand what makes a good shot, and to have a clear knowledge of how to accomplish it, than to dream of the ideal bow or more-perfectly matched arrows. We already know where the solution to that problem leads us. We might just as well mount the arrow in the barrel of a rifle and propel it with gun powder and have done with it. The object of archery is to shoot the bow, and too much time wasted in reinventing the implements of the sport is time better spent shooting.

Pick up a bow and admire it. It should have pleasing lines and feel good in the hand, balanced and not awkward. No need to be overburdened or to accept clumsiness or unattractiveness. Beauty, of course, is in the eye of the beholder, but there is a classic beauty of grace and simplicity that is universal. I have always thought that recurve target bows, with their elegantly shaped limbs and long slender stabilizer rods protruding in front of the handle, are quite beautiful; and seen in the act of shooting, or pitched gracefully forward in the archer's hand during the follow-through, they unquestionably are. My own attraction to the longbow was shaped by the countless hours I spent in my youth shooting them and admiring their clean, simple lines and pleasing symmetry. I never see the pale crescent of the waning moon at dawn, or the new moon shining in the twilight, without being reminded.

Slowly pull back the string. It should be possible, but not too easy; there should be a sense of pride in the muscles for a feat accomplished. Hold the bow at full draw while muscles and tendons warm to the task and the string cuts into the tips of the fingers through the shooting glove. Now take it out and shoot it, first at some nearby target too close for there to be any sense of delay between releasing the string and the impact of the arrow. Experience the recoil of the bow and the reaction of muscle and bone that serves as a constant reminder to the archer that he is an integral part of the shot. As my bow kicks in my hand, the response of my entire body, of arms and backs and legs, joins me to the act of shooting, and my mental impression is one of reaching out across the intervening distance and driving the arrow through the center of the target.

Now shoot toward some more distant object, such as a clump of grass or a low bush, so that you can see the flight of the arrow and observe where it lands. Bring the bow to full draw and aim it, stepping once again into the shot itself and searching in the mind's eye for a picture of arrow and bush that will cause the two to converge at the precise point in space. Remain immobile after the release and watch the arrow fly: this follow-through is the most pleasurable part of shooting. You can savor the satisfied feeling of tense muscles slackening and the sight of an arrow speeding along its curved trajectory in response to the unmistakable impression of a shot well executed.

Dust kicks up in front of the bush, so you nock another shaft and shoot again, elevating the bow a bit higher and aiming until that exact instant when mind and muscle and sight all come together and the release occurs automatically, triggered by something indistinct and indefinable. This time there is the instant realization born of long experience that everything was solid and the aim correct. You stand riveted, every muscle motionless and every nerve on end, at the mounting expectation of seeing the arrow find its mark.

Suddenly, you are on the field at Crecy or Agincourt, firing bodkin-pointed shafts aloft in volleys of thousands at long lines of knights advancing in chain mail armor; or watching with heart stopped as the arrow speeds toward a bounding deer; or standing on the line at a double York round seeing the shaft strike in the center of the gold one hundred yards away. As the arrow swoops down upon the bush, a sudden spasm of exhilaration explodes in every nerve and fiber, a sensuous celebration of sight and sound and feeling that makes shooting the bow an intensely physical and emotional experience. Those who have experienced it know that the elation and satisfaction of a good shot as quickly turns to the frustration made even more acute of those that go astray. One is not encountered without the other, and both are merely differing aspects of the same peculiar fascination that is archery.

Shooting the bow will forever remain a contest, a physical and mental confrontation matching the archer against the limitations of bow and arrow and the demands of a perfect shot. No amount of technology can change that or decide the outcome. Shooting the bow is not a technological challenge but a human one. It is a quest in which one competes against one's own will and determination and failings, and in which only varying degrees of perfection are possible.

Few who have ever pulled a stout bow and watched the speeding shaft fly true to the mark will easily forget the basic animal satisfaction of muscle and sense at feeling the shot and seeing the arrow converging with its target and hearing it solidly strike. It can be felt long afterwards at the core of one's being, like some echo from out of the dim genetic past, and it persists in an elemental way that betrays the superficiality of more sophisticated emotions—persists and brings us back to experience it again and again. The witchery of archery, we might label it, or perhaps more appropriately, the sensuality of archery. At least that is what it will always be for some of us, who afterwards are never able to put it completely aside.

# About the Author

Thomas Grissom has been a lifelong archer. He began shooting a bow at age eight and has been doing so, or thinking about it, in one form or another ever since. A bowhunter, he has taken small game, wild boar, deer, and elk with a bow and arrow. In 1968 he was the men's combined champion of the Southern Archery Association. He is also a bowyer, designing and making his own laminated recurve bows. He was awarded a PhD in physics by the University of Tennessee in 1970. For fifteen years he was a member of the technical staff and a department manager at Sandia National Laboratories in Albuquerque, New Mexico. He is Emeritus Member of the Faculty at The Evergreen State College in Olympia, Washington, where he taught physics, mathematics, philosophy, and literature from 1985 to 2007. He is the author of several works of fiction and non-fiction, including four collections of poems also published by Sunstone Press. He resides in Albuquerque.

CPSIA information can be obtained
at www.ICGtesting.com
Printed in the USA
BVOW09s0729290517

485399BV00002B/425/P